The Mt. Pleasant Public Library
PLEASANTVILLE, NEW YORK

GIFT OF

READER'S DIGEST

THE AEGEAN CIVILIZATIONS

The Making of the Past

The Aegean Civilizations

Peter Warren

938
w

Peter Bedrick Books
New York

Advisory Board for
The Making of the Past

Frontispiece: a 19th-century sketch of the acropolis of Mycenae.

AN EQUINOX BOOK
First American edition published in 1989 by
Peter Bedrick Books
2112 Broadway
New York NY 10023

First edition © 1975 Elsevier Publishing Projects SA, Lausanne
Second edition © 1989 Equinox (Oxford) Ltd

Library of Congress Cataloging-in-Publication Data
Warren, Peter (Peter M.)
    The Aegean civilizations/Peter Warren. — 1st American ed.
      p. cm. — (The making of the past)
    "An Equinox book."
    Bibliography: p.
    Includes index.
    ISBN 0-87226-304-5
        0-87226-213-8 (pbk.)
    1. Civilization, Aegean. I. Title. II. Series: Making of the
past (New York, N.Y.)
DF220.W36 1989
938'.01—dc20
                                              89-32102
                                                CIP

Printed in Yugoslavia

Contents

Maps

Preface to the series

This book is a volume in The Making of the Past, a series describing
in comprehensive detail the early history of the world as revealed
by archaeology and related disciplines. Written by experts
under the guidance of a distinguished panel of advisers,
it is designed for the layman, young people, the student, the
armchair traveler and the tourist. Its subject is a *new* history –
the making of a *new* past, freshly uncovered and reconstructed
by skilled specialists like the authors of these volumes. Since these
writers are themselves leaders in a rapidly changing field, the
series is completely authoritative and up-to-date; but it loses
nothing of the excitement of earlier discoveries. Each volume
covers a specific period and region of the world and combines a
detailed survey of the modern archaeology and sites of the area
with dramatic stories of the pioneer explorers, travelers and
archaeologists who first penetrated it. Part of each book is
devoted to a reconstruction in pictures of the newly revealed
cultures and civilizations that make up the history of the area.
As a whole, the series not only presents a fresh look at the most
familiar of archaeological regions such as Egypt and Classical
Greece, but also provides up-to-date information and photographs
of such archaeologically little-known areas as the Islamic world,
the Far East and Africa.

Preface

The brilliant civilizations of the Aegean Bronze Age have excited interest ever since the initial discoveries of Heinrich Schliemann at Troy, Mycenae and Tiryns almost a hundred years ago. Schliemann was inspired by his love and knowledge of Homer to seek the monuments of the pre-Classical, Heroic Age. It was his achievement to lay before an astonished and often skeptical world evidence that an entire civilization, to be called Mycenaean after its capital at Mycenae, existed long before Classical Greece, a civilization which provided a material basis for the tales of the Trojan War and the house of Agamemnon which had for so long been enshrined in the creative literature of Europe. In a similarly radical spirit Arthur Evans went to Crete in 1894. He believed that a form of writing existed in the island long before Greek. His successful travels there led him to concentrate on Knossos, where he uncovered the center of a civilization older even than Schliemann's Mycenaeans and which again suggested historical credence for the legendary stories of Minos, Pasiphae and Ariadne.

In recent years the spate of discovery has been no less intense and hardly less spectacular. The Mycenaean palace of King Nestor was excavated at Pylos in Messenia by Carl Blegen; a new Minoan palace at Zakro in southeastern Crete is still rewarding its discoverer and excavator, Nikolaos Platon, after more than ten seasons in the field. Meanwhile at Akrotiri on the Cycladic island of Thera the enormous forces of nature, which had enveloped the landscape with meter upon meter of volcanic ash and pumice, have proved unique agents of preservation. For eight seasons Spyridon Marinatos brought to light a settlement which enjoyed the closest links with Minoan Crete. From the ruins have come thousands of objects, exquisite and plain domestic items, and above all a series of largely complete wall paintings of unparalleled beauty and interest. Their preservation gracefully places Thera alongside Mycenae and Knossos for our understanding and appreciation of the prehistoric peoples of the Aegean.

In this book therefore we attempt a study of the Aegean Bronze Age which takes into account the most recent discoveries as well as those of earlier explorers. The work is addressed to any reader or Aegean visitor who, while not a specialist in the subject, is questing to develop his or her interest in what those early Aegeans achieved. Their products can be visited today at dozens of sites and museums; among the latter those of Athens, Nauplion and Herakleion display the major collections.

The region with which we are concerned coincides closely with modern Greece and the western coast of Turkey. The Minoan civilization developed in Crete and extended its influence to Rhodes and throughout the Cycladic islands – themselves centers of the earliest urban development in the Aegean in the 3rd millennium BC, before the palace period of Crete. The Mycenaeans occupied what is now southern and central Greece, the long island of Euboea and eastern Thessaly. In western Greece there was much Mycenaean contact with Epeiros, while recent discoveries have shown that these contacts extended well up into what is now Albania. The Ionian islands of Ithaka, Kephallenia and Lefkas were most noticeably influenced by the Mycenaeans towards the end of the Bronze Age. But further west there were strong trading links with southern Italy and Sicily at the height of the Mycenaean period in the 14th and 13th centuries BC, as well as outlying links with the western coast of Italy, the Aeolian islands and Sardinia.

The northern Aegean regions of Macedonia and Thrace were beyond the bounds of Mycenaeans or Minoans, but not so the ancient city of Troy. Here stood an important center of Bronze Age culture for northwestern Anatolia, one always in close contact with the peoples of the Aegean. Further down the western coast of Anatolia Minoans and Mycenaeans forged trading links and perhaps planted settlements at sites like Miletos and Iasos. The eastern contact zone for the Aegean was first the island of Cyprus, with its own prehistoric cultures but populated by Mycenaeans in the 12th century, and before that in close relations with both Crete and the Argolid, and second the Levant coast, where imported Mycenaean pottery has been found on dozens of sites. With Egypt the Minoans enjoyed centuries of contact before the Mycenaeans followed them with exports of pottery to Amarna and other cities of the Pharaohs.

Examination of a map or, better, travel in the region itself will soon show that it was the natural divisions of Aegean physical geography which determined the pattern of settlement and maritime connections outlined above. Major Bronze Age sites all lie within regions bounded by mountain masses like Pindos, Parnassos, Olympos and the central Peloponnesian ranges. The regions being therefore geographically defined, were potentially transformable into distinct political units, kingdoms and states – once given suitable development and organization. Within them settlements were placed to exploit fully the naturally advantageous Mediterranean environment of good adjacent soils and with easy access to sea communications.

How the palaces and other centers made such successful use of their surroundings and why; by what combination of processes the cultures to which those centers gave expression may properly merit the term civilization, are questions we shall explore. But we may appropriately begin by investigating the graphic story of how these abundant remains were brought to light.

Chronological Table

PERIOD	DATES BC	KEY SITES
Palaeolithic and Mesolithic	<40,000–6500	Epirus caves, Thessalian sites below later Peneios river, Franchthi cave (Argolid)
Early Neolithic	6500–5500	Nea Nikomedeia (Macedonia), Elateia (Phokis), Franchthi, Corinth, Lerna (Argolid), Knossos
Middle Neolithic	5500–4500	Sitagroi (E. Macedonia), Sesklo, Elateia, Khaironeia, Corinth, Lerna, Saliagos, Emborio (Chios), Knossos
Late Neolithic	4500–3700	Dikili Tash, Sitagroi (E. Macedonia), Dhimini, Elateia, Corinth, Saliagos, Emborio (Chios), Knossos
Final Neolithic	3700–2900	Sitagroi, Rhakmani, Larisa, Eutresis, Kephala (Kea), Kum Tepe (Troad), Emborio (Chios), Poliochni (Lemnos), Knossos, Phaistos, Partira (Crete)
Early Bronze Age	2900–2000	Sitagroi, Eutresis, Orchomenos, Tiryns, Korakou, Zygouries, Lerna, many Cycladic sites, Troy, Thermi, Poliochni, Knossos, Lebena, Mochlos, Myrtos, Vasilike (Crete)

MM, LM Middle, Late Minoan pottery phases;
MH, LH Middle, Late Helladic (Mycenaean) pottery phases.
All dates approximate.

	PERIOD			DATES BC	MAJOR ASPECTS
	Crete	Greece	Troy		
MIDDLE BRONZE AGE	MM I A	MH	VI	2100/ 2000	
	MM I B			1930	First Cretan palaces built. Crete's wide links overseas. Troy VI. Phylakopi (Melos) Second City
	MM II			1800	
	MM III			1700	Cretan palaces destroyed and rebuilt
LATE BRONZE AGE	LM I A	LH I		1550	Shaft Graves of Mycenae. Great Age of Crete: Second Palaces, towns, villas. Minoan settlements abroad
	LM I B	LH II A		1500	Destruction of Thera
	LM II	LH II B		1450	Destruction of Minoan and Cycladic sites
	LM III A	LH III A		1400	Fall of Knossos. Mycenaean palace civilization and wide expansion of Mycenaean commerce
	LM III B	LH III B		1300	Destruction of Troy
			VII A	1200	Destruction of Mycenaean centers and (again) of Troy
	LM III C	LH III C	VII B		Continuity and new features in Mycenaean world
	Sub-Minoan	Sub-Mycenaean		1070	

Introduction

In the summer of 1975 an important sanctuary of the Late Bronze Age was defined on the island of Melos, the first excavations began at Assiros in central Macedonia, and a 12th-century BC settlement, its rooms filled with destruction debris, came to light on another Greek island, at Koukounaries on Paros. These three discoveries exemplify the main point of this new introduction – to examine, appreciate and assess the astonishing amount of new information, undiscovered and unknown in 1975, about the lives of the early Aegean peoples. The material is organized thematically. First, the settlements and the evidence they offer for economic life and forms of society are considered, then the varied and intriguing new evidence for religious belief and practice, and finally trade, both within the Aegean and with neighboring Mediterranean cultures and with states of the Near East. The chronological and regional framework of the main text is maintained, but since we shall as far as possible avoid repetition of what is discussed in the chapters that follow, new readers may prefer to turn straight to the main text and afterwards return here and read about what can now be added.

Many exciting and informative individual discoveries besides the three sites mentioned above will be noticed here. First, however, it is worth drawing attention to three important general developments in Aegean archaeology during recent years. They have all promoted new levels of understanding of the early Aegean civilizations.

Intensive surveys involving fieldwalking by teams over selected zones or transects of landscape, to discover evidence of every kind of human activity and occupation throughout the entire past, now take place in all parts of the Aegean. In every case dozens of new sites are discovered. These may be villages or small towns, but more commonly are small hamlets or farmsteads. Thus a more complete picture of ancient occupation and changes in the relationship between urban and rural communities can be obtained, as well as changing relationships between larger, independent territories (recently discussed as a model entitled peer polity interaction).

A second general development has been the application of theory and models to enable better understanding of different patterns in the organization of trade, or of forms of "colonial" settlement or types of economic production. It is fair to say that such theoretical modeling has not advanced far in the Aegean. It is equally true that such approaches have brought about more rigorous and systematic excavation and fieldwork, designed to investigate specific problems.

The application of techniques from the physical sciences for solving archaeological problems, our third recent development, is not at all new. But it has achieved most important advances. Above all there is now available the globally valid adjustment or calibration of radiocarbon dates, based on C-14 dating of annual rings of trees back to the 6th millennium BC. This means that we have an established timescale based on physical measurements, even though the range or dating band from most calibrated samples is often rather wide for the archaeologists' purposes. Sometimes, indeed, we can get closer absolute dates through links to the historical chronology of Egypt. But for the 3rd millennium BC and earlier in the Aegean, sequences of calibrated radiocarbon dates are fundamental.

The other main scientific advance is in the characterization of materials, chiefly pottery and metals, through analyses of their trace elements or their radioactive isotopes, notably of lead. Much more will be achieved in these areas in coming years and valid statements about the provenance of pots, metals, pumice and other stones will be added to what we know already. Thus trade and exchange patterns will be more accurately understood. Finally, we may notice systematic and excellent new work in palaeobotany, not only the identification of grains, seeds and crops, but also forms of crop processing and storage.

Settlement, economy and society. Remains of Palaeolithic communities and activities have come to light in remarkably varied locations. There are mine shafts for red ocher at Tsines on Thasos, stone tools on the acropolis of Nauplion, in a cave on Mount Phangos and in a valley north of Thespiai, both in Boeotia, in the Nemea valley of the northeast Peloponnese and on Kephallenia. The most interesting Palaeolithic site, because of meticulous excavation and recording of thousands of tools, bones and other objects, is the Klithi rock shelter on the steep face of the Voidomatis gorge and river in northwest Greece. This place proves to have been a station for hunters of ibex, chamois and beaver, and occasionally of lion, lynx, red deer, wolf, marten and badger. The hunters lived for the most part from 10,000 to 8000 BC, a millennium before Neolithic farming settlement. Far to the south, on the island of Crete, the finding of small tools of chert near Samaria in the great gorge of that name may (when published) indicate pre-Neolithic settlement, the first known from Crete.

New discoveries of the Neolithic period have been

fewer, but a site near Serres in Macedonia is said to be one of the largest Neolithic settlements in the Balkans. To the south in Thessaly, whose fertile plains bore the densest concentration of Neolithic communities in the Aegean, the discovery of Early Neolithic cremations in pots at Souphli and Zarkos suggests a very much longer tradition for this funerary and burial practice than previously imagined. Rougher pots, perhaps offerings, accompanied the burials. The discovery of a foundation offering of a house model filled with small human figurines and miniature pots in a Late Neolithic house at Zarkos in Thessaly suggests another custom with beginnings much older than previously known.

The Early Bronze Age on the Greek mainland, the 3rd millennium BC or Early Helladic period, has been greatly enriched by new discoveries, both from intensive surveys and at individual sites. Survey has revealed a pattern of small, dispersed settlements, as on the peninsula of Methana, in the Nemea valley and in Lakonia, east of the river Eurotas. At Astakos, off the coast in northwest Greece, underwater survey indicates an Early Helladic (EH) town of about 50,000 square meters; publication of EH Lithares in Boeotia shows this too was a large community, up to 40,000 square meters in area at the beginning of the Early Bronze Age, with a road at least 66 meters long and houses opening off it. Across the narrow channel dividing Boeotia from Euboea there was a vast settlement (and cemetery) of the same early date at Manika, just north of Khalkis. It was importing much obsidian from Melos and turning it into tools in its own workshops. Further south, the village of Tsoungiza near Nemea was another well-developed community, careful excavation having recently revealed occupation throughout the Early Helladic period, with a cistern, houses and pits. Reinvestigation of the great EH circular building at Tiryns has confirmed a construction with two floors, horseshoe-shaped compartments and terracotta roof tiles. It may well have been a communal granary. Other buildings at EH Tiryns include an obsidian workshop, and lead was in use. Exploitation of lead and silver at Thorikos in south Attica (two veins in mine 3) has recently been demonstrated already in the Early Bronze Age. Later, in Mycenaean times, lead has been shown to have been in abundant use at Dendra, Mycenae, Tiryns and Gla.

Recognition of these large communities from such an early date, around 3000 BC, on the Greek mainland will provide a new basis for understanding the form, structure and organization of Early Bronze Age (EBA) society, to be integrated with the evidence of sites such as Lerna, Eutresis and Akovitika. Centralized administrations, large, socially undifferentiated villages and dispersed hamlets and farmsteads all appear to have covered the mainland landscape. An EBA site of different character and of international importance, Pefkakia on the Thessalian coast, will be noticed below.

In Crete at this time current excavation of a little hill-top site near Trypete on the southern coast has revealed a village considerably smaller than but with rooms resembling Early Minoan Myrtos: Phournou Koryphe. Defense must have been a factor in location, while seeds of fruits and cereals and shells reveal local exploitation. The village's long-plundered communal round tomb lies well off the hill, nearer to the sea.

In the following Aegean period, the Middle Bronze Age, new discoveries of very different kinds are important. On the mainland burials in tumuli are now seen to have been prominent in the northeast Peloponnese, with a line of such mounds along the east flank of the Aspis Hill at Argos, just as they have long been known to be characteristic of the western Peloponnese. Here in the west reinvestigation of the Mycenaean tholos tomb at Voidokilia shows it to have been set down within an older, Middle Helladic tumulus. This suggests continuity of burial place by means of a very different architectural form. Perhaps the local population had not changed, but had adopted a funerary structure of Cretan origin, as elsewhere in Messenia. The tumulus itself is now revealed, most interestingly, to have been built on top of a substantial Early Helladic settlement. It would appear, as too at Lerna, that a new population was, so to speak, negating the previous one. Meanwhile later Middle Helladic burials at other sites offer confirmation of the emergence of social ranking and powerful warrior leaders previously seen at Mycenae. Thus we now have a warrior burial at Thebes with sword, spear, one-edged knife and arrowheads, and another and richer one at Aigina: Kolonna, in a shaft grave, with sword, spear, dagger and pottery from the Cyclades and Crete, as well as from Aigina itself. A tomb of about 1600 BC at Peristeria in Messenia was equally rich, with a gold kantharos, rosettes and papyriform pendants.

This demonstration of social status through deposition of wealth in burials continued in the Late Helladic or Mycenaean period, as we know from the Shaft Grave circles at Mycenae and from numerous tholos tombs. In this period too, moreover, new discoveries amplify the picture, as in a tholos tomb at Kokla near Argos, with one gold and seven silver vases, spearheads, other bronzes, sealstones and an ivory plaque, the finds recalling the contents of the Dendra tholos tomb. Kokla dates to about 1400 BC. From outside the citadel of Mycenae has come a grave with an inhumation burial accompanied by 21 bronze double axes and with a bronze tripod caldron as grave marker.

In contrast to this recent mainland cemetery evidence for technology and social structure, Crete in the Middle Minoan period has produced two sites of the living, each of exceptional interest. One is Aghia Photia, on the north coast just east of Siteia. Here is a rectangular building, 27 by 18.5 meters, comprising some 36 rooms on a single alignment around a central court, itself aligned east–west. In plan, therefore, the building gives every appearance of having been carefully designed in advance, and closely resembles a small Minoan palace. So its early date of c. 2000–1900 BC (Middle Minoan I A–?B) is of great importance. In function, however, it seems not to have been a palace, since the groups of rooms form separate, self-contained units, as if for families or other small social groups; but these were in close contact through the communal central court. Stone tools and pottery suggest no functional differences between the groups of rooms. Storage, at least in the customary large pithoi, does not appear to have been a major function.

In some ways Aghia Photia resembles the oval building at Khamaizi, west of Siteia, with its rooms radiating off a communal central area (with a cistern). Khamaizi was protected by its hilltop location and strong outer wall; Aghia Photia was also defended, most surprisingly by a freestanding wall with solid semicircular bastions, which recall Cycladic defense walls of the Early Bronze Age. One says defense at Aghia Photia, but it is not clear that the wall ran around the whole building. It survives on the seaward side and may have served for protection against the strong northern winds which blow over the exposed coast here. The greatest interest of the site is the social information it may yield, after publication and analysis of its unique plan and the contents of the rooms. The site is also important for a further reason. Directly over it, after it had passed out of use as early as 2000–1900 BC, was built a circular construction with an entrance on the east. This closely resembles the Early and Middle Minoan circular tombs, though at Aghia Photia there were no traces of bones or other funerary remains. Pottery associated with the circular building indicates a date of about 1900–1700 BC (not later than Middle Minoan II).

The second Middle Minoan site with remains important for their apparent social information is Mallia. Here the group of large buildings known as Quartier Mu, west of the palace, proves to have had built beside it a series of workshops, with debris from and equipment for seal carving, pottery making and bronze casting respectively. The size of these workshops, with two or three rooms each, suggests that they were family ateliers and, like the size of houses at Early Minoan Myrtos, that the family was the basic social unit.

Knowledge of the Minoan achievement when the civilization of Crete was at its height, from about 1700 to 1450 BC, has been increased at several sites. Of the towns with palaces Mallia has been mentioned, and we may add that new investigations in the palace show that a building with monumental rooms existed already before 1700 BC. At Knossos recent work has brought to light remains of buildings immediately preceding the first palatial constructions, but located some 350 meters west of the palace. This may help to suggest that the Minoan palaces evolved within a preexisting urban environment, through social reorganization and emergence of power-ful families. But these changes must have occurred with the cooperative acceptance of the community, since the monumental constructions which we call the first palaces were centrally located and undefended. We do not in fact know precisely who was responsible for these monumental, central buildings. The powerful family model, though suggestive (and we must not forget the Greek tradition of King Minos), is not proved; a person or body sanctioned by religion could have exercised control from the buildings; it is not impossible that they were non-residential buildings, intended to function for the community as cathedral, civic center, storage center and high-technology factory combined. But any explanation must surely accept as certain a high degree of planning and organization of building and contents, and thus a person or group responsible for that organization.

At Zakros continued excavations have revealed much more of the town, enabling economic distinctions to be drawn between production of foodstuffs in most houses and of specialist objects, metal tools, stone vessels and luxury goods such as ivories, within the palace. Among other Minoan towns we are currently learning more of Khania at the time of the great Minoan destruction around 1450 BC, with the uncovering of several town houses. Their contents included Linear A tablets and clay seal impressions made from rings engraved with cult and other scenes, serving administrative functions. In east Crete reexcavation of Pseira and Palaikastro and excavation of Petras near Siteia should contribute much on the nature of coastal towns combining maritime interests with agricultural production. The Late Minoan I Cyclopean walls of Petras invite attention. In central Crete the splendid constructions of ashlar masonry under the modern village of Arkhanes imply a building with important status, as does the group of male figurines of ivory within it. One of the greatest surprises has been in southern Crete, at the harbor town of Kommos, where an enormous building of ashlar blocks has come to light. It is a stoa 55·4 meters long, with an open front of columns facing onto a courtyard more than 1100 square meters in area. The building is beside a fine paved road leading directly to the sea from inland central Crete.

The island has also produced three new country mansions or estate centers of great interest: Nerokourou, because it is the first known from west Crete; Zominthos, because it stands at an altitude of 1187 meters at the junction of three routes high on Mount Ida, perhaps to control seasonal movements of men and flocks; and Makrygialos on the south coast of eastern Crete, because it is a Minoan "villa" with a palatial plan, that is it has a central court, a west court and a monumental west facade.

Economic and political relationships between the Minoan centers at this time are being investigated through new and precise work on clay sealings from Khania (see above), Aghia Triadha, Knossos, Phaistos and especially House A at Zakros. The pieces of clay impressed with seals or rings have string marks on their backs and shapes indicating that they sealed jars or tiny, folded objects of leather or conceivably linen or papyrus. Such objects must surely have been written documents, presumably accompanying goods arriving or for onward dispatch. The very closely similar devices on seals which were used to impress the face of the clay sealings suggest specific groups of administrators or producers controlling and organizing the flow of goods.

Outside Crete perceptive insights into the nature of Aegean society are being gained through continued discussion of the wall paintings at Akrotiri on Thera, notably the miniature fresco or fresco of the ships from the West House. Debate here centers both around specific interpretations, from booty raiding (the clearest among several depictions of a general phenomenon) to navigation festival, and on general principles of Aegean iconography, notably underlying themes such as aggression; the latter is expressed directly or symbolically through the actions of animals and birds.

Investigation of the cause or causes of the catastrophic destruction of Crete around 1450 BC (Late Minoan I B) continues to focus on two possibilities: invasion by Mycenaeans from the mainland or the effects of the great eruption of the volcano of Thera. (The following summary replaces the account on p. 104.) If the effects of the Thera eruption were the cause of destruction the mechanism will have been severe accompanying earthquakes and possibly sulfurous and other gases temporarily poisoning land, vegetation and livestock in eastern Crete. The distribution of ash fallout from the eruption is now known to have lain mainly east and northeast of Thera, with only a thin level on eastern Crete. By contrast, layers up to 1 meter thick have been found on Rhodes and up to 0·6 meter on Kos. A layer of ash from the eruption has also been found recently in Lake Gölcük, 90 kilometers inland from Izmir on the Turkish coast. Damage from ash fallout must therefore have been severe on the east Aegean islands and western Turkey. But whether this cataclysmic event occurred at or near the time of the destruction of Akrotiri on Thera (in Late Minoan I A) or later, to cause the Minoan and Rhodian destructions of Late Minoan I B around 1450 BC, is still unresolved. Frost damage to trees, likely to have been caused by a temporary lowering of the earth's temperatures as a result of a dust veil caused by major volcanic activity, around 1626 BC, and a high acidity level, caused by volcanic discharge, in one of the annual layers of ice in a core from south Greenland, around 1645 BC or up to 20 years earlier or later, have each been linked to the eruption of Thera. But the suggested frost-damage correlation has statistical problems in the quality of the correlation of data for frost damage to trees with dated eruptions, and the ice-core evidence needs much independent support from further work. Calibrated radiocarbon dates from grain samples and other short-lived organic remains from jars in the destroyed houses of Akrotiri suggest a high, late 17th-century BC date for the destruction; but some of the calibrated dates are compatible with a traditional date around 1500 BC. As stated above, the destruction of Akrotiri occurred before those of Crete. The dating evidence of crosslinks to and from Egypt and its historical chronology for both destructions, that is for the Late Minoan I A and I B periods, supports the traditional, lower dates, around 1500 and 1450 BC respectively, with some leeway for each. Solutions to these highly stimulating scientific and historical questions – the destruction of the independent Minoan civilization – may well be forthcoming from the spate of current research.

A separate, but no less important historical question, namely the date of the final destruction of the palace of Knossos, with its Linear B tablets in Mycenaean Greek, has continued to be much debated. Several archaeologists have supported L.R. Palmer's case for a "late" date, around 1200 BC; others have accepted the traditional date around 1400 BC or soon afterwards. The writer's view is that a date near the traditional one, around 1375–1350 BC, is correct, but that a significant amount of the material taken by Evans and others as reoccupation after the destruction and by Palmer as part of the destruction, was indeed part of the destruction, but can be dated around 1375–1350 BC rather than 1200 BC.

Meanwhile for this period of Mycenaean control of Knossos and for post-palatial Crete of the later 14th and 13th centuries BC recent work has demonstrated the great importance of Aghia Triadha, with its central building over the ruins of the great Minoan "villa," its public shrine and its public building with rooms opening onto a long court. This building is often called a stoa, with a commercial function; storage and assembly rooms for chariots may be suggested as an alternative. New discoveries at Knossos and other Cretan sites which flourished in the 14th and 13th centuries will be discussed below, for their contribution is to enrich our understanding of religion within Crete and of trade beyond the island.

On the Greek mainland these two centuries were the zenith of Mycenaean civilization. Small kingdoms were based on the natural geographical units of central and southern Greece, and were tightly organized and controlled from their palace centers. Three sites have given important additions to knowledge, while the excavations at Tiryns have exceeded all expectations.

On the foothills above the east bank of the Eurotas river, south of Sparta, a major Mycenaean settlement has emerged: a substantial building with corridors had a short life in the later 15th century, to be replaced by another mansion around 1400 BC, also short-lived. Those buildings were near the later Greek shrine of Menelaos and Helen and others stood on an adjacent hill. After an apparent gap the sites were reoccupied before the end of the Mycenaean palace period and destroyed in the earlier

12th century BC. The buildings are not palatial in the Mycenaean architectural sense, but the later association of the spot with Menelaos, together with the absence of post-Bronze Age remains (before the shrine), recalls the situation at Pylos and Mycenae and may be thought to offer some support for a historical, Bronze Age basis for Homeric geography and political organization. Equally, however, knowledge of Homer may have caused later Greeks to identify an area of old remains or associations with Menelaos.

In Boeotia Thebes has given yet more evidence of its rich Mycenaean past, with a jeweler's workshop destroyed within the palace period and other locations there destroyed later, around 1200 BC. Nearby Orchomenos has a major Mycenaean building to accompany the great tholos tomb. From the building have come pieces of wall paintings depicting a boar hunt.

At Tiryns a whole sequence of buildings on the lower ground within the citadel, north of the palace, has revealed the history of the town from the Early Bronze Age (see above), through the palace period and down to the end of the Bronze Age. The sequence of construction of the great fortifications is now clearly documented. The Cyclopean walls existing today were built late in the palace period, 13th century BC, but replaced an earlier fortification built around 1300 BC or earlier (beginning of LH III B) on a different line. This early wall had itself been rebuilt with a mudbrick superstructure including casemates. Within the walls very fine Mycenaean pottery, including pictorial scenes with human figures, and abundant use of lead (as in the Early Bronze Age) characterize some of the rooms. Beside a hearth of about 1200 BC (LH III B 2) in one room was a complete vase of the so-called Barbarian Ware, dark-burnished, non-Mycenaean pottery from northwest Greece or Italy. Evidence for religion, of great interest, is discussed below. Finally, continued finding of stray fragments of Linear B tablets at Tiryns has enabled the important conclusion to be drawn that here too, as at Mycenae, Pylos and Thebes, there was originally a full archive of written records. This requires new assessment of the status of Tiryns in relation to Mycenae. With its own administrative archive it is not easy to see Tiryns as a seaward dependency of its inland neighbor. If it was an independent state it would have controlled Mycenae's access to the Aegean Sea.

The excavators of Tiryns consider that the final destruction of the site as a palace center, around 1200 BC, was caused by earthquake. This is also the view of current excavators from their discoveries at Dendra and Mycenae, and at the Menelaion and Aetos Hill site near Sparta. The consequences are that the destruction of the Mycenaean citadels cannot be attributed to attack by other Mycenaeans or by foreign enemies, although the walls themselves, including that across the isthmus of Corinth, were certainly built against the possibility of human attack. It might be expected that destruction by earth-quake would be followed by rebuilding and continuation of the same social and political structure. Such, however, was not to be the case.

Before turning to the following, 12th century we may notice important results from work at the tell site of Assiros in central Macedonia. A destruction level of about 1350 BC, when Mycenaean pottery was being imported and imitated locally, has produced rich evidence for agriculture. Einkorn, broomcorn millet and bitter vetch were stored separately in individual containers (pithoi, clay bins and perhaps sacks), as probably were bread or macaroni wheat and hulled barley; emmer wheat and spelt were grown and stored together. Storage was in a unit for the whole community – none of the rooms sampled held all of the crops – and the produce was perhaps acquired by obligation from and was for return to the population as payment for communal work, a redistributive system. Here too was excellent agricultural practice, since the different crops have slightly different sowing and harvesting times and would have provided for varied nutritional needs as well as being an insurance against individual crop failures. The whole system, reconstructed from very detailed recovery of samples, is well seen by the team of excavators as an instructive indication of how the more developed, centralized agricultural economies of the Minoan and Mycenaean worlds to the south could have come into being.

The period after the Mycenaean destructions around 1200 BC may now be substantially reassessed as a result of recent work. The long-known population movement from central into outlying Mycenaean areas such as Achaea, the Ionian islands and Cyprus, with renewed Mycenaean influences on Crete, must now be balanced by clear evidence from Mycenae and Tiryns for extensive occupation throughout the 12th century, and at Argos until after 1200 BC. Political organization had changed, however, because the 12th-century towns were no longer controlled by palace authorities. Who did control or organize these 12th-century nucleated towns such as Mycenae, Tiryns and Lefkandi, whose populations were quite densely concentrated, and towns inferred from their cemeteries, such as Perati and Ialysos on Rhodes, is therefore a question of considerable interest.

The presence of northwest Greek or Italian dark-burnished pottery, which had begun already before the destruction of Tiryns but increased in the 12th century (Aegira, Lefkandi, Korakou, Menelaion, Tiryns), may indicate the arrival of some newcomers. But the contexts seem entirely peaceful, and perhaps suggest an enclave of Italian merchants in this period at Khania in Crete. Abandonments and perhaps destructions do, however, mark major changes in the 12th century. Argos and the Menelaion site can now be added to those that ended then, as can the recently excavated and remarkably preserved little citadel (about 625 square meters) at Koukounaries on Paros, and Phylakopi with its sanctuary on

Melos. Koukounaries is considered by its excavator to have been destroyed by human attack and burning. Tiryns and Mycenae lasted on to the sub-Mycenaean period of the 11th century.

Beyond the northern boundaries of the Mycenaean world there is also new evidence for change. South Balkan incised pottery at Assiros and Bulgarian and Trojan or Thracian (Troy VII B2) pottery in a cemetery at Tsiganadika on Thasos suggest incursions of new people onto the north Aegean coastlands, as at Troy to the east. But any such movements do not appear to have penetrated to the remnants of the Mycenaean heartland to the south, where continuity from the 12th century through the 11th and into the Greek Iron Age is further evidenced by new work on the Athenian cemeteries.

Religion. More than any other single aspect of Aegean civilization, religion has been enriched by new discoveries in recent years. From all this new evidence we not merely know much more about cult places and their contents, both ritual equipment and offerings, but interpretation can begin to concentrate more effectively on reconstructing ritual practice and the sequence of actions carried out in shrines to express wishes and belief. In particular, sacrifice (human as well as animal) and initiation rituals are beginning to be understood, though some would see initiation as expression of social stages rather than as a religious operation.

In Crete the mountain shrine of Kato Syme had a building with at least 17 rooms in the palace period, destroyed by a landslide of boulders (earthquake-induced?) in Late Minoan I. Soon afterwards a large stone platform was built, surrounded by an enclosure wall which was flanked by fine paved roads. Between wall and platform were remains of countless animal sacrifices, stone offering tables and clay chalices for liquid offerings to the divinity. The monumental platform, enclosure wall and paved roads indicate that the shrine had far more than local status. It was succeeded by another complex of rooms. In post-palatial times a series of long terraces with further sacrificial remains begins and continues into the Greek Iron Age.

At Anemospelia, on the northern slope of Mount Juktas, a remarkable three-roomed shrine contained many offerings of fruits and cereals. In the central chamber was a pair of life-size terracotta feet. They may have supported a cult statue made from other materials. In the destruction debris of the building were four human skeletons, one of which, on a low table, appeared to be a human sacrifice being enacted when destruction came, perhaps about 1600 BC.

At Knossos remains of several children in the basement of a building also appear to be from sacrifices, made at the time of the great Minoan destruction about 1450 BC. Many of their bones bore knife-cut marks, showing that flesh had been removed. The evidence suggested that this might have been for cooking, which in turn may mean consumption to achieve communion with the divinity.

Mountain-peak sanctuaries have also produced rich remains of equipment and offerings, especially at Juktas with its stone altar and terraced buildings, at Vrysinas in west central Crete and at Modhi and Prinias in the east. The great cave of Zeus high on Mount Ida has yielded in recent excavations, besides thousands of Greek and Roman finds, a sealstone of rock crystal, a sard pendant, bronze daggers and a double axe, suggesting cult already in the Late Minoan period. The Idaean cave may have succeeded the Kamares cave on the south side of Mount Ida, sacred in Middle Minoan times.

Two individual finds of the finest workmanship are also important for Minoan religion. One is a triton shell in dark serpentine from Mallia. Natural triton shells and imitations in clay, faience and fine stones were often used in Minoan religion. The new one is unique in that its exterior is carved in relief, with marine rockwork enclosing a scene of two Minoan "demons," standing figures with lion head and scaly back; they face each other, with one pouring liquid from a ritual jug over the paws of the other. Such demons are seen elsewhere watering plants or other objects in fertility ritual. This is the first time they have marine associations, which is additional evidence for the essential unity of Minoan religion.

The second object is a statuette of a male figure from the main destruction level, c. 1450 BC, revealed in new exacavations at Palaikastro. The preserved parts comprise a splendidly modeled torso of ivory, the upper part of the head with exquisitely rendered shaved top and single crest of hair, in serpentine, two rock-crystal eyes, part of the ivory face and ears and ivory feet. The legs, not yet found, may have been of a more perishable material, probably wood. Many accompanying fragments of gold leaf indicate clothing or body adornments originally. Given its exotic materials and size, about 0·4 meter according to the excavators, the figure may have been a cult statuette of a young male divinity, fallen from a shrine, rather than a worshiper, though the arms bent across the chest represent a pose adopted by worshipers on other male figures (pp. 67–68).

At Akrotiri on Thera sustained work on wall paintings from the fine building of ashlar masonry called Xeste 3 has established very important iconographical data for understanding the use of lustral basins. These underground tanks, entered down an elegant staircase and with stone slabs or dadoes around their walls, are not uncommon in Minoan palaces and houses. The basin in Xeste 3, unique outside Crete, had above its dado course a painted scene of women in ceremonies, one, with an olive spray in her hair, seated and clutching a bleeding foot. Two loose crocus stamens by her foot suggest she may have been a crocus gatherer like the marvelously dressed and bejeweled young women in the painting of the room on the floor directly above the lustral basin. These women gather and present the stamens to a seated goddess. Down below, in the basin scene, a woman beside the seated lady looks back to an altar dripping with blood. Dr Nanno Marinatos has plausibly argued that these are scenes of initiation rituals in the presence of the goddess. Rituals would have taken place in the tank and adjacent rooms, but the altar and outdoor location of the goddess on an elaborate seat in the painting imply other locations too for the actual events.

Cleaning of paintings from the adjacent space on the ground floor of Xeste 3, where a pit or tank may have repeated the function of the women's lustral basin, has revealed equally superb paintings of male figures, an older, seated man with a white loincloth, pouring from a large jar, and two naked youths or boys, one holding out a golden cup, the other holding a long piece of colored cloth. Initiation ceremonies with liquids suggest themselves in these paintings too. Professor Christos Doumas would see the ceremonies as essentially social or secular, Dr Marinatos as essentially religious rites of passage.

At Knossos, during the time of Mycenaean control in the earlier 14th century BC, three remarkable circular

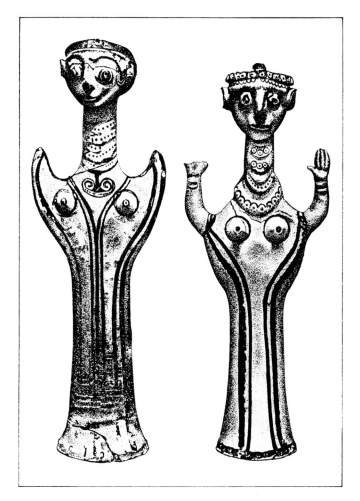

Two cult statuettes from a 12th-century BC shrine on the acropolis of Tiryns. They have rich painted decoration to indicate jewelry.

stone platforms have been found, some 350 meters west of the palace on what appears to have been open ground. The largest, 8·38 meters in diameter and with steps onto its top surface, is best understood as a place for dances in honor of the great Minoan goddess. Homer describes a dancing place built by Daidalos for Ariadne at Knossos (*Iliad* 18.590ff.). The two smaller platforms could also have been for dancers or musicians.

Finally from Crete there is the very recent discovery, at Vronda near Kavousi, of a Minoan shrine from the end of the Bronze Age. It had contained many statuettes of one or more female divinities, together with terracotta snake tubes for use in ritual. The types are known from other late shrines at Gazi, Gournia and Karphi (p. 109), but not in such numbers, except at Kannia.

On the Mycenaean mainland a hilltop sanctuary of the 16th–15th centuries BC above Epidauros marks local cult, but with Minoan characteristics both in its mountain location and its offerings. By contrast a series of shrines against the citadel walls within the town of Tiryns is wholly Mycenaean, with exquisite statuettes of a divinity (or several). They are painted to show their robes and jewelry and with them were many terracotta figurines of offerings. These shrines date both to the final palace period, 13th century BC, and to the subsequent period after the destruction around 1200 BC. Also located against the inner face of the city wall, and so also for the protection of the city, was a 12th-century BC sanctuary at Phylakopi on Melos. Its statuette of a goddess is Mycenaean, but the offerings of terracotta bull figurines and nude male figurines have parallels of the same late date in Cretan shrines. The eclectic character of the Phylakopi sanctuary is enhanced by bronze Reshef figurines from the Near East.

Trade. New information about Aegean trade with bordering lands has been extraordinarily prolific in recent years, and has promoted much debate and models for the organization and networks of such exchanges. In Thessaly Pefkakia proves to have been an international port already in the Early Bronze Age, with pottery imports from the Macedonian coastlands, southern Greece and, towards the end of the 3rd millennium, from western Anatolia. Early Minoan Knossos has been shown to have been importing hippopotamus tusk from Egypt or the Near East, adding to the older evidence of incoming Egyptian stone vessels. Dr Olga Krzyszkowska has demonstrated the different technologies required for hippopotamus and elephant ivory working. In addition to new evidence for the production of silver, lead and probably copper at Thorikos-Lavrion in south Attica and of silver on Siphnos, exciting indications of an origin for tin have been forthcoming from Turkish survey work in the Bolkardag mining district of the Taurus mountains, 100 kilometers north of Mersin and just north of the Cilician Gates. It appears that deposits of argentiferous galena

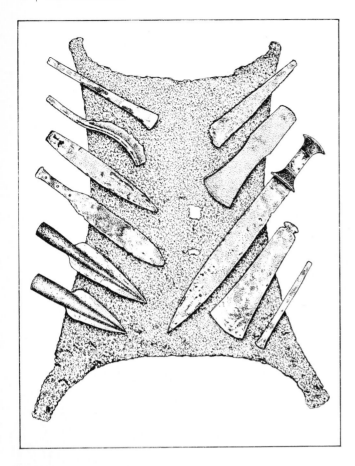

A copper ingot, weighing over 27 kg, and bronze tools and weapons from the Ulu Burun shipwreck off southern Turkey. 14th century BC.

ores have significant levels of stannite tin. Cassiterite is also reported, as also lead, zinc, silver, gold, iron and arsenic. The deposits and mines are accompanied by archaeological sites dating from the Neolithic period onwards.

In Crete, recent excavations at Kommos, on the coast not far southwest of Phaistos, have produced a building dated to the time of the Myceanaean control of Knossos, around 1400 BC. It was constructed over the site of the huge building T (see above, p. 3) and is even more astonishing. This is building P, 35 meters long and nearly 30 meters wide. It is divided into five narrow chambers, 35 by 5·6 meters, plausibly argued by their excavators, Professors Joseph and Maria Shaw, to have been shipsheds. A commercial fleet based on Kommos (controlled by Kommos, Aghia Triadha or Knossos?) and trading with the eastern Mediterranean and Egypt, and perhaps first with the station at Marsa Matruh on the north African coast, would accord with the wide range of imported pots at Kommos and with the broader picture of Mycenaean trading patterns.

The port of Khania also enjoyed international status in the 14th and 13th centuries, with ceramic imports from Cyprus and exports of oil jars to the Mycenaean mainland. In the 12th century a colony of Italian merchants with their dark-burnished pottery appears to have settled there. The Mycenaeans themselves have recently been shown to have had links even further west, with the discovery of Late Helladic III pottery (from over a hundred vessels) in Nuraghe Antigori in Sardinia. Dr Birgitta Hallager has argued that some of the pottery is Minoan and of west Cretan types. It is probable that pottery was exchanged for Sardinian copper, in the form of ingots.

But the most remarkable discovery of recent years in all Aegean prehistory is the shipwreck off Ulu Burun, near Kas on the southern coast of Turkey and nearer to Rhodes than to Cyprus. The vessel, which appears to have been built of fir wood with tenons and pegs of oak, is still under excavation by Professors George Bass and Cemal Pulak. But a mere list of its main contents shows the exceptional potential of the cargo for illustrating the nature, purpose and organization of international trade in the Late Bronze Age of the Aegean, Cyprus and the Near East. It may be that this was not a free-lance merchant ship, but a cargo specifically destined for a Mycenaean palace center, ordered, so to speak, by a Mycenaean ruler.

The main cargo was metal, currently estimated as 200 ingots of copper, with others of tin. There were also over 100 Canaanite amphoras, many containing resin. The cargo in fact included nearly a ton of terebinth, an aromatic resin suitable for use in perfumery and incense. Seeds of fig, grape, olive, almond, sumac, coriander, pistachio and safflower have also been skillfully recovered. One large pithos had been filled with pomegranates. Logs of African ebony (*Dalbergia monoxylon*) are another find of the greatest interest, since ebony has long been thought from Linear B tablets at Pylos to have been used in Mycenaean furniture. Other exotic contents of the cargo were hippopotamus and elephant ivory (raw material), ostrich egg shells and cobalt blue glass ingots, the latter doubtless for use in Mycenaean jewelry. There was too an abundance of bronze tools and weapons, axes, adzes, chisels, drill bits, tongs, swords, daggers and arrowheads. Balance pan weights in animal form, gold and silver jewelry and scrap metal, beads of stone, faience and amber, shell rings, Near Eastern cylinder seals and a gold scarab of Nefertiti, the wife of Akhnaten, rhytons of faience, a gold chalice and an ivory-hinged wooden frame for a wax writing tablet amplify the astonishing list of items. Hundreds of lead weights for nets and hooks give evidence for fishing and many stone anchors for ballast and control of the ship are more humdrum, but no less significant finds. Pottery from Cyprus and the Near East and particularly several Mycenaean pieces (LH III A 2) give a provisional dating for the ship in the 14th century BC, perhaps no later than about 1350 BC.

The Ulu Burun ship and her contents are a most powerful and exciting demonstration of what is still to be found and interpreted, year by year, for the advancement of knowledge of the Aegean civilizations.

Peter Warren

1. The Discovery of the Bronze Age

The so-called mask of Agamemnon. A gold funerary mask uncovered by Schliemann in Shaft Grave V of Circle A at Mycenae. 1550–1500 BC. Ht. 26 cm.

The ruins of Gortyn. A drawing made by Pitton de Tournefort who visited Crete in 1700.

Discussion of Aegean prehistoric civilization today is conducted in terms of a body of knowledge based on a hundred years of discovery. But how were the monuments of the past found? What were the motivations, excitements and achievements of the early explorers and archaeologists? It is to this fascinating story, the continuing discovery of the remote past of Greece, that we now turn. A connecting thread of at least two strands runs through the story – the gradual increase of factual information from material remains, which the mere passage of time provides, and the more accurate understanding and appreciation of the marvelous achievements of the early Aegean world which come from the researches of archaeologists and related scholars, developing and building on the work of their predecessors.

The story is twofold in another sense also. What an archaeologist finds when he goes out to dig a new site, until that point an unknown factor, is in part the gift of fortune. Schliemann could never have predicted the quantity of wealth he was to find at Mycenae; at Knossos the surface indications and preliminary diggings gave Evans a reasonable confidence that he was to be involved with an important site, but the hundreds of inscribed tablets and exquisite treasures that poured from the ruins, so near to ground surface and the chances of destruction through the centuries – all these were far beyond his expectation. From previous investigations Marinatos knew that Bronze Age buildings were well preserved under the pumice of Thera, but who could have foretold the astonishing quantity and beauty of the wall paintings which have come to light, still in position upon the walls?

So much is good fortune. But at the same time the selecting genius of the archaeologist plays a part. The probability of success is increased by deep prior study and knowledge, in the field and in the library, of the cultural questions to be investigated. The preceding scholarship is the crucial guide in the choice of a specific site for excavation. Troy, Mycenae, Pylos, Knossos, Zakro and Thera were not found or investigated by accident.

Travelers and the tradition. The belief that behind the intellectual and artistic splendors of Classical antiquity there lay a heroic past with achievements of its own was never lost. The Homeric poems sang of the war at Troy waged by leaders from Greece in times long before recorded history, while in the 5th century the historians Herodotus and Thucydides knew that once King Minos of Crete had controlled the Aegean. Herodotus wrote:

"Of old they [the Carians] were subjects of Minos and were called Leleges. They inhabited the islands [Cyclades], paying no tribute as far as I can determine in all my enquiries. Instead, whenever Minos required it, they manned his ships."

"Polykrates is the first of the Greeks we know who planned to rule the sea, apart from Minos the Knossian."

The traveler and explorer Pausanias, who lived about 150 AD, could verify the legendary past by visits to monuments remembered locally as prehistoric. At Mycenae he was shown the so-called treasuries of Atreus and other legendary figures, and he learnt of the murderers of Agamemnon.

"Klytaimnestra and Aigisthos were buried a little way outside the wall, for they were not thought worthy to be within, where Agamemnon lay and those who fell with him."

But the Lion Gate, the walls and tombs of Mycenae were

only one group among many monuments recorded by Pausanias. Travelers to Greece and Crete and Asia Minor in the medieval and later periods were interested in the ruins of Classical antiquity. For example, the great French botanist Pitton de Tournefort was in Crete in 1700 and drew a picture of the antiquities, mainly of Roman date, at Gortyn. But it is true that in Crete all were shown the famous labyrinth built by King Minos. W. Lithgow in *The Totall Discourse* (1632) wrote:

"I saw the entry into the Laborinth of *Dedalus*, which I would gladly have better viewed, but because we had no Candle-light, we durst not enter: for there are many hollow places within it; so that if a man stumble, or fall, he can hardly be rescued: It is cut forth with many intricating wayes, on the face of a little hill, ioyning with Mount *Ida*, having many doores and pillars. Here it was where *Theseus* by the helpe of *Ariadne* the daughter of King *Minos*, taking a bottome of threed, and tying the one end at the first doore, did enter and slay the *Minotaurus*, who was included there by *Dedalus*."

Yet this lay not at Knossos, but near Gortyn, and it had been known since Pierre Belon's work (1553) to be simply

Heinrich Schliemann (1822–90). A great linguist, he realized his childhood dreams of rediscovering the Homeric world of Troy and Mycenae.

Mrs Schliemann shared her husband's enthusiasm for archaeology and took an active part in the excavations. She is seen wearing the so-called Priam's Treasure from Troy, 2200 BC.

the stone quarry from which Gortyn, the Roman capital, was built. In matters legendary and pre-Classical the antiquarian scholars confined their knowledge to the literary evidence of the ancient authors, Homer, Plutarch and the Romans, Ovid, Pliny and Vergil.

In the 18th and early 19th centuries travelers to Greece were naturally impressed by the great walls of Mycenae and Tiryns, still standing and known from Pausanias to have been built by the legendary and giant Cyclopes. Edward Dodwell's *View and Descriptions of Cyclopian, or, Pelasgic Remains in Greece and Italy*, published in 1834, has fine views of Mycenae and Tiryns, and Robert Pashley sketched prehistoric walls on Mount Juktas to the south of Knossos. Yet none of these scholars and explorers was concerned with pre-Classical history, with proving the relation of the legends of the heroic age to the visible monuments, by the clear evidence of excavation. For this an entirely new mental attitude was required, not that of antiquarianism, but of archaeology. It came with Heinrich Schliemann.

Heinrich Schliemann. He was born in 1822 in the Duchy of Mecklenburg-Schwerin in Germany. The family was poor (his father was a pastor) and the death of his mother when he was nine made education difficult. At 11 family

circumstances compelled a move from his classical school to a commercial one. Thereafter for 33 years, to 1863, he engaged in commerce. It is clear that he was a man with extraordinary business ability. After starting as an almost penniless errand boy he became, in 1846, at the age of 24, the agent of a Dutch firm in St. Petersburg. In that city he soon built up his own business which he extended to Moscow. Through the indigo trade, sales of military stores in the Crimean War, and finally with dealings also in cotton and tea he amassed a considerable fortune. He was also a brilliant linguist and, apart from his native German, rapidly learned Dutch, Spanish, Italian and Portuguese to add to the Latin, English, French and Russian he had acquired knowledge of in his youth before being sent to Russia by his employers in Amsterdam.

In his earliest years Schliemann had been introduced by his father to Homer. His passion for the Homeric epics was to motivate him for the whole of his life. In his business activities it was his intention to make enough money to allow an early retirement. In this he would first complete his study of Greek and then reveal, by excavation, that very Troy of which Homer sang. After traveling to China and Japan in 1864, he settled next year in Paris, where he devoted himself to the study of archaeology and Greek. In the summer of 1868 he visited for the first time the sites which he was to make famous. The explorations produced a book the following year with French and German editions, *Ithaca, the Peloponnesus, and Troy*. It was an important work, since his previous study and investigation on the spot – the selecting genius we suggested above – enabled him to expound two fundamental theories which were to determine the major course of his archaeological life. First, with Pausanias before him, he came to the conclusion that the graves of Agamemnon and the other Atreidae must lie inside and not outside the citadel wall at Mycenae. Second, this time with Homer in hand, he located heroic Troy on the Hellenistic and Roman site of Ilion, a low hill called Hissarlik near the coast, and not – as contemporary scholars who cared to consider the matter held – on the steeper heights of Balli Dagh near Burnarbashi, five miles to the south. Thus his intention was clear: he would excavate at Mycenae to find the famous burials, at Ilion to find the buildings consumed in the flames of Troy's fall.

Troy. In April 1870, when one Arthur John Evans was 19 and finishing his education at Harrow School, Schliemann first sank his spade into the soil of Hissarlik. This season was a preliminary test and revealed the extent and great depth of the remains. No ancient wall appeared until 16 feet down. Full excavation was needed and this required

Turkish permission. So major work began in October 1871 and lasted until November 24. Inscriptions and a building, the Bouleuterion or Senate House of New Ilion, Hellenistic Troy, were revealed, then primitive walls and stone implements at a depth of 33 feet. Excavation began again in March 1872 with up to 150 workmen and a host of new English wheelbarrows, pickaxes and spades. A huge platform, 233 feet wide, was trenched from north to south across the site. It was soon realized that the lowest deposits could not be reached over so vast an area, so a broad trench was sunk within the platform. Work continued right through until August 14. Many remains of walls appeared, but their relation to each other was uncertain. Schliemann knew he must continue, and the following year, 1873, he began on February 1. The weather was bitterly cold and living conditions for the excavators – Schliemann being accompanied since 1871 by his Athenian wife Sophia – were primitive. By day things were bearable but in the evenings "we had nothing to keep us warm except our enthusiasm for the great work of discovering Troy."

Then one day in May came remarkable success. Town walls and a great gateway were being uncovered. Nearby, at the foot of the wall, Schliemann caught a glimpse of a "large copper article of the most remarkable form, which attracted my attention all the more as I thought I saw gold glimmering beneath it." Schliemann called the lunch break

A 19th-century engraving of Schliemann's great trench through the hill of Troy. Work began on the site in October 1871. Greek buildings are visible here in the upper levels and workmen are digging the prehistoric levels below.

early so that he could "cut out the treasure with a large knife," undisturbed by workmen. Sophia stood by and gathered the countless jewels, bars, tools, weapons and vessels of gold, silver and bronze in her shawl. They had saved the treasure for archaeology, Schliemann wrote, though a half should, by the terms of the excavation permit, have gone to the Turkish Government.

Schliemann's enthusiasm unfailingly spurred him on to the fundamental requirement of an excavator, to publish his results. *Trojan Antiquities* appeared immediately, in 1874, in French and German. More important than the excavator's Homeric claims that he had found the treasure and Palace of Priam and the Skaian Gate was the basic revelation of a very early settlement, with at least three superposed cities, datable to the Bronze Age, long prior to the historical periods. There were walls and a ramp and gateway of architectural magnitude, as well as an unbelievable richness of metalwork.

Mycenae. In the same year that his first book on Troy was published Schliemann turned to Mycenae. A lawsuit brought at Athens by the Turkish Government over the removal of the Trojan treasure resulted in his having to pay 10,000 francs compensation. Instead Schliemann sent 50,000 francs for the funds of the imperial museum. Meanwhile he was sinking trial pits within the citadel of Mycenae and he began full operations in July 1876. We have noticed what guided his choice of a place to excavate. The graves of Agamemnon and his contemporaries must be within the circuit wall. Just inside the Lion Gate remarkable stone grave stelae began to appear. They had sculptured faces with scenes of hunting from chariots and a border of spirals. Surrounding them was a large double circle of upright slabs. On November 24, 1876 the first telegram to *The Times* (London) was transmitted at Argos, to be published next day, Saturday 25:

"In the great circle of parallel slabs beneath the archaic sepulchral stones, considered by Pausanias, following tradition, as the tombs of Atreus, Agamemnon, Cassandra, Eurymedon, and their companions, Dr. Schliemann has discovered immense tombs containing jewelry. He found yesterday in one portion of a tomb human bones, male and female, plate, jewelry of pure archaic gold weighing five kilogrammes, two sceptres with heads of crystal, and chased objects in silver and bronze. It is impossible to describe the rich variety of the treasure."

Scarcely had English readers taken in these words when a second telegram, sent from Argos on the 25th, was published two days after the first, on Monday November 27, and further telegrams came in and appeared in *The Times* on November 30 and in the early days of December. Schliemann himself wrote to a friend in Leipzig on November 24, on the day the first telegram was sent. The letter was published on Thursday, December 7, and ended:

"I have now the firmest conviction that these are the tombs which, as Pausanias writes, belong, according to the accredited tradition, to Atreus, Agamemnon, Cassandra, Eurymedon etc. But how different is the civilization which this treasure reveals from that of Troy! I write in the midst of the greatest turmoil."

On December 13, along with Schliemann's own report on the Treasury of Atreus, came a letter to the Leipzig correspondent, dated Mycenae, November 27, and greatly expanding the telegram printed on that day:

"You will soon receive a more complete report; but, in the meantime, a foretaste of what is to come may be agreeable. In the same tomb of which I wrote to you in my last letter, I have just discovered what I took to be the skeleton of a woman, judging from the small teeth and the female ornaments with which the bones were covered. The two earrings are treasures in themselves. There were besides pendants of precious stones (red), hundreds of large and small leaves of gold, every one entirely covered with spiral ornaments and circles. When, after having dug out mountains of earth, I began to remove the stones and rubbish of the lower layer, I struck on the large gilded silver cow head [*sic*] with two golden horns, one large δέπας ἀμφικύπελλον of gold with a pigeon on each handle (who does not think of Nestor's cup?), three δέπαες [goblets] with only one handle, and an enormous vase of pure gold, richly ornamented. I found about 200 gold buttons, very large, and splendidly engraved, an immense golden τελαμών [baldric], richly ornamented, which I first mistook for a belt, nine silver vases, one or more of them gilded, ten very large vessels of bronze. All this was found before hardly one third of the tomb had been emptied. The bones which I found are like the bones of giants, of extraordinary size, and the teeth very large. There were close to them two large heaps of lances and swords of bronze. Many swords showed the remains of wooden handles, ornamented with innumerable gold pins (χρυσόηλον). The handle of one sword was entirely of gold. There is no end of smaller objects, all of gold, which had been scattered over the richly-embroidered clothes of the Royal deceased. . . . The tomb is the tomb which the tradition of the ancients assigned to the 'ἄναξ ἀνδρῶν' ['king of men'], the εὐρυκρείων 'Αγαμέμνων [wide-ruling Agamemnon], to Cassandra, to Eurymedon, and their companions. I can say no more at present."

Whether or not Schliemann had gazed upon the face of

Opposite: a general view of the acropolis of Mycenae.

Right: a magnificent imported Minoan rhyton or vase in the shape of a bull's head, found by Schliemann in Grave IV of Circle A at Mycenae. 1550–1500 BC. Ht. with horns 31 cm.

Below: the so-called cup of Nestor found by Schliemann in Shaft Grave IV at Mycenae. Note the two birds on the lip. Ht. 14.5 cm. 1550–1500 BC.

Agamemnon, king of men, the effect of these discoveries upon the antiquarians and scholars of England was no doubt considerable. The excavation continued until December, 1876. Articles by Schliemann appeared in *The Times* of December 22 and 27 and January 3, 1877. They form the basic text of a richly illustrated account of the astonishing finds, which appeared in 1879. *Mycenae* was published in London and New York, and a French edition came out the following year in Paris. Mr. Gladstone, the British statesman, like Schliemann a keen Homeric student, wrote the Preface.

The excavator had naturally claimed the graves were those of Agamemnon and other Atreidai. But many decades of scholarship had to pass before the historical sequence could be established, by stratification and style, to show that if one accepted a historical Agamemnon fighting at Troy, the occasion had to be somewhere in the 13th century BC, while the graves and treasures of Mycenae were some 300 years older. But in 1876 Schliemann could at least demonstrate to the world that the visible ruins of Mycenae, the capital city of the Achaians of Homer, were not only datable to the Bronze Age but, like Troy, housed people of unbelievable wealth and splendor.

Before going back to the Troad Schliemann made a return visit to Ithaka. Here he explored a site on the summit of Mount Aetos with the remains of many houses; he thought the central summit area had been occupied by the palace of Odysseus. But his aim of further investigation at Troy could now be carried out, and excavations were renewed in 1878 and 1879. The town walls of the second city were fully exposed, as was the contemporary, so-called Priam's palace along with them. Two eminent scholars, Virchow from Germany and Burnouf from France, assisted Schliemann and the work assumed a more scientific aspect. Burnouf made plans of the buildings and Virchow gathered much geological, botanical and meteorological information throughout the Troad. Schliemann was able to incorporate the results of all his investigations to date in his great book, *Ilios: The City and Country of the Trojans*, which appeared at the end of 1880 in English and German.

While *Ilios* established the high antiquity of Troy, its author was busy from 1880 to 1881 uncovering one of the finest monuments of the Greek Bronze Age, the great bee-hive tomb at Orchomenos in Boeotia. It had been known since Pausanias as the treasury of the legendary King Minyas, like the great underground Treasury of Atreus at Mycenae. But still Troy demanded more work and Schliemann began his third period of excavations on March 1, 1882, accompanied by Dr. Wilhelm Dörpfeld, a field archaeologist of marvellous skill who had taken part in the great German excavations at Olympia. In this year the long halls of the second city were uncovered beside that previously known as Priam's palace, and Dörpfeld began to understand the stratigraphy of Troy, which he was later to present in full order and detail. A new and large book, *Troja*, was promptly written by Schliemann to include the latest researches and it appeared at the end of 1884, in English and German. Dörpfeld's collaboration now demonstrated that the four cities of Schliemann's earlier work were in fact seven, superposed and interwoven in great complexity.

Tiryns. But already in 1884 Schliemann had returned to Greece to investigate a site which he knew should be contemporary with prehistoric Mycenae and Troy. Within the Cyclopean walls of Tiryns he and Dörpfeld uncovered what could hardly have been hoped for, an entire palace centered on a long hall, with porch and vestibule just like those found two years earlier at Troy. But this palace once had rooms decorated with brilliantly colored wall paintings of richly dressed ladies in procession, hounds hunting a wild boar, an acrobat leaping over a charging bull, a floor painted with panels of abstract motifs and stylized dolphins and octopuses, as well as a wall fresco of great figure-of-eight shaped shields like those described by Homer. The results of these excavations, which included the great walls, gate and vaulted galleries seen and sketched by earlier visitors, were once again rapidly published. *Tiryns* appeared at the end of 1885, with important chapters on the architecture written by Dörpfeld.

Schliemann was now 63, fully active and ready to tackle new sites. In 1887 he went to Crete, sensing that at Knossos a palace would be found comparable to that of Tiryns. But negotiations with the Turkish owners of the ground proved impossible to complete – time and chance were soon to bestow that gift elsewhere – and Schliemann went away. In 1888 he carried out excavations on Kythera to find the temple of Aphrodite at the church of St. Kosmas, investigations which have been successfully renewed and published by a British team in 1973. Then he worked on the shore of Pylos and the island of Sphacteria to find the fortifications used by the Spartans in the Peloponnesian War campaign of 425 BC. But still Troy called. In 1890 at the age of 68 he went out again with Dörpfeld for further excavations. But in December at Naples he underwent an operation for deafness. As a result he was affected by cold and on the 26th he died suddenly.

Schliemann's aim was simple, to verify Homer in stone and gold. His methods in the beginning were of the crudest, the vigorous removal of everything in the way of reaching Homeric Troy which, since he believed it to belong to remotest antiquity, must lie at the base of the hill. But later, guided by Dörpfeld, the work became more scientific, with careful recording of the remains. When Schliemann died it was clear that his aim had been achieved in a general way, but major problems of chronology remained. The palace of Tiryns had a central hall like those of Troy, which suggested a similar age for both of them. But his Homeric Troy was clearly associated with pottery far older than that of Tiryns; so which site was Homeric, and how did the treasures of the Shaft Graves relate to either site?

Yet we must stress Schliemann's achievement, which in just 20 years, to 1890, was vastly greater than he had aimed at, or perhaps even realized. His brilliant successes at Troy, Mycenae, Orchomenos and Tiryns and his full and prompt publications had established the actual, material existence of prehistoric Greece. There could be little doubt that the Homeric poems were a reflection of this past, though actual detailed correspondences with archaeological material, such as the grave of Agamemnon, were and will remain open to discussion.

Had Schliemann lived only a few years more he would have enjoyed the satisfaction of seeing the great heroic age he had unearthed begin to be understood, not just as one long period but as a series of sequential developments. Dörpfeld continued at Troy to find the mighty walls and gate of the Sixth City (close to the time of Homer's Troy), with which went another of the long halls or megarons, and it contained Mycenaean pottery like that of Tiryns. Here then was a great Homeric equation, which Dörpfeld could explore in his monumental publication of the site, *Troja und Ilion* (1902). Meanwhile in 1891, only months after Schliemann's death, Flinders Petrie was finding

Above: an early drawing of the Lion Gate at Mycenae. Two lions are disposed heraldically against a column, their forepaws on two altars. 13th century BC.

Below: Edward Dodwell's view (1834) of the Cyclopean walls of Tiryns which were to be excavated by Schliemann and Dörpfeld in 1884. Their operations brought to light an entire palace.

Mycenaean pottery not unlike that of Troy or Tiryns in the palace of the Pharaoh Akhenaten, which he was excavating at Tell el-Amarna in Egypt. As a historical date is known for the reign of Akhenaten – approximately the second quarter of the 14th century BC – the prehistoric age of Greece thus received an absolute date.

Schliemann's contemporaries. Other important finds had come to light in Schliemann's time. As early as the 1860s quarrying on the island of Santorini (Thera) for pumice to make cement for the Suez Canal had revealed well-preserved rooms at a vast depth, with beautiful fragments of wall-paintings and pottery of unknown age. Stamatakis had excavated a sixth shaft grave at Mycenae for the Greek archaeological authorities and in 1878 had cleared the so-called Treasury of Atreus. In the same year a certain Minos Kalokairinos had excavated some huge store jars with Mycenaean pottery at a site called Knossos, south of Herakleion. A beehive tomb with Bronze Age burials had been found by Lolling at Menidhi just north of Athens in 1880, thus establishing the prehistoric date and function of these great monuments.

Then Christos Tsountas, a Greek archaeologist, began to make major contributions to prehistoric knowledge. In 1886, the year in which Furtwängler and Loeschke published a corpus of Mycenaean pottery, Tsountas excavated another large beehive tomb at Vapheio south of Sparta. It contained astonishingly rich finds of engraved gems and metal weapons and vessels. Tsountas' chief find was the famous pair of golden cups with bull scenes in relief, objects to rival (and, many would think, surpass) anything from the Shaft Graves. In the same year Tsountas worked within the citadel of Mycenae and found not only great houses but the remains of a palace similar to that at Tiryns which Schliemann and Dörpfeld had uncovered two years before. In 1887 and 1888 he opened 52 chamber tombs outside the circuit wall of Mycenae. The pottery found with the burials compared well with that of Tiryns. Subsequently he turned his attention from the Peloponnese to the Cycladic islands.

The English traveler James Theodore Bent had dug 40 graves on the little islet of Antiparos in 1884 and there were reports of looting on other islands. On Naxos, Syros, Paros, Siphnos and Amorgos, Tsountas excavated literally hundreds of simple earth or stone slab-lined pit graves, containing pottery and metalwork reminiscent of Schliemann's deepest finds at Troy, and with them a wonderful series of white marble bowls and human figurines. He also investigated a contemporary settlement with a circuit wall of bastions near Khalandriane on Syros. His standards of recording were good for his time and his reports appeared in the Greek Archaeological Society's journal. The problem of dating Cycladic graves received some help from the first British excavations in the Aegean, from 1896 to 1899, at the settlement site of Phylakopi on Melos. Here three superposed settlements were found, the latest with My-

cenaean pottery, the earliest with material akin to objects from Tsountas' graves. An early horizon, contemporary with early Troy, was emerging. The British team on Melos was fortunate in having Duncan Mackenzie, who perfected a system of pottery correlation with stratified levels.

By the end of the century Schliemann's great discoveries had not only been supplemented and expanded, particularly by the many excavations of Tsountas and the British work on Melos, but a prehistoric chronological sequence was beginning to emerge. There was a Mycenaean period, possibly earlier remains at Thera, and clearly earlier cemeteries in the islands and in the cities at Troy. In all of this, however, one area was still almost a total blank.

Evans and Crete. Arthur Evans went to Athens in 1883 and saw the exhibition of Schliemann's treasures. At that time and on his second visit ten years later he was fascinated by a special problem. He wrote:

"In the absence of abiding monuments the fact has too generally been lost sight of, that throughout what is now the civilized European area there must once have existed systems of picture-writing such as still survive among the more primitive races of mankind."

From the evidence of engraved sealstones he had examined in Athens, Berlin and Oxford Evans considered that the island of Crete, so prominent in legend, might be an early center of one such pre-alphabetical writing system. With the aim of collecting seals with engraved signs he first went to Crete in 1894.

Evans was then 43. He already had a distinguished reputation in several fields. An expert in Greek and Sicilian coinage, he had published a large and important article, "The Horsemen of Tarentum" in the *Numismatic Chronicle* of 1889. He had traveled widely through Europe and knew the Balkans intimately. Here his interest was twofold: passionately in favor of the independence of the Balkan peoples, he distributed relief supplies among those who suffered during the Austro-Hungarian and Turkish conflicts in the 1870s. At the same time he sent lengthy dispatches to the *Manchester Guardian* telling of the miseries and poverty of the Bosnians and Herzegovinians. For a time the Austrians imprisoned him at Ragusa (the modern Dubrovnik).

His other Balkan love was the coinage and antiquities of the region, which resulted in a fundamental work, *Antiquarian Researches in Illyricum* (*Archaeologia*, 1884–1885). As the son of Sir John Evans, wealthy paper manufacturer and one of Britain's foremost antiquarians and prehistoric scholars, Evans naturally developed a deep interest in prehistory. He was intimate with Schliemann's work and in 1892 was visiting Sicilian tombs which were being opened by Orsi. One of them contained a true Mycenaean vase. A few days before, he had met Federico Halbherr in Rome. That great scholar had traveled all over Crete to record Classical antiquities and inscriptions, and must have stimu-

One of two Minoan gold cups discovered by Tsountas in a beehive tomb at Vapheio near Sparta. This cup shows the capture of a Cretan bull in a rope net fixed to a tree, but not before the bull has disposed of two of his captors. 1500–1450 BC. Diameter 10.8 cm.

lated Evans' enthusiasm for the island, almost unexplored for prehistoric remains. So Evans took with him to Crete in 1894 a specific interest, the origins of European writing, and a far wider vision than Schliemann's – a genuine desire to discover the importance of the Bronze Age in Crete for its own sake, whether or not it fitted the details of legend (these would be welcome extras). There was, moreover, the whole question of the origins of the rich Mycenaean culture of Greece. But there was Knossos too, the legendary home of Minos, already fruitfully tested by Kalokairinos and the American consul, Stillman.

Evans arrived in the little harbor of Candia (now Herakleion) on March 15 and at once set to work on his two tasks. Dr Joan Evans' excellent biography of her half-brother (*Time and Chance*) records from his diaries: . . .

"Arrived considerably the worse for voyage. Juno, Austrian Lloyd, bad. 24 hours voyage from Peiraeus . . . Able to visit bazar: found Chrysochoi and a man from whom I bought 22 early Cretan stones at about 1½ piastres apiece . . . Joubin had 'prospected' Knossos for the French and come to an agreement with one proprietor, but the pretensions of the other were too exorbitant . . ."

Then, four days later, came Evans' first visit to Knossos. "Mar. 19. . . . The site of Knossos is most extensive and occupies several hills. The Mykenaean akropolis however seems not to be the highest but that to the south west, nearest to the gorge, which on this side divides the rich undulating site of the chief Cretan city from the limestone steeps beyond. Here at a place called τὰ πιθάρια (tà pithária) are the remains of Mykenaean walls and passages (where the great pots, Pithoi, were found) noted by Stillman and others. They are very complex as far as one can judge from what is visible to the eye, but were hardly as Stillman supposes the Labyrinth itself (Later: No, on further examination I think it must be so). I copied the marks on the stones, some of which recall my 'hieroglyphics' . . . The Pithária lie in the village of Makroteichos, and here, enquiring for antikas, I was brought a remarkable fragment of a black basalt vessel. At first I thought it was a bit of some kind of Roman relief ware, but to my astonishment I found it was Mykenaean, with part of a relief representing men perhaps ploughing or sowing – an altar? – and a walled enclosure with a fig tree: a supplement to the Vapheio vases and contemporary in style! . . . From a school-master at Makro-

teichos I obtained two Mykenaean stones. . . . The site of Knossos brilliant with purple, white and pinkish anemones and blue iris."

Here, in this record of his first day at Knossos, are the elements of all that was to come in Evans' discoveries and writings: his sense of landscape and topography, the Palace of Minos (for that is what the tà pithária site turned out to be), the Minoan scripts and engraved symbols, the fragment of a Late Minoan stone vase with a relief scene, and finally Evans' abiding love and knowledge of the Cretan flora of all periods.

With the help of Joseph Hatzidhakis, founder and president of Candia's collection of antiquities, Evans began to negotiate for the purchase of Knossos from the Turkish owners. Without the continued efforts of the Cretan scholar, later to become a distinguished archaeologist himself, Evans would never have completed the transaction. Even so the matter was to take more than five years.

In 1898 Crete became free of the Turkish yoke which had lain upon her for 230 years. Evans in England and Hatzidhakis in Crete had been busy collecting funds for the victims of the preceding insurrections, but now the way was clear for excavation. The following year, 1899,

Hatzidhakis and Stephanos Xanthoudides, secretary of the Collection of Antiquities, had drawn up a proposed law which was favorable to foreign excavators. Evans was to dig on the Kephala hill at Knossos and the British School at Athens would excavate elsewhere at Knossos and on other, now famous sites like Palaikastro, Zakro and Praisos.

Work began on March 23, 1900, directed by Evans with the assistance of Duncan Mackenzie, whom we have mentioned, and as architect Theodore Fyfe, an excellent team for recording, planning and evaluating any finds that might come up. After only five days Evans was able to record in his notebook:

"The extraordinary phenomenon: nothing Greek – nothing Roman – perhaps one single fragment of late black varnished ware among tens of thousands. Even geometrical fails us – though as tholoi found near central road show a flourishing Knossos existed lower down . . . Nay its great period goes at least well back to prae-Mycenaean period."

Here then was the fundamental fact, that the great building at Knossos was older than the civilization of Mycenae. Soon the details started appearing, the preserved top of what Evans considered the central building, the walls blackened by the fire destruction, the rims of the huge store jars. Then on March 30 he found:

"[A] kind of baked clay bar, rather like a stone chisel in shape though broken at one end with script on it and what appear to be numerals. It at once recalled a clay tablet of unknown age I had copied at Candia, also found at Knossos."

Finds of every sort, frescoes, molded plaster reliefs, tablets and pottery were appearing and considerable care was being taken.

"Ap. 10. Interesting discoveries in the N.E. chamber early this morning. The earth here now is passed through a sieve so that every bit goes through a double and even triple examination and every scrap is noticed and set apart. One result was the discovery of what I had always hoped to find: the clay impression of a Mycenaean signet. It bore a bold but somewhat imperfectly executed design of a lion in a contracted position."

On April 13 we have these first words describing what the world now knows as the throne of Minos, set against the wall of the throne room.

"The chief event of the day was the result of the continued excavation of the bath chamber. The parapet of the bath proved to have another circular cutting at its East end and as this was filled with charred wood – cypress – these openings were evidently for columns. On the other side of the North wall was a short bench, like that of the outer chamber, and then separated from it by a small interval a separate seat of honour or throne. It had a high back, like the seat of gypsum, which was partly imbedded in the stucco of the wall. It was raised on a square base and had a curious moulding below with crockets. (Almost Gothic!) Probably painted originally so as to harmonize with the fresco at its side."

News of the discoveries had been telegraphed to *The Times* and Sir John Evans had sent his son £500. In reply Evans wrote on April 15:

"The great discovery is whole deposits, entire or fragmentary, of clay tablets analogous to the Babylonian but with inscriptions in the prehistoric script of Crete. I must have about seven hundred pieces by now. It is extremely satisfactory, as it is what I came to Crete seven years ago to find, and it is the coping stone to what I have already put together. These inscriptions engraved on the wet clay are evidently the work of practiced scribes."

Evans lost no time in writing up his discoveries. An excellent, detailed and well-illustrated report of 70 pages appeared early in 1901 in the *Annual of the British School at Athens*, and similar detailed accounts were to follow in the next five years. In the year 1901, the second at Knossos, the east wing of the palace began to be investigated and Evans' letter of May 4 to his father evokes the magical freshness of those famous moments.

"Digging is now in full swing on the East side and two first rate finds have just been made. One is the king of Mycenaean stone vases, decorated with fine spiraliform reliefs, and so large that it took eleven men with poles and ropes to remove it from the site. The other is the remains of a royal gaming table, about a metre by fifty centimetres. It is set with crystal and ivory mosaic with gold settings and silver lining under some of the crystal plaques. At one end is an arrangement of circles for the Egyptian game of

Opposite: early excavations at Knossos. Sir Arthur Evans' wager system with teams of workmen competing (for wagers) in the excavation of the Little Palace.

Right: the uncovering of the western storage magazines in March 1900. Note the stone walls fortunately preserved to just above the tops of the great storage jars.

A Middle Minoan cup found by Evans at Knossos. The fluted rim is probably copying a metal original. 1800–1700 BC.

draughts.... Then follows a kind of labyrinth of crystal ... and four large inlaid rosettes follow, magnificent specimens of jewelry.... Getting it out was a matter of enormous difficulty as the perishable framework lay in loose earth above a somewhat irregular pavement. But we made a wooden frame round the sides and plastered them round and gradually introduced slips of wood with plaster below. But it took two days to get through with it, and it suffered no further harm."

The archaeologist was enjoying unimaginable good fortune. The transference of his finds to orderly analysis in published form immediately occupied the scholar. A large Minoan cemetery to the north of the palace was dug in 1904. One tomb, at Isopata, was rich in architecture and alabaster vases from Egypt. All the graves were published in a long and magnificently detailed article in 1905 (*Archaeologia* 59). Already in 1901 Evans had addressed the British Association at Glasgow on Neolithic Knossos, classifying the remains into a Neolithic period, followed by three of the Bronze Age. The classification was expanded for an International Congress at Athens in April, 1905, where he first defined the Minoan Bronze Age with periods of early, middle and late, each subdivided into three. In the 70 years since this scheme was proposed, based on the stratigraphical and stylistic development of the pottery, it has needed almost no modification, and is still the most accurate and detailed way of describing the successive phases of the Bronze Age – though it has to be appreciated that major points in Minoan history do not always coincide with the beginning or ending of the three major periods.

After the first six seasons Evans re-applied himself to the problem of the scripts in particular. The result was a great volume, *Scripta Minoa I*, which was published in 1909 and treated the three early forms of Minoan writing. These were the pictographic, hieroglyphic and early Linear (Linear A) systems. All the knowledge from the engraved seals was here combined with that of inscribed tablets, bars and labels from the palace excavation, together with the author's own wide scholarship in primitive writing systems.

The operations at Knossos were not the only ones then starting in the island. Halbherr and his colleagues began on the lovely site at Phaistos in the same year as Evans and immediately found another Minoan palace with a magnificent wide stone staircase. It was a fitting rival to the grand staircase of five flights which the Knossian excavator was finding so well preserved as to justify the great expense of reconstruction. In eastern Crete the British School had taken up its options. Hogarth went at once to Zakro, where the finds proved to be Minoan, a fine series of mansions with hoards of bronze tools and clay sealings with the impressions of many curious engraved seals. We may note today that Hogarth came within a few yards of the Minoan palace with its wonderful finds which Professor N. Platon has been bringing to light over the last ten seasons. The British School also began to reveal the large Bronze Age town at Palaikastro, one of whose excavators, Marcus Niebuhr Tod, could still, at the age of 94, describe the digging and excavation life to the author in 1972.

Meanwhile, still in the east of Crete, an American lady of remarkable courage, wide humane interests and meticulous archaeological skill found and dug what is still the most completely preserved Aegean Bronze Age town. Harriet Boyd, with the assistance of Edith Hall and others, uncovered Gournia and promptly published her findings in 1908. *Gournia* remains to this day one of the finest pieces of Minoan scholarship. Working near Miss Boyd was another American archaeologist, Richard Seager. In 1904 and 1906 he uncovered a settlement at Vasilike which was seen to be of great importance: it belonged to the period before the palaces, the Early Minoan age of Evans, and was comparable in date with two large round tombs which the Italian team had just opened at Aghia Triadha near Phaistos. Seager, a scholar with a fine feeling for stratigraphy, was also sensitive enough to appreciate the beauty of the exquisite gold jewelry and polychrome stone vessels, again Early Minoan, which he soon went on to find in the stone tombs built into the little cliffs of the adjacent islet of Mochlos.

Later Aegean archaeology. Archaeology in the Aegean since Schliemann and Evans has experienced a prolific development along four main lines. First, discoveries of great richness have continued to expand our knowledge. In 1901 Staes and Tsountas had found a fortified town of Late Neolithic date at Dhimini and still earlier remains at Sesklo, both near Volos in Thessaly. In the second decade of the century Xanthoudides found and cleared in the Cretan Mesara a large number of round communal tombs of the Early Bronze Age. Hatzidhakis found the mansions of Tylissos and the palace of Mallia. He excavated the former and ceded Mallia to the French School at Athens.

On the mainland Blegen was uncovering the now famous Bronze Age settlements at Korakou and Zygouries near Corinth, and a huge Mycenaean cemetery at Prosymna in the Argolid. Just before the war a new Mycenaean palace came to light near Pylos in Messenia and this was uncovered by Blegen and his American colleagues through the 1950s.

Within the last ten years a Bronze Age settlement, rich in Minoan influences through its later phases, has been excavated in the bay of Aghia Eirene on Kea by John L. Caskey, while Platon has excavated the Minoan palace of Zakro, unplundered since its day of destruction, and Marinatos was still, at the time of his death, uncovering at Thera buildings, objects and wall paintings as magnificent as the products of Mycenae and Knossos. Moreover these discoveries we have cited are only the most brilliant jewels in the crown. Each year the soil of Greece and Crete yields a truly amazing quantity of sites and artifacts assignable to the ages of stone and bronze.

Following the discoveries have come publications. After his great series of early articles and *Scripta Minoa* I, Evans spent the next 25 years producing his monumental account of the excavations of Knossos, incorporating evidence of every Minoan find in Crete and many of Bronze Age date elsewhere in the four volumes of *The Palace of Minos*. Volume I appeared in 1921 when he was 70, volume IV in

Sir Arthur Evans handles a copy of the stone bull's head rhyton from the Little Palace at Knossos at the 1936 exhibition staged in London by the British School at Athens.

1935. Then he and Dr. Joan Evans published the index volume, itself a compendium and reference source of all Minoan knowledge, in 1936. Meanwhile at Mycenae Alan Wace meticulously organized his researches and excavations on the citadel and in the great beehive tombs into volumes 24 and 25 of the *Annual of the British School*, which appeared in 1922 and 1924. The many chamber tombs he had dug were published in 1932 and his exemplary detail was followed in Blegen's *Prosymna* (1937). A few years earlier a monumental work had appeared. Nearly 80 years after Schliemann opened the Shaft Graves, Georg Karo gave them in 1933 the publication they merit. The excellence of these Mycenaean works had made a great corpus of excavated pottery available, which the Swedish scholar Arne Furumark was able to order and analyze in 1941. *The Mycenaean Pottery* remains the basic major work for its subject. The tradition of fine scholarship in presenting the achievements of the Aegean Bronze Age continues. Through the 1930s Blegen and his American colleagues had re-excavated Troy. The great volumes which appeared from 1950 presented in final detail the complicated history of that settlement, a coping stone to Dörpfeld's achievement in *Troja und Ilion*. In our own day it is fitting to mention the exemplary standards of the Greek scholars in the presentation of their results in major volumes, that by M. Andronikos of the rich early Iron Age cemetery at Verghina in Macedonia and S. Iakovidhes' huge work on the tombs of the final years of the Bronze Age at Perati in eastern Attica.

Pylos and Linear B. The third main line of development has been quite different. On Tuesday April 4, 1939, Blegen sunk his first trial trench into the hill of Ano Englianos near Pylos and recorded in his notebook:

"Dark and threatening weather. McDonald and I go out to Ano Englianos. Lv. 7:30. Arr. 8:15. We find Charalambos and many men. . . . Lay out long trench approx. N–S, ca. 50 m. long, 2 m. wide. . . . 5 sections ca. 10 m. long each. McDonald takes charge of trench. . . . Looks like walls of big building. Earth black and red, all burned. Sherds few but look LH III. In section A found ca. .30 deep a deposit of inscribed tablets, plano-convex in shape. Lined out on flat side and inscr. w. Minoan (?) signs. Workman gets out two. Mac and I three more – all complete. One more at least left, but we leave and cover, for a drizzly rain sets in and hard to photo and to get out."

Thus in precise, unadorned notes was the first record of inscribed tablets from the mainland of Greece, their contents destined to inspire thousands of learned publications. Then came the war and excavation had to await its conclusion. But soon came an electrifying new stage. Michael Ventris, an English architect with a brilliant genius for cryptography, had heard Sir Arthur Evans' lecture in 1936 when he, Ventris, was 14. Before and after the war he worked on the few published tablets and from 1950 to 1952 circulated detailed notes of his work to specialist scholars

A Linear B tablet from the palace at Knossos. Scholars were puzzled by the script until it was discovered to be an early form of Greek and deciphered by Michael Ventris. This tablet records chariots and horses. 1400 BC.

all over the world. The final note, dated June 1, 1952, is entitled "Are the Knossos and Pylos tablets written in Greek?" Ventris had been asked by the B.B.C. to speak on the recent appearance of *Scripta Minoa* II in which Sir John Myres, with immense labor, put together Evans' papers prepared for the publication of the Linear B tablets of Knossos. Ventris discussed the whole problem of the scripts and towards the end made an announcement with momentous implications for the history of Greece and the Greek language:

"During the last few weeks, I have come to the conclusion that the Knossos and Pylos tablets must, after all, be written in Greek – a difficult and archaic Greek, seeing that it is five hundred years older than Homer, and written in a rather abbreviated form, but Greek nevertheless."

John Chadwick, who collaborated with Ventris from the moment after the decipherment was put forward, has excitingly and skillfully set out the whole story in his book *The Decipherment of Linear B*. That the Linear B tablets from the destruction levels of Knossos, Pylos and the houses of Mycenae (with more recently from Thebes) are in fact an early form of the Greek language is now accepted by the great majority of those philologists and linguists who are qualified to judge. It was what Evans had devoted much of his career to solving and, in opening up the whole world of Mycenaean palace and state organization, has been one of the greatest contributions towards our understanding of the Bronze Age.

Archaeology comes of age. Fourth, the story of the discovery of the early Aegean has in the last 15 years been taking a new and probably significant turn. While meticulous digging and recording have been carried out, sometimes followed by definitive publication, at the same time we are seeing a new application of a wide range of pure sciences to archaeology. It is no exaggeration to say that this use of often highly sophisticated techniques, knowledge and equipment is transforming not only our ability

to obtain important information from excavation but also our entire approach to the subject. This has come about largely through investigation of the Neolithic period, for which it has been traditional discipline to strive as much for evidence of the agricultural and industrial economies as for artifacts in themselves.

The application of biological sciences, the study of faunal and floral remains, did not of course begin with the recent excavations of Vladimir Milojčić at the Neolithic sites of Thessaly, or the work of Robert Rodden and a Cambridge University team at Nea Nikomedia in Macedonia in 1961. Taramelli had carefully recorded the species of animal bones when he dug the late Neolithic cave at Miamou in southern Crete in 1897 and any glance at the Index volume of *The Palace of Minos* will reveal the attention paid to floral remains. Thus by 1936 Vickery was able to produce an excellent monograph on *Food in Early Greece*. But the recent Neolithic excavations in Thessaly, Macedonia, Saliagos in the Cyclades, Knossos in Crete and Franchthi in the Argolid have made it a prime aim to see how much new information can be gathered, not just on the subsistence pattern of a settlement but on its use of and

Modern methods of excavation. A building beside the Royal Road at Knossos. Observe the various books for recording the finds.

adaptation to its whole environment. The find of a single grain of wheat or the stone of an olive may tell us more about the life of an early Aegean settlement than the discovery of a dozen beautifully painted pots, though the realization of this potential economic understanding has yet to penetrate to all areas of Bronze Age studies, let alone to later investigations.

Another important new aspect of the applications of pure science is apparent in dating. For the Early Bronze Age, and periods further back in time, radiocarbon dating of organic samples (e.g. wood, bone, plant remains, shell) has provided a sure means of dating cultural sequences, and therefore of reconstructing the pattern of our earliest history. As a single date may be in error because of contamination or inadequacy of the sample, while the dates themselves as usually expressed have only two chances in three of falling within the range of years quoted, care must be taken to obtain as many dates as possible from stratified contexts at different sites in order to arrive at an accurate time-range for a site. Radiocarbon dates must be translated into calendar years. It had been assumed that the two were the same, but recent research on the radiocarbon dates of tree rings (whose precise calendrical date is known because one ring represents one year) has shown that radiocarbon dates become too "young" as one goes back in time. To a radiocarbon date of about 3000 BC, for instance, about 600 years must be added to obtain an approximate calendrical or historical date. Together with radiocarbon dating another technique, thermoluminescence, to determine the age of the fired clay of pottery, is being made available by colleagues in the pure sciences, together with a battery of chemical and physical methods for establishing just where an object was made.

Finally the realization of how much new information, waiting in the ground, is to be gained from the judicious employment of such techniques is beginning to provoke a fundamental reconsideration of our explanations for the Aegean civilizations. Great joy has and will be obtained from the discovery and description of the countless objects of beauty and skill which document the civilization at its height. But the beginnings of civilization, questions of origin and of why (as well as how) the processes started which lead on to the palaces are of equal interest. The explanation of cultural change is proving as demanding and as fascinating as are descriptions of cultural stability.

The new emphasis today on high recovery and recording standards in excavation allows for abundant collection of biological data. From the study of these data by specialists there arises a proper emphasis on the settlement in relation to its local and wider environment, an emphasis that tends to suggest that local, environmental factors, such as climate or soil and other resources, influence development or promote change to a greater degree than had been realized. Previously sought explanations of change,

such as invasions of people or ideas from external sources, often still best suit the evidence – for example burnt destruction levels at the end of the Early Bronze Age on the Greek mainland. But other hypotheses, of the kind employed in our next chapter and favoring locally inspired development, should not be neglected.

Today Aegean prehistorians are in the fortunate position of being able to promote a felicitous union of science and art. Only the use of these two in combination can yield the widest human understanding which the early Aegean civilizations merit. The fresco masterpieces of Thera, for example, must now be studied by the botanist and zoologist as well as by the historian of art. No one would have

Terracotta figurines of gods and goddesses are revealed: a recent discovery by Lord William Taylour in a shrine on the citadel at Mycenae. 13th century BC.

felt more at home in such an atmosphere than Sir Arthur Evans. In describing the Minoan pottery from the cave on Juktas Mountain, he included learned botanical paragraphs on the history and use of *Origanum dictamnus* (Cretan dittany), a lovely plant that grows in the environs of the cave, while upon that very mountain, he explained, religion and mythology combined to locate the burial place of Zeus.

The Tombs of Mycenae

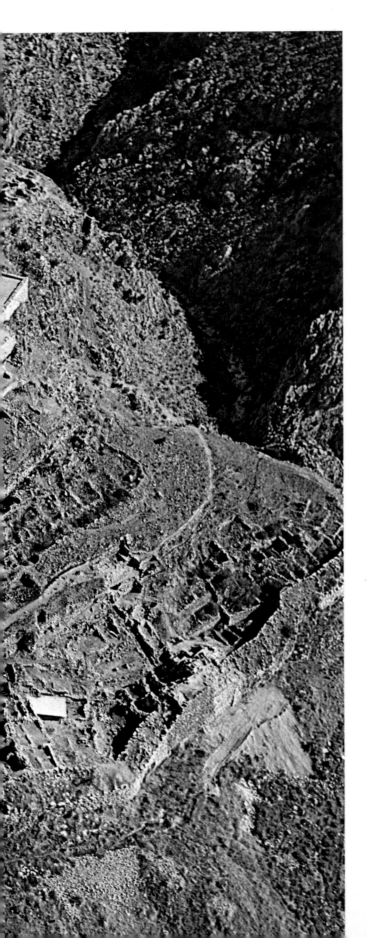

Mycenae's fortunes are precisely reflected in the many tombs located on and around the citadel hill. In the Middle Bronze Age a cemetery had occupied the western slope. Within this area a special plot was marked out with a small circuit wall to house a group of graves and soon this was extended to a larger stone circle enclosing 24 graves. This is Circle B (c. 1650–1550 BC) in which the burials, found unplundered about 20 years ago, must be of the ruling families. Fine pottery drinking vessels, vases of precious metal and stone, weapons, jewelry and engraved gems, a death mask of electrum and, probably, a wooden scepter with bone mountings like those from a rich burial of the Wessex Culture of Early Bronze Age Britain were placed on or beside the bodies in deep, slab-lined (cist) graves covered over by stone slabs. While this grave circle was in use another group of deep shaft graves was constructed a little higher up the western slope. These are the famous tombs found by Schliemann, which were to be included about 300 years later within the fortification wall of Mycenae and also given their prominent circular enclosing wall of upright slabs. This group of graves was used from c. 1600/1550 to 1500 BC and the countless treasures in gold, silver, bronze, stone, pottery, ivory, faience, amber and other materials from the burials (18 or 19) in the six tombs have pride of place in the National Archaeological Museum in Athens. The men buried therein, although their names are unknown, must have been the warrior kings of Mycenae (and the females their queens or daughters). The final burial, a woman in grave I, is dated c. 1500–1450 BC, during which time a splendid stone keel-vaulted tomb was placed in the older circle, B. From c. 1500 BC, however, a new type of tomb began to be built at Mycenae, the great beehive-shaped corbeled stone vault, called a tholos tomb. The architectural origin of the type may well have been in the round tombs of Crete, from where it may have come first to the southwestern Peloponnese. About 80 are known from mainland Greece and at Mycenae nine were built. Two of the latest of these, probably constructed in the early 14th century BC, are the so-called Treasury of Atreus and the Tomb of Klytaimnestra. These are two of many famous names located at Mycenae in legend.

This dramatic aerial view of the acropolis of Mycenae shows the palace halls in the upper area and the dozens of well-built houses of the 14th and 13th centuries BC. In the lower area stands the great circle of Shaft Graves excavated by Schliemann.

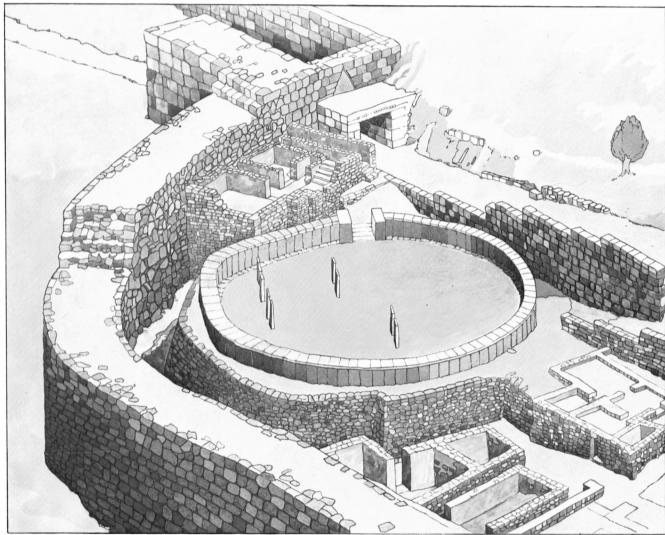

Top: a drawing from an early photograph marking the beginnings of prehistoric archaeology in Greece. It shows Schliemann's excavation of the Shaft Graves in 1876. The 13th-century BC ring of parallel slabs encircling the 16th-century BC graves is seen as it was found. Sculptured stelae or markers stand over the graves in the center. Horses and carts are present to remove the heaps of earth and some of the 125 workmen employed stand on the ramp above. From within the graves Schliemann removed the thousands of precious objects with extraordinary skill and care, recording them and their find spots with meticulous attention to detail, which he promptly published in his *Mycenae*.

Center: in the 13th century BC the kings of Mycenae built a circuit wall 900 meters long round their city. On the west it swung out to enclose the old Shaft Graves with their sculptured marker slabs. A special wall of upright slabs was also built round the six graves, with a monumental entrance which is seen here in the reconstruction. The entrance lay just off the ramp which proceeded from the famous Lion Gate, whose interior is visible here, up to the palace. The 13th-century arrangements for the protection of the Shaft Grave area can only mean that the rulers of the time knew this to have been the royal burial place of their predecessors some 250 years before.

Above: a gold signet ring, from Shaft Grave IV, depicting a battle scene. The warriors wear helmets of boars' tusks and elaborate kilts, carry long swords or spears and are protected (here unprotected) by tower-like body shields such as Homer describes. *Right*: gold death masks were placed on the faces of five kingly burials in Shaft Graves IV and V of Circle A. This mask of electrum, a natural alloy of gold and silver, comes not from Schliemann's Circle A, but was beside the head of one of the three burials in Grave Gamma in the slightly older Circle B.

Above: this magnificent 16th-century diadem of decorated gold was found in Circle A. *Left*: one of the finest treasures came from Shaft Grave V, twelve applied gold relief plaques on a six-sided box, probably of wood. This one shows a lion attacking a horned animal (antelope, deer or goat) and incorporates a stylized bull's head.
Above left: one of 701 decorated gold disks found by Schliemann in Grave III.

Above: below the Lion Gate stands a beehive tholos tomb, traditionally known as the Tomb of Klytaimnestra. It was first excavated by Mrs. Sophia Schliemann (seen here) in 1876.

Below: the so-called Treasury of Atreus before the clearance of the dromos. The tomb chamber was emptied to ground level by Veli Pasha early in the 19th century.

Opposite: the Treasury of Atreus is architecturally the finest of the tholoi at Mycenae. The facade (*top*) today looks bare and the triangle above the door gapes open. Originally it was decorated in a way befitting the tomb's importance, as shown in this reconstruction. The axonometric view (*center*), after Hood, demonstrates how tholos tombs were constructed. A great passage was driven into the hillside and a circular shaft excavated at its end. Within the shaft the corbeled vault was built in regular ring courses, with the hole at the top covered by a capstone. *Below*: a plan and cross-section of the tomb, after de Jong.

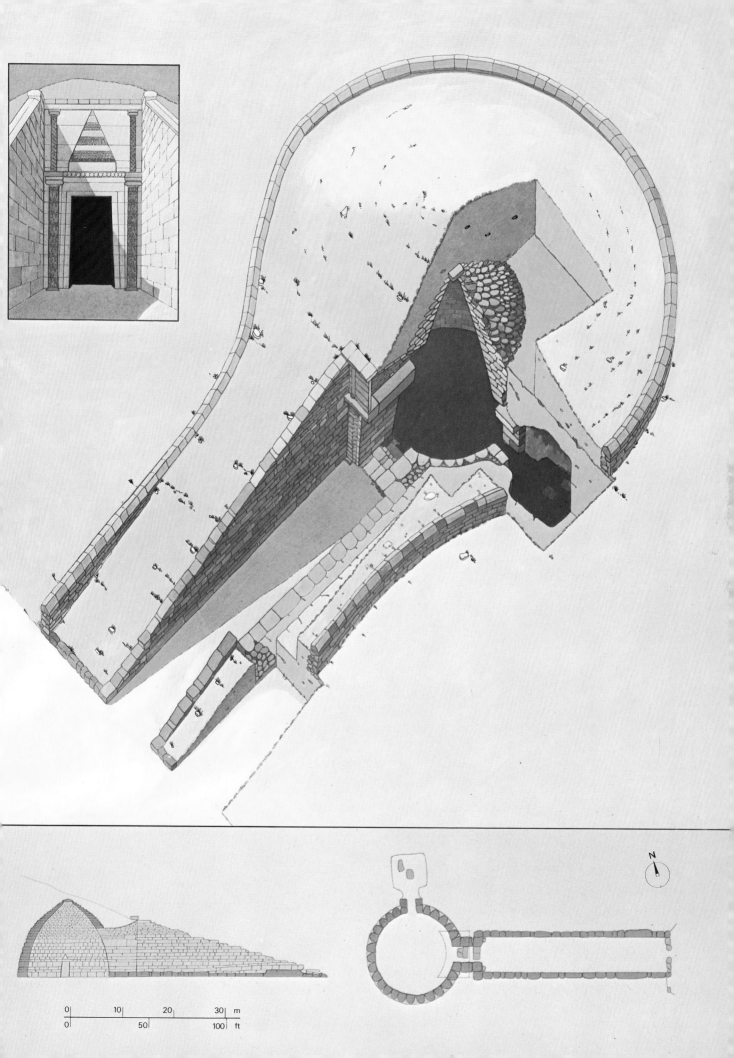

0   10   20   30   m
0   50   100   ft

Above: the Treasury of Atreus as seen today. It was probably built in the 14th century BC. The approach is by a passage or dromos, 36 meters long and 6 meters wide, with dressed stone masonry over 10 meters high, and the entrance is through a monumental doorway 5.40 meters high. Burials were made in pits in the rock-cut side chamber, but they have long since been plundered. Funeral ceremonies would have been held in the dromos. After burial the doors were closed (in less grand tholoi they were simply walled up) but the monumental facade and approach suggest the passage stayed open between burials. In smaller tombs it was blocked up with earth.
Left: a view of the interior as seen by the English traveler Edward Dodwell.

2. Civilization in the Aegean Bronze Age

The plains. The River Peneios in Thessaly, one of the few perpetual rivers in Greece. It provided fish and a route to the mountains and east to the Aegean coast. The richest Neolithic cultures in Greece sprang up beside the river and over the great Thessalian plain.

The coast. A view of the palace of Zakro in eastern Crete. A long beach suitable for drawing up ships lies beyond the palace. Communication by sea was of fundamental importance to the Minoan civilization. At Zakro Middle Minoan occupation has been found below the Late Minoan palace, but we do not know if there was a palatial building in the earlier period. It remained the social and economic center of the district throughout the Second Palace period.

Among the collective human achievements of the world to which we give the name civilizations, those of the Minoans and Mycenaeans are generally agreed to have a place. How and, more basically, why did they achieve so much? If we are to gain some understanding of the pre-historic Aegean as a whole, these brief but fundamental questions must be examined first. The core of the matter is the human response to the physical geography, environ-ment and resources of the Aegean region. It is the inter-action of environment and humanity through time that we must study, since the long process was to result in a complex and beautiful palace on the Kephala hill at Knossos and in the royal citadel and tombs of Mycenae. The first stage then is to appreciate the physical environ-ment.

The setting. Geographically the Aegean divides into five major regions and these are basic to our understanding of the growth of Aegean civilization: northern Greece, with the large and fertile plains of Macedonia and Thessaly being well suited to grazing and the growth of cereal crops; the central area, comprising Boeotia, the long island of Euboea, Phokis, Attica and the Peloponnese, all with smaller plains and valleys kept distinct by mountain masses and able to support olives, vines and other fruits, cereals, sheep, goats, pigs and cattle; the Aegean islands, in easy communication with each other and the mainlands of Greece and Anatolia (Turkey), blessed with fertile slopes, indented coasts and beaches for shipping; Crete, over 150 miles long, geographically similar to the Peloponnese with large, gentle bays and rich coastal plains (and occasional inland plains) backed by mountain ranges which divide off the fertile areas from each other; and lastly, the western coastal region of Anatolia, again divided into fertile plains from north to south, though in this case drained by major rivers flowing down from the high Anatolian plateau to the east. In Greece and the islands, rivers and streams are mostly seasonal and relatively unimportant, save larger ones like the Axios and Haliakmon in Macedonia and the Peneios in Thessaly. These were not navigable but yielded fish and provided routes through to the west and the Balkans to the north.

These regional configurations carry several implications for the pattern of human settlement. The massive moun-tain chain running down from Albania in the north through western Greece, where it is called the Pindos range, effectively cuts off the coastal lands of northwest Greece, and they are not relevant to the main development of Aegean civilization. Mainland geography gives an eastward orientation to the settlement pattern, with the major cultivable areas and their gentle coastlines lying east of the Pindos and directly open to Euboea and the central Aegean islands. Thus communications, by land or sea, are particularly easy around the eastern mainland and Cycladic islands and over to the Anatolian coast. Such geographically-encouraged communication bears a potential for the ready transmission, not just of manufactured objects but of ideas.

Second, as we shall examine in chapter 3, the suitability of the northern plains for cereal crops contrasts with that of south Aegean slopes and soils for the olive-vine-cereal triad. This agricultural contrast has an important bearing on the ability or otherwise of the occupying cultures to develop beyond subsistence. Third, the geographical similarity of Crete and the Peloponnese (medium and small cultivable plains with streams, surrounded by soil-retaining hill slopes with frequent springs and paths of access, often to shorelines) carries, I think, a profound significance. Such land, if carefully developed, together with its adjacent, timber-clad hills, can make its occupants – provided they are not too numerous – self-sufficient in food supplies and in many required natural resources. It

was to be in just these two regions that Aegean culture was to find its richest expression.

Lastly, the physical geography might and in fact at all times in the ancient world did substantially influence the political structure. It was natural for small local centers or kingdoms or city states to arise, in control of their fertile territory defined by mountains and shores. Mediterranean geography is often not greatly dissimilar elsewhere, as we shall note, and the geography of the Aegean was not therefore the determining factor in the rise of civilization. But, for the reasons given, it certainly held within it a potential for civilized development.

The climate of the Aegean, other than in the higher mountains, is a normal Mediterranean one with fairly hot, dry summers and mild winters; the rain falls mainly from October to March, often in heavy downpours. We have no precise information on the Bronze Age climate, but we may reasonably infer that with a recurring settlement pattern of prosperous agricultural communities it cannot have been greatly different from that of today.

The natural resources of the region available to the peoples of the Bronze Age were primarily the plains we have discussed above. Their fertility and clay soil made them ideal for cultivation and for pottery making. Adjacent hills provided an abundance of timber and building stone, while obsidian (hard, black, volcanic glass) came from the

A cup of olives, 3,400 years old, found in the palace at Zakro in 1964.

Cretan Olive trees, flanked by vines and cereals. The three products formed the basis of the Minoan agricultural economy.

island of Melos and served for thousands of years as the precursor of metal for all cutting operations. There were a few deposits of metallic ores: surface copper, lead and silver-bearing galena in the Cyclades and Crete. Lead and galena were found also in Attica, and the copper of the Thessalian mountains may also have been used. There is no evidence that the gold-bearing rocks of mount Pangaion in Thrace were exploited. Alluvial tin might have come from western Anatolia, where there is an early concentration of tin-alloyed objects, but no direct evidence survives. Finally we may note exotic and attractive rocks exploited for art and luxuries, or for industrial tools: marble, porphyry, serpentine, steatite and emery. To augment the food supply the mountain regions maintained a variety of animals for hunting and the sea was exploited as an abundant source of fish, tunny for example being caught in the Cyclades during Neolithic times.

It is clear then that the Aegean was well provided with most basic resources for prosperous development, with the single exception of its poverty in metals. These, particularly copper, were second in importance only to land for those cultures aspiring to civilization.

The Aegean response. Given the physical environment we have described, what was the human response to it? We may speculate first on what might have been expected. If we consider geographically similar areas bordering the Mediterranean on the north – Spain, southern France, Italy, the Dalmatian coast of Yugoslavia, and if we include islands comparable to Crete in size, Sardinia, Sicily, Malta and Cyprus, we find there existed through the Neolithic and Bronze Ages well-developed cultures with some notable achievements. The stone-built round tombs of Los Millares in Spain, the temples of Neolithic Malta, the plentiful and varied bronze tool metallurgy of Italy and the elaborate terracotta models depicting Cypriot religion and daily life come to mind. But in none of these regions can we speak of civilizations in the sense of Minoan Crete or Mycenaean Greece. What in fact developed in the Aegean, with a geography and resources not unlike those of the areas mentioned, was an incomparably greater flowering of the human spirit.

The evolution of Aegean civilization is considered in detail in subsequent chapters. We must now discuss how and why the response to the environment was so distinctly different from those of other prehistoric Mediterranean cultures.

The time factor. The first and rather obvious point in this brief chronological summary is that civilization developed gradually in the Aegean area and did not, like one of its goddesses, Athena, spring fully formed into life. Human occupation in the Aegean has been traced back to nearly 40,000 BC. From then until the mid-7th millennium Palaeolithic and Mesolithic hunters and gatherers of food occupied caves and open sites over most of the Greek mainland. Before 6000 BC new groups began to arrive from Anatolia, introducing the Neolithic way of life which was dependent on permanent settlements practicing the domestication of crops and animals. For some three thousand years Neolithic farming skills established a successful agriculture and stock-raising which were to form the basis of life, though much augmented, throughout the Bronze Age. Meanwhile, in the 4th millennium BC, the extraction of metals from their ores was slowly beginning to be understood.

Then for some four centuries, c. 2600–2200 BC, in the mid-3rd millennium, there was a formative urban period in which the potential of combining a mixed farming economy, based on the Mediterranean triad of the olive, the vine and cereals, with craft specialization based primarily on metallurgy was understood and exploited. From the rapid success of this new, Early Bronze Age living system came the first palaces of Crete (c. 1900–1700 BC).

A crucial factor for Minoan development was that nothing interrupted it. The material culture of the First Palace Period evolved directly from that of the Early Bronze Age. Although the only two substantially excavated Early Minoan II settlements, Myrtos and Vasilike, were destroyed by fire there is no sign here or elsewhere of invaders. Vasilike continued to be occupied and in the case of Myrtos the settlement at Pyrgos continued in prosperity after adjacent Fournou Korifi had perished. The palaces themselves may be seen to have much in common with the Early Minoan settlement type, both economically and in their architectural arrangements.

Myrtos (Fournou Korifi) was a large single-building complex of cellular form divided by passages; near its center was an open area reached by two passages and used as a court. At Vasilike there was a paved court on the west side of the many-roomed building. The Myrtos settlement had well-defined areas of use with several magazines of big storage jars in the southeast corner and northwestern area. Elsewhere were kitchens, living and working rooms and a domestic shrine. All the features we have noted occur later in the palaces, and the Early Bronze Age storage magazines are clear precursors of the rooms with this function in the first palace of Phaistos and the great row of magazines at Knossos.

Burial methods illustrate another aspect of the uninterrupted Cretan development. Round communal tombs and rectangular enclosures for bones continue from Early into Middle Minoan. In the wide range of ceramic forms there is also gradual evolution; many of the classic shapes of the First Palace Period have prototypes in the Early Bronze Age. This is true of other classes of artifact: metalwork, engraved sealstones and stone vessels – evolution and improvement in technique within a firm tradition. Nor is there evidence of newcomers in Crete at the time of the destruction of the first palaces around 1700 BC. The economic and architectural reconstruction in palaces, towns and villas is on the same lines as before and the

Above: Linear A tablets from Aghia Triadha, c. 1450 BC. The predecessor of Linear B, this script has yet to be deciphered, but about two-thirds of its signs were taken over in Linear B. *Below left*: engraved seals were impressed on clay producing sealings such as this one from the palace of Knossos. We see here perhaps a portrait of a Minoan king with an elaborate hairstyle and, below, an example of the earliest form of Minoan writing which was hieroglyphic. The inscription may perhaps give the king's title. 18th–17th centuries BC. *Below right*: a companion sealing from Knossos shows a young boy, perhaps a prince; such representations are very rare.

A view of the palace and courtyard crowning the site of Gournia on the north coast of Crete. 1700–1450 BC.

artifacts develop from earlier types. In metalwork, for example, the triumphs of the swordsmiths of Mallia at the close of the First Palace Period are now developed further in the long swords of the following age. In another important matter recent discoveries have given a vital indication of continuity. At Phaistos, in a room of the first palace, a few tablets in the Linear A script were found with a hoard of clay seal impressions. This suggests that the Minoan writing system, so characteristic of the Second Palace Period when the Minoan civilization was at its height, had already begun to be developed at the time of the first palaces, perhaps from the Minoan hieroglyphic script.

Minoan civilization suffered a huge disaster around 1450 BC, after which it never regained its former brilliance. After the disaster newcomers, Mycenaeans, are found in control of the palace at Knossos and, according to their inscribed Linear B tablets, of much of the island. They are the first new cultural group for which there is clear evidence in Crete since newcomers came, probably from western Anatolia, in the centuries round 3000 BC. The Minoans, for so we may call the culturally unified stock from the start of the 3rd millennium, enjoyed close on 1,500 years of development.

On the Greek mainland the situation through this long period was quite different. In the late 3rd millennium the successful Early Bronze Age proto-urban culture of the Argolid and central Greece, evidenced in the palatial "House of the Tiles" at Lerna, was destroyed, and there are clear signs of newcomers. New house types appear, long

houses with straight or curved (apsidal) ends. Pottery types show many connections with western Anatolia. It looks as though some groups were moving thence west across the Aegean. They may have been responsible for the destruction of the flourishing centers at the end of the Early Bronze Age II and during the Early Bronze Age III (2200–2000 BC), or have arrived in the wake of the destructions. In any case the disturbed pattern of life at the end of the 3rd millennium leads into the Middle Bronze Age culture of the mainland. At Lerna in the Argolid and at Pefkakia near Volos the inhabitants at this time were importing pottery from Middle Minoan Crete; but this was not a period of high civilization on the mainland, though the culture of the Cycladic islands flourished.

The interruptions at mainland centers in the late 3rd millennium in effect delayed the attainment of civilization there for some four centuries. But it cannot have been an entirely unfruitful delay. The sudden and extraordinary richness of the Shaft Graves of Mycenae, beginning at the start of the Late Bronze Age, around 1550 BC, at one time suggested to scholars the explanation that there must have been a big break between the Middle and Late Bronze Ages on the mainland, with newcomers, the people of the Shaft Graves, introducing the Mycenaean civilization. But the discovery of a second grave circle, less rich in the contents of its tombs and slightly older in date than Schliemann's circle, has indicated that the rise of Mycenaean civilization was not so sudden as it had seemed.

The new circle extended back in date into the late Middle Bronze Age and was begun around 1600 BC. It has

The town of Gournia. Note the paved roads among the houses with their small ground-floor rooms.

many links with Crete and the Cycladic islands. Minoan artistic and technological influences were undoubtedly powerful in these formative stages of Mycenaean civilization, but the social and economic basis of its coming into being is to be seen as a development through time, with the gradual formation of strong centers like Pylos, Mycenae, Orchomenos, Eutresis and Lefkandi through the Middle Bronze period, when local chieftains or families acquired distinctive power. The outcome of this hypothetical development is seen in the warrior rulers of the Shaft Graves, powerful in their own territory, trading, very probably for metal, with Epeiros, modern Albania and the Lipari islands (perhaps en route to Tuscany and Sardinia), and ready to derive artistic and cultural advantage from the rich flowering of the Second Palace Period of Crete, which began after 1700 BC.

The documentation of development over a long period of time makes it easier to understand how and why civilization was attained, by gradual capitalization on skills gained and environments more fruitfully used. But this is still a far from sufficient explanation. Other cultures had time for development, but no such spectacular achievement ensued. We should therefore look more closely into the Aegean cultures as systems of living, that is, how a whole cultural unit, like the palace civilization of Crete or of Mycenaean Greece, worked as a complicated system in operation. This is of course only one (rather fashionable) way among many of looking at a culture or civilization, but it does have advantages in trying to understand what was going on. The living system clearly had many distinct

but interrelated activities or subsystems. Let us visualize some.

Living systems. The Early Minoan settlement at Fournou Korifi near Myrtos stands at the formative stage of Aegean civilization, in the 3rd millennium BC. The main components of the way of life of the inhabitants were mixed farming and industrial activities. Agriculture involved the growing of barley, wheat, olives and vines; the stock raised were sheep, goats, pigs and cattle. There is only slight evidence for exploitation of the sea for food, but on land wild fruits, nuts and herbs would have been collected. These separate and distinct activities together made up the food supply subsystem. At the same time extractive industries involved other forms of exploitation of the environment, providing clays for pottery-making, timber, building and artifact stones, lime for plastering, and earths and plants for paints and possibly dyes. These raw materials were then put to use in a wide range of manufacturing industries – pottery, figurines, loom-weights, buildings, stone tools, sealstones, stone figurines, pot decoration, textiles, bone tools and wall plaster. The extractive and manufacturing processes together comprise the industrial subsystem. Religion, trade (import of obsidian and stone vessels, possibly of metal tools, possible export of pottery and textiles) and the organization of the water supply were other distinct and important activities, definable as further subsystems. The complete way of life of the settlement consisted of the obvious interdependence of these separate activities.

The basic structure of the Myrtos living system is paralleled in dozens of contemporary proto-urban settlements throughout the Aegean, with variations such as greater emphasis on objects of wealth, external connections, metalworking or hunting. The Aegean 3rd-millennium pattern as a whole is later repeated on a much larger and more complex scale in the Cretan palaces.

The palaces are the core of the system, as great redistributive centers organizing agriculture and stock-raising and storing the products to ensure a food supply for a hierarchical society, which included experts in many crafts. The growth and developing complexity of the Minoan system are documented by the coastal and inland settlements and the country villas, living units with local economic independence yet in some measure linked by mutual supply and demand to the palace centers. The industrial subsystem was intricately developed and varied, with a wealth of manufactured products in clay, stone, metal, ivory and faience. To supply the raw materials for these activities one subsystem (external connections or trade) had to be greatly expanded from its Early Minoan beginnings; hence in part, Minoan links in the palatial age with mainland Greece (fine stones for vases and seals, silver and lead); the Aegean (possibly marble and emery); Anatolia (probably fine black obsidian); Cyprus (copper); the Levant (probably lapis lazuli and ivory), and Egypt (raw alabaster, finished alabaster vases, ivory and possibly gold). In return, fine pottery, metal and stone vases, seal-stones and probably craftsmen, textiles and spices went out from the palaces.

The living system of the Mycenaean civilization was broadly similar to the Minoan, based on palaces as major redistributive centers with elaborate agricultural, industrial, trading and religious subsystems. Within the basic similarity of structure there are naturally differences of emphasis from the Minoan: for example, the direction of trade (interest in the Adriatic and central Mediterranean as well as the Levant and Egypt), the apparently greater preference (in relation to other crafts) for a ceramic industry producing huge quantities of attractive but not outstanding pottery vessels, major differences in burial customs and the apparently closer control of territory directly from the palaces, with no subsidiary organization of country mansions. But the basic system is akin to that evolved by the Minoans. In each we find multiple interactions of home agricultural and industrial activities, with a vigorous subsystem of external exchange. The pattern had clearly evolved in the less complex living systems of the 3rd-millennium settlements like Lerna, Myrtos, Thermi on Lesbos and the second city of Troy.

In looking at the living systems of the prehistoric Aegean in this way we not only observe civilization in operation through its various component parts, but we must stress the interaction and interdependence of the parts or subsystems. These interactions have been searchingly and brilliantly explored in *The Emergence of Civilization* (1972)

A magnificent rock-crystal rhyton found at Zakro. 1500–1450 BC. The vase is formed from a single crystal with a crystal ring of separate pieces capped with gold, and a handle of crystal beads threaded with a bronze wire. Ht. 20 cm.

by Professor Colin Renfrew, who has proposed their multiplier effect, each subsystem both dependent for its resources on and at the same time responsible for the operation and expansion of other subsystems. For example, agriculture a) needs tools, which are manufactured from extracted metals or gathered stones, which may come by trade (copper, obsidian); b) is protected by religion; c) provides food, which is stored and cooked in pots made from extracted clays. A palace goldsmith needs food, extractive industries and an exchange system (trade) to supply him with raw materials, which would not in turn be extracted unless gold vessels or jewelry were part of the demands of would-be possessors. These are simple series of linked and interacting processes. The great palaces as redistributive centers are multiple and complex instances of precisely the same processes.

Over a long period of time there developed in the Aegean an increasingly complex response to a potentially excellent environment, culminating in the civilizations under study. More and more resources were exploited with increasingly elaborate skills centered on great palatial organizations. In some measure this explains Aegean civilization. But the analysis is still as much descriptive (how civilization worked) as causative. We have still to ask what sets these processes in motion. Why should the subsystems interact, producing such splendid results? We come in the end to an essentially causative hypothesis – individual and collective human abilities.

The human factor. The initial stimulus which set Mycenaean civilization on its way was certainly Minoan, though the stimulation would have been ineffective without a receptive, potentially transformable and hierarchical Middle Helladic society. The products of this society can be seen in the Shaft Graves of Mycenae, where warrior leaders of society were buried with weapons and gold death masks, completely non-Minoan in appearance, surrounded by glorious artifacts to a large extent imported from or artistically indebted to Crete. Thereafter the historical development of Mycenaean civilization involves it in even closer fusion with, and finally control of Crete in the later 15th century BC, before it flourishes with its own specific character through the next two centuries. But in all this time, particularly during the palace period from about 1400 to 1200 BC, the Mycenaean people displayed powerful collective abilities in maintaining such elaborate, mutually dependent subsystems in an effectively unified organization, centered on their palaces.

By the pure chance of their survival these collective, organizational abilities are illuminatingly displayed for us in the records and inventories of goods, produce and people on the Linear B tablets – though these abilities might well have been inferred from the other material remains. Within the living system as a whole individual ability clearly existed. The traditions of artistic and manufacturing skill had long ago been learned, ultimately from the Minoans, in a variety of crafts. But to develop rather than simply repeat these craft products, individual craftsmen of genius were required. The ivory carvers are exemplars, continually producing exquisite yet stylistically different inlays and statuettes of human figures and animals through the palace period. Metalworkers, particularly those skilled in the technology of inlaying different metals into other metals, further demonstrated brilliant individual achievement.

While the Mycenaeans received initial stimulation, both aesthetic and technical, from the Minoans, the latter developed their civilization with extraordinarily little dependence on external abilities. Foreign goods were indeed

Above: an ivory group from Mycenae. It shows two women guarding a child. They may be goddesses (Demeter and Persephone) and wear rich dresses of Minoan style. The Mycenaeans were especially skilled in carving ivory. 13th century BC.

Below: the famous pendant from Mallia, two wasps sucking a drop of honey. Metalworkers displayed brilliant individual achievement. Here techniques of granulation and wire-working are used on an object only a few centimeters in size. 1700 BC.

sought after, particularly ivory and the metals, but foreign ideas are hard to identify and, when traceable, seem to have been rapidly adapted and transformed by the Minoans. For example, from about 2500 BC, they began to carve stone and ivory seals, perhaps getting the basic idea and a few designs from contact with Anatolia, the Levant coastal cities and Egypt; but their seals were soon transformed into the wide range of shapes and elegant varieties of motif found in 3rd-millennium tombs. Among the Minoans we find extraordinary generative powers constantly displayed, which could only have been the result of brilliant individual craftsmen within a richly developing tradition.

The tradition, the interaction of the subsystems developing through time, was one of technical skill and aesthetic appreciation. It is probable that aesthetic sensibility was greatly influenced by the requirements of Minoan religion, for so many of their finest products seem designed for a part in or as a portrayal of ritual activity. But the constant numinous spirit of religion in Bronze Age Crete did not prevent, rather it seems to have inspired the individual genius. Let us examine, individually and then collectively, instances of these human abilities, for they are the distinctive core of the Minoan achievement.

In the 18th century BC the palace workshops at Knossos and Phaistos were producing an abundance of pottery. Some cups and bowls had very slim walls, sometimes of almost eggshell thinness, and were painted to produce a black iridescent surface. To this were added patterns in white, red, orange and occasionally purple. But some of the potters were craftsmen or craftswomen of genius. They possessed the ability to prepare clay which would mold and fire to an incredible thinness and they could relate the color and decorative design to the surface shape of a vase in exquisite proportions; a single large rosette or a highly complex spiraliform pattern would be perfect in size and positioning for the surface curvature.

In the 15th century, 300 years later, the pottery tradition had taken a different turn. Surfaces of fine wares were now a lustrous pale buff. On this a few artists, probably members of a single workshop at Knossos, were painting a variety of naturalistic marine motifs, shells, octopuses, rockwork, seaweed, nautiluses. The understanding of design in relation to shape, the skill in naturalistic representation and the sense of a unified composition in a large, free field are again remarkable. A huge and lifelike octopus amid a wealth of seaweed and rockwork will wriggle its body and tentacles over the strongly curved surface of a closed vase or dominate the flatter surface of an amphora, with the painter in total control of his creature's position in the area defined.

Makers of stone vases practiced throughout the pre-palatial and palace periods. Among the hundreds of attractive but simply-shaped Early Minoan vessels placed in tombs we find the work of at least one lapidary of arresting sensitivity. He made two cylindrical boxes, found at Mochlos and Zakro, of a green stone called chlorite,

covered them with an incised decoration of triangles, and carved as the handle of each lid a long, lean dog, stretched-out as you would find one in any Cretan village today. The naturalism is delightful; so too are the scale and proportion in relation to the box as a whole.

In the Second Palace Period craftsmen in stone of remarkable ability were at work. From the villa or small palace at Aghia Triadha comes a vessel in imitation of a dolium shell, 28.5 centimeters high, carved from a single piece of obsidian. This volcanic stone, black with white speckles, comes from the islet of Yiali in the Dodecanese and is very difficult to work, being brittle as well as very hard. The result is an individual craftsman's triumph of naturalistic representation and technical ability. The same site yielded three vessels in bluish-black stone, a mixture of steatite with serpentine, carved with scenes of human figures in relief. The stylistic similarity of the three pieces is close and all may be the work of a single craftsman-artist.

But the individual who made the so-called Harvester Vase – probably portraying a procession of men going out to sow their land – created a masterpiece. Here are 27 figures marching around a ritual vase a few inches high, figures carved in a field only a few millimeters in depth and yet sometimes rendered four deep across the line of the procession, with a gradual lowering of relief at the side of the procession furthest from the viewer to form a kind of perspective. The figures are bound together as a rhythmic unity by the regularity of their ranks and marching; yet the unity is varied by the clashing interplay of the poles and osiers and the changes in stance and posture of one or two participants. The artist has momentarily captured an intense Minoan delight in action with more than photographic accuracy and detail.

At least two more stone vase-makers left masterpieces in the palace of Zakro. Among the 30 or more vessels of outstanding beauty and technical skill from the site are two rhytons, ritual vases with holes at top and bottom for pouring offerings. One is 31 centimeters high and covered all over with a relief scene showing a mountain peak sanctuary set in a rocky landscape. There are no human figures, but the craftsman has set beautiful clumps of crocuses and Cretan wild goats over the scene. One animal leaps over rocks, another stops to investigate the shrine, others sit peacefully over its doorway, while birds are atop of sacred poles at the sides of the building. The rendering of the whole scene, a summit shrine amid rocks gently falling away, seems deliberately impressionistic in technique, a clear but momentary vision. The subtlety and smoothness of the surface gradations were originally enhanced by a covering of gold leaf, of which a few traces have survived.

The second Zakro vase, of green chlorite like the peak sanctuary rhyton, is a model bull's head. This work is smaller than the conical Peak Sanctuary rhyton and has a hole in the top of the bull's head for pouring in libations, with egress through another hole in the mouth. It is carved

being taken by might and main, caught in a net after flooring at least one hunter; the gentle suasions of a female are used to decoy the other, in which calm state his hoof is easily knotted to a stout rope by his capturer. On each cup we may suggest that the artist understood and chose a narrative treatment, portraying the capture of each animal by successive stages. The scenes are held to a unity by bordering rockwork and trees. As with the sowers' procession on the Aghia Triadha vase, we are given a wonderful sense of space through the balance of arrest and movement.

A precisely similar achievement is found on another masterpiece of this period, a cylindrical box of ivory with a carved relief scene showing another bull capture with one figure leaping down from a tree. This ivory was found in a tomb of slightly later date, around 1400 BC, at Katsamba, the harbor town of Knossos, but belongs stylistically with the creations we have been discussing.

Yet another individual of genius is known to us through two female statuettes of faience. This is a silica-based paste with separately added colored glazes or other coloring agents, which requires a technical mastery of firing conditions. The core is normally fired first and then fired again after the surface glazes and decoration have been added. The two statuettes were found in a shrine repository in the palace at Knossos and are dated around 1600–1550 BC, probably a generation or two older than the creations of

Above: a vessel in the shape of a dolium shell from the Minoan villa at Aghia Triadha, carved from a single piece of obsidian. 1550–1450 BC.

Right: the so-called Harvester Vase, carved in a serpentine-steatite stone and showing a procession of men probably going out to sow their land. Diameter 11.5 cm. 1550–1450 BC.

with great delicacy, the life-like strength of the head and throat contrasting with the idealized rendering in relief of curling hair on the crown and face. The artist had studied and understood the Cretan bull. He or a fellow master craftsman had also made the larger bull's head, of dark blue serpentine with an inlaid band of white shell around the nostrils and eyes of painted rock crystal and red jasper, found in the Little Palace at Knossos. Like that at Zakro it originally bore horns of gilded wood and was a work of equal power and beauty.

In the same period, 1700 to 1450 BC, goldsmiths and silversmiths were also productive. The well-known gold cups from the beehive tomb at Vapheio in the southern Peloponnese are the work of a master of the highest ability. Though found in this mainland tomb, the burial place of a local prince, they are Minoan in style to the smallest detail and must have been imports from Crete. The two drinking cups form a pair: each has a highly naturalistic relief scene in repoussé technique portraying the capture of a bull. One is

A detail from the cup of Vapheio. A highly naturalistic relief scene in repoussé technique portrays the capture of a wild bull by using a cow as decoy. This is perhaps the finest surviving picture of a Minoan male. 1550–1450 BC.

individual artists previously described. They are taken to represent a snake goddess and a votary or possibly two votaries. One holds snakes in her outstretched hands, the other has them crawling over her arms and neck. The latter figure wears a prominent headdress surmounted by a cat, and she may be intended to represent a goddess. In each figure the artist has produced a marvellous representation of Minoan female beauty, with prominent exposed breasts, narrow waist held tight by a high bodice, girdle and long flounced dress. The dresses are decorated with exquisite small-scale patterns, including borders of crocus flowers. The impression given by each work is one of a craftsman's assured technical mastery of materials, combined with an artist's feeling for beauty to serve a ritual function.

As a last example of individual creative ability among the Minoans we may cite an architect and a stonemason. Professor J. Walter Graham showed some years ago that the Minoans had a standard unit of measure, which has been called a foot, equivalent to 30.36 centimeters (nearly 12 inches). He had discovered that the palaces at Knossos, Mallia and Phaistos all had their major dimensions, such as central court and west building block, laid out in specific proportions in whole numbers of Minoan feet. The central courts at Mallia and Phaistos measure 170 by 80 Minoan feet, that of Zakro 100 by 40. The west wing at Phaistos is 100 feet wide at its northern or largest end, while at Mallia the same block measures 150 feet.

The palace of Zakro was discovered after Graham's theory was advanced and its major dimensions confirmed it. It is more than likely that an individual architect, or a small number trained in a single school, devised and planned the palaces according to specific measurements. This is no mean achievement. The executant of the work would have been the architect himself or a master mason. One of the latter built the fine stone keel-vaulted tomb known as the Royal Tomb at Isopata, situated between Knossos and the sea to the north. The monument was totally destroyed in the last war, but Sir Arthur Evans' fine plans, section and elevation, drawn by Theodore Fyfe after the excavation in 1904, show the excellence of the dressed stone and the skilled building techniques used to construct the vault. Ashlar masonry of this type is also frequently found in the palace and surrounding mansions at Knossos. Highly trained and able masons must have prepared it.

Time and again through their history the Minoans produced persons with inherited skills who could express their individual talents, not in just one or two but over an astonishingly wide range of crafts and materials. But individualism is a two-sided coin. While we may feel that the maker of the Vapheio gold cups can properly be called by us a craftsman and artist of genius, there is little or nothing about the Minoan masterpieces to suggest that the craftsmen regarded themselves as distinct individuals, achieving personal works of art like artists since Classical times. These works of art are without signatures in any sense, products

of brilliance and naturalism within a defined tradition – what was required to be made rather than what an artist individually decided to experiment with. And yet the results which have survived make it hard for us not to credit these great craftsmen with some deserved feelings of personal satisfaction when they had finished their masterpieces.

Human initiative and direction are also patent in the collective abilities of the Minoans. Their agricultural system has been described, but as we bring to mind the big clay storage jars for oil, wine and cereals in the magazines at Myrtos (2200 BC), at Phaistos (1700) and at Knossos (1400), we may reflect on the organization required to achieve these results and the subsistence on which the civilization depended. In the second palatial age, 1700 to 1450 BC, as among the Mycenaeans later, the organization of the agricultural and industrial subsystems was aided and controlled by another achievement, writing. We think therefore not only of skilled and trained scribes but of the sense of collective ability implied by the tablet records. At least some Minoans clearly understood the benefits to be derived from the detailed organization and planning by quota of agriculture and industry.

The famous snake goddess or her votary from Knossos (c. 1600–1550 BC). She holds two snakes and has a cat, perhaps a royal symbol, on her head.

Above: a Kamares-style pithos from Phaistos (1900–1700 BC). Notice how the design, probably intending to show fish caught in nets, harmonizes so well with the shape.

Right: the sculptured ceiling of the side chamber in the royal tholos tomb at Orchomenos. 14th century BC. It is similar to painted designs in contemporary Egyptian tombs.

We may also observe collective human initiative in another area. It was the concern of Minoan religion to ensure fertility of crops, animals and the human population and to protect against natural disasters – drought, disease, earthquakes. Deities were given offerings of food or goods in household and rural shrines, sacred caves and mountain peak sanctuaries. Sacred caves, like the Diktaian above Lasithi and the Kamares cave on the south side of mount Ida, must have been collective cult centers, probably for regular ritual performances; the many peak sanctuaries must also have been built and used by the nearest Minoan settlements in the period of the palaces. There was individual worship, as we know from a clay seal impression of an adorant before a mountain goddess and from a single visitor to a shrine, portrayed on a relief stone vase fragment; but religion must have been corporate too, in

uniform sanctuary types for the collective projection of beliefs, fears and hopes.

Few will agree upon what makes the difference between a culture and a civilization. In the case of the Minoans and the Mycenaeans, to summarize our conclusions, there existed a potentially excellent environment of fertile soils, abundant resources (except in copper, tin and gold), a desirable climate and relatively easy land and sea communications. In response to this environment the Aegean peoples developed, over a long period of time, a living system of great richness and complexity. The crucial stage was the Early Bronze Age, the 3rd millennium, when the advantages and potential of combining mixed farming with new, wealth-supplying industrial activities, particularly metalworking, were first understood. From these proto-urban experiments came a whole system based on great palatial centers, with writing as the material, religion the spiritual unifier.

The system comprised distinct groups or subsystems of activity whose growth and essential interdependence produced a balance of man and his environment, with vigorous but not excessive exploitation of resources. This interaction and growth within the system promoted civilization. The causative mechanism, that which frequently set in motion the many processes of interaction between the different aspects of the living system, appears to have been extraordinary individual and collective human abilities. These began to make their mark, simply but imaginatively, in the achievements of the Early Bronze Age peoples and were thenceforward continually at work within a long tradition of inherited skills and aesthetic sensibility.

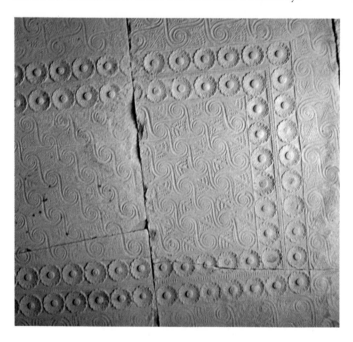

3. Early Farmers and Metalworkers 6000-2000 BC

A Cycladic female figurine in white marble. A strong contrast with
the corpulent creations of the Neolithic period, these standing
figures with folded arms date from the middle phases of the Cycladic
Early Bronze Age (2600-2200 BC).

In the centuries around 6000 BC major changes occurred in the pattern of human settlement in the Aegean. On the Greek mainland the population, dating back to at least 38,000 BC, had relied for subsistence on hunting wild animals, gathering fruits and nuts, and on fishing. Occupation sites with chipped flint tools and animal bones are known in the Louros river valley of northwest Greece and in caves southeast of the lake of Ioannina. Elsewhere they have been traced in Thessaly, around lake Copais in Boeotia, on the northwest Peloponnesian coast in Elis and in the Franchthi cave at the tip of the Argolid peninsula. Settlement may have been widespread, though none has been found in Crete or the islands, in spite of searches, apart from possible traces on Euboea and Skyros.

In the later 7th millennium new population groups arrived and introduced a quite different way of life: permanent settlements on open ground, located in areas where the domestication of animals and crops could be practiced. These Early Neolithic sites have a markedly eastern distribution, being found (from north to south) on the Haliakmon river in Macedonia, along the Peneios river, around the gulf of Volos, the Copais basin, Euboea, the coasts of Attica, the Corinthian region at the head of the gulf of Argos and in the southeast Peloponnese. In Crete there was Early Neolithic occupation from the same date, before 6000 BC, at Knossos and possibly at Katsamba to the north.

The area from which the new population groups came lay to the east of the Aegean, as the eastern distribution of the sites suggests. It may have been Anatolia rather than the Levant or further east, since clay figurine types, stone "ear plugs" and bone "belt hooks" are closely similar in both the Anatolian and Greek Early Neolithic areas. The bull cult was prominent in Minoan religion, as it was at the Neolithic site of Çatal Hüyük in Anatolia; but there is a huge time gap between the Early Neolithic and the earliest evidences for the cult in Crete, in Early Minoan times.

The evolution of settled life. The Early Neolithic settlements, discontinuous with the preceding Mesolithic and Palaeolithic, established a pattern of life – farming communities with communications by sea and land throughout the region – that was to last, basically unchanged, for three millennia. Shipping and land routes are best documented by the collection of obsidian from the island of Melos and its distribution to most Neolithic sites for cutting, boring and scraping tools. The use of obsidian, and thus the presumed existence of some form of shipping, is in fact known now at the Franchthi cave in the Argolid from at least 7000 BC, in the pre-Neolithic levels (possibly the earliest shipping in the world). The basic farming pattern was naturally subject to development in animal and crop husbandry, as well as to fluctuation with the possible arrival of new population groups. These seem to have come during two periods – towards the end of the Early Neolithic in Macedonia and Thessaly, where monochrome pottery with impressed decoration appears which

has Balkan and west Greek connections, and second, towards the end of the Middle Neolithic period, around the mid-5th millennium in Greece generally. Dark burnished wares with Anatolian links and stone arrowheads are new at this time.

The next main development appears gradually, through the later 5th and the 4th millennia. This is incipient metalworking. Five copper hooks and pins were found at Sitagroi in east Macedonia, a gold ornament at Dhimini, silver and copper objects in the Alepotrypa cave of the southern Peloponnese (though their find places within the cave are not known), and a flat copper axe at Knossos, while there were traces of metal smelting in the settlement at Kephala on the island of Kea, datable to about 3500 BC.

In the centuries around 3000 BC – conventionally but very imprecisely termed the beginning of the Bronze Age – new groups seem to have reached at least some parts of the Aegean and to have come from western Anatolia. Along the north Aegean in Thrace and eastern Macedonia pottery forms display similarities with those of early Troy. In the Cyclades the earliest Bronze Age groups, called the Grotta-Pelos culture after sites on Naxos and Melos, used bowls with heavy rims closely related to those of Kum Tepe in the Troad; while in Crete there are very many close pottery parallels between Early Minoan I and contemporary cultures in northwest Anatolia.

Towards urban life. A new farming pattern soon developed in this Early Bronze Age. It was based on the exploitation of the olive and the vine together with the traditional cereals. Olives and vines require much less working time for their cultivation than does a wholly cereal agriculture. Thus the labor force is more freely available for other work, a factor not unimportant in the development towards civilization.

Along with these new agricultural developments there occurred a fairly rapid expansion of metallurgy. In comparison with Early Bronze Age I, the range of tool types produced in the next period, Early Bronze Age II, is striking. The Cycladic and Early Minoan graves have produced most of these copper and arsenical or tin bronze artifacts, but the few hoards and settlement finds show that the tools were also intended for use in daily life. Their

potential value for farming and all types of building and woodworking is enormous when compared with the range of the stone tool kit.

These two developments, in agriculture and metallurgy, play a major part in the evolution of the first urban phase in the Aegean in the mid-3rd millennium BC. Other factors were involved, as we saw in chapter 2, but the very long tradition of Neolithic skills and practices was not canceled or replaced; for example chipped and ground stone tools continued in common use through the whole Bronze Age, and the cellular structure of the Early Bronze Age building complex at Myrtos has much in common with that of Late Neolithic Knossos. Rather, the Neolithic inheritance was transformed, with new agricultural and industrial adaptations which were to determine the subsequent development of the Aegean Bronze Age.

Dating. The varied aspects of the life of the early farming communities and first metallurgists may now be examined in more detail, but first it will be useful to summarize the dating structure of the four millennia from about 6000 to 2000 BC. Our means of dating are stratification – superposed occupation levels – and radiocarbon determinations. Through a study of stratification we can build up a relative structure of dating – the relation of a level at one site to those preceding and following it and then the relation of that stratified level or levels to those of other sites. To these relative dates are added the absolute dates provided by the radiocarbon method. By 1974 there were more than 110 dated samples for the Aegean from the beginning of the Neolithic through the Early Bronze Age, and they cohere remarkably well with the relative sequence constructed

Opposite: a clay figurine of a woman found near Pharsala in Thessaly from the Middle Neolithic period (5th millennium BC). These Neolithic terracotta sculptured Venuses emphasize fertility.

Right: an Early Cycladic sauceboat or drinking cup (2600–2200 BC) from Spedos on the island of Naxos. Length 27.7 cm. The type is common in Greece and the Cyclades in the Early Bronze II period.

from the stratified levels. As a result of correlating radio-carbon and tree ring dates we have the following approximate dating structure for the Neolithic and Early Bronze Ages in the Aegean.

Settlements. Although settlements are found all over the Aegean in the Neolithic period, their distribution is not uniform. From western Greece few sites are known, though there was occupation in the Ionian islands; again almost nothing has been found in the Cyclades except for Saliagos and a few associated sites in the Middle and early Late Neolithic, and Kephala (on Kea) in the Final Neolithic. Apart from Knossos there was little occupation in Crete until the Late and Final Neolithic periods. By contrast, eastern Greece was extensively occupied, as we have seen above. In the east Aegean there was occupation at the Aghio Gala cave on Chios in the Middle Neolithic, and from then on through the Early Bronze Age at Emborio on the same island. Occupation began at Poliochni on Lemnos, in the Troad and probably on other east Aegean islands in the Final Neolithic, around 3500 BC.

In the Early Bronze Age there is a radical shift in the occupation pattern. While Boeotia, the eastern Peloponnese and east Aegean continue to support many flourishing settlements, northern Greece loses most of its importance; the Early Bronze Age in Thrace, Macedonia and Thessaly is a paltry affair in comparison with the achievements of its Neolithic period. But in contrast the Cycladic islands and Crete are covered with settlements and cemeteries evincing a material life of richness and variety. A major factor in the change was agriculture: the plains of northern Greece are best suited to cereal crops, the marginal lands and smaller plains of the south to the olive and the vine, with cereals interspersed among them.

The Neolithic population occupied two main types of site, caves and settlements on the open ground. The latter gradually assumed the shape of large mounds as new buildings were erected over those which had passed out of use. Caves provided ready-made shelter, could be spacious like Alepotrypa in southern Greece, usually had that vital commodity, a water supply, and were normally adjacent to cultivable or pastoral land or usable coast, like Franchthi in the Argolid. If the cave had natural divisions, a common feature in the limestones of Greece, some could be used for living, others for burial. A settlement on open ground would be located to take best advantage of natural features, like Nea Nikomedeia and Servia which were near or on the Haliakmon river and adjacent to fertile plains.

On open sites in northern Greece the free-standing houses had a timber frame with vertical posts supporting wattle and daub walls. These had a smooth white plaster coating inside. An internal row of posts would support a pitched roof. Very recently remarkably well-preserved remains of a floor and a roof have come to light. At Servia in west Macedonia there was a Late Neolithic floor with a hard plaster surface which had a substructure of parallel logs set in hardened mud. At Prodromos near Karditsa in Thessaly a wooden roof more than 10 by 10 meters in size, from the Early Neolithic period, was found in 1970, completely preserved. It was made of trunks and branches, some in their natural logged state, others worked into rough planks, all fastened together by large wooden nails. Internal fittings within the houses consisted of domed clay ovens, slightly raised hearths and clay storage bins.

At Sesklo however, and elsewhere in Thessaly, there was a different building technique. In the Middle Neolithic period square or trapezoidal houses had well-built walls of stone with mud-brick forming the upper parts. Cobbled courtyards and passages surrounded the houses, and the settlement, in plan and building methods, seems to have been similar to that of Haçilar level VI (Late Neolithic) in Anatolia. Internal buttresses at Otzaki and Tsangli are similar to those found in houses at contemporary Çan Hasan, again in Anatolia.

At Knossos the buildings were similar to those of Sesklo. We find a complex of several rectangular rooms and little cobbled areas forming a cellular structure. Walls were of stone in the lower part, up to a meter high, with baked mud bricks or pisé (rammed earth) above. Internal fittings included a cobbled bench, a clay platform bordered by stones and a cupboard; outside were hearths, storage pits and cooking holes.

During the Early Bronze Age we find the Neolithic tradition of timber-framed long houses continuing in north Greece while houses of similar plan but of stone construction appear in the eastern Aegean at Troy, Poliochni on Lemnos and Thermi on Lesbos. The sites where these houses are found, however, represent a much more advanced architectural and social achievement than anything in the Neolithic. We are concerned now with small towns fortified by strong stone walls and bastions. In the south Aegean smaller fortified sites are found at Lerna and on Syros, Naxos and possibly Siphnos in the Cyclades. The island house architecture so far known is unimpressive: small single or two-room rough stone dwellings of little constructional merit. But at Lerna the House of the Tiles was a substantial building of stone and mudbrick, 12 meters by 25, with many rooms and corridors, staircases to an upper floor and a pitched roof with terracotta and stone tiles. Other houses at Lerna were also of a substantial size.

At Eutresis in Boeotia House L was of Early Bronze II date like the House of the Tiles and consisted of three rooms, one with a fine circular hearth with raised edge and a stone bench. At Aghia Eirene on Kea there is a well-built group of rooms of the same date with a raised hearth like that at Eutresis. In Crete the buildings at Myrtos are not

Opposite: a marble figurine of a woman from the Early Neolithic period (6th millennium BC), found near Sparta. This is the most complete example of Neolithic stone sculpture from anywhere in Greece. Here too corpulence is probably suggestive of fertility.

Above: a view of the House of the Tiles at Lerna, c. 2200 BC. It is the most complete building of the Early Bronze Age on the Greek mainland.

Right: Early Bronze Age rooms at Aghia Eirene on Kea: well built but on a smaller scale than the House of the Tiles at Lerna. 2600–2200 BC. The houses are very similar to those in the Greek islands today.

unlike those of Neolithic Knossos, but some walls were completely of stone and the masonry of the later, Early Minoan II phase is often good. At Vasilike there were timber supports in the stone and mud-brick walls and a fine, red plastered finish to the surfaces.

Domestication. In the 7th millennium BC the first Neolithic settlers introduced a mixed farming system based on the domestication of plants and animals. The pattern is clear from faunal and floral remains in the earliest levels of newly occupied sites, while at the Franchthi cave there is a clear faunal change from the Mesolithic and earlier assemblages. On present evidence we must conclude that new settlers brought with them domesticated animals and seeds.

The Thessalian sites have produced evidence of einkorn wheat, millet, oats, vetch and peas, and acorns were collected. At Knossos the earliest level gave a grain sample consisting almost entirely of bread wheat, with emmer wheat, einkorn, hulled and naked barley present in small quantities. Lentil and weed seeds also occurred. Before the end of the Neolithic period figs, grapes, almonds and pistachio nuts were being collected. At Sitagroi the transition from wild to domesticated vines can be observed in the grape pips and stalks recovered in the excavations. This transition had taken place by 3000 BC. As yet we know little of the purity of individual fields of crops, but the Knossos sample suggests the deliberate growth of a fairly pure wheat crop as early as the 7th millennium.

In the Early Bronze Age we have noted a significant agricultural development. The south Aegean sites changed over to a system based on the olive, the vine and cereals. At Myrtos nearly 80 per cent of the wood charcoals analyzed were olive wood, probably the remains of branches after pruning. A single olive stone was found and another was reported from an Early Minoan I well at Knossos. Charcoals, probably of domestic olive wood, were found in the Early Bronze I settlement at Thermi on Lesbos. Again, at Early Minoan II Myrtos remains of grape pips and stalks, probably from wine-making, lay in two jars. New evidence from Debla indicates that einkorn, emmer wheat, oats and barley were grown in western Crete in the Early Bronze Age. But Lerna has provided the fullest evidence: almonds, barley, broad beans, brome grass, einkorn, emmer, figs, grapes, lentils, oats, peas, strawberry tree fruit and vetches were all grown or collected for food in the Neolithic period and Early Bronze Age.

The domesticated animals of the earliest Neolithic settlers were primarily sheep and goats. They make up about three-quarters of the animal bones in the first Neolithic phases at Knossos. Most of the remainder were from pigs and seven per cent were of small cattle. The same species, and in similar proportions, are found at Nea Nikomedeia in Macedonia and Argissa in Thessaly. At Knossos there is a steady rise in the proportion of cattle through the Early Neolithic period. Their value as a source of meat, milk and hide was increasingly realized. A few canids, probably jackal or domestic dog, were also present. Hunting did not of course cease in the Neolithic period or Early Bronze Age. Deer, hare, rabbit and wild fowl were caught. Shellfish were collected and fishing was practiced. At Saliagos bones of tunny, an excellent source of meat, were found in abundance. At Troy dolphins, tunny and other fish augmented the food supply.

The best faunal evidence available comes from Lerna. From the Neolithic and Bronze Ages as a whole no less than 23 species of animals were recorded. In the Neolithic period the following were known and probably eaten: domestic dog, red fox, European hare, wild boar, pig, red deer, sheep, goat, wild ox, domestic cattle and several species of birds. In the Early Bronze Age we find all these plus the ass, badger, beech marten, common otter, roe deer and wolf. Finally in the Middle Bronze Age, brown bear, lynx and horse were added.

Unlike agriculture, animal husbandry underwent no major change in the Early Bronze Age. Sheep and goats continued to predominate, while cattle and pigs remained secondary, as is still the situation today. But a single cow and even one pig always provided much more meat than a sheep or goat.

Arts and crafts. After an initial phase, when containers must have been made of leather, wood or plaited basketry, the Neolithic people began to produce fired pottery, soon after 6000 BC. Alongside red or dark monochrome wares some attractive painted styles developed, especially in Thessaly. Here in the Middle Neolithic or Sesklo period vivid red motifs, especially a flame or dog's-tooth pattern, were painted on a cream surface. In the Late Neolithic or Dhimini period bold checkerboard, zigzag, meander and spiral designs covered open bowls. In northern Greece at Sitagroi we find graphite-painted ware with dark, silvery gray spirals and swirls on a black surface, while in the Cyclades at Saliagos dark monochrome goblets are enlivened by white-painted designs. Shapes meanwhile were conservative and functional – store jars and bowls and footed goblets for eating and drinking.

Figurines of clay and stone were either schematic, or lifelike representations of the human form. Of the latter most are female, with emphasis on breasts, buttocks and genital organs. A clay statuette from Lerna is, to modern eyes, one of the most attractive. Male figurines also occur, though far more rarely. A fine piece, smoothly sculptured in a white, marble-like limestone, comes from Early Neolithic Knossos. It is, however, the Thessalian sites which have produced the most examples. One from Prodromos

indicates the moment of birth. At Nea Nikomedeia a clay female figure was originally constructed from separately made parts. Sitagroi has produced many arresting works reminiscent of the rich Balkan figurine art of the Vinča period. Detail was usually added by incision, painting and applied pieces of clay.

Craftsmanship also found expression in the banded marble vessels of Nea Makri in Attica and in exquisitely carved ornaments like the greenstone frogs of Nea Nikomedeia. Nor must we forget the scores of ground and polished stone axes, found on every site, or the spherical, pierced maceheads of Knossos, often in hard and attractive stones. These everyday tools were also skilled pieces of workmanship.

We do not know if in the Neolithic period there were specialist craftsmen or women making only one kind of object, such as figurines or pottery. But the modest degrees of skill and mastery of materials suggest that there was no rigorous specialization, save possibly among the stone bowl makers of Nea Makri. But in the Early Bronze Age specialist groups seem to have existed, on the evidence of the quantity of production, especially of grave goods, the wide variety of crafts and the resulting technical knowledge. It is not known whether each settlement had its own metalworkers, potters and stone workers or whether particular places specialized in one product and distributed it widely through the Aegean. Eventually scientific analyses of trace element composition patterns will throw light on these questions of provenance and distribution.

For the moment we rely largely on style. Some groups of objects, such as the mottled Vasilike ware or the fine

A clay jar from Dhimini, of the Late Neolithic period, c. 3000 BC. Bowls of this period in the Dhimini style display bold checkerboard, zigzag, meander and spiral designs.

gray incised pottery of Crete, some varieties of Cycladic white marble figurines, or complicated methods of gold-work, are so similar wherever they appear that they might well have originated from one or a very few workshops and have been distributed by exchange. Or else they may be the works of locally based craftsmen or women closely in touch with the ideas, methods and products of their fellows elsewhere in the Aegean.

Potters were active everywhere in the Early Bronze Age. On the mainland they were content with jugs, cups, bowls, jars in monochrome, painted or burnished wares, while dark-on-light painted patterns were rare. One popular shape, probably a drinking cup, is named the sauceboat after its resemblance to the modern form. In the Cyclades, unlike the mainland, the pottery comes mainly from tombs. In Early Bronze I footed jars, pyxides (cylindrical boxes with lids), globular bottles and shallow dishes (now called frying pans), are all dark monochrome with incised or impressed patterns. These are developed in Early Bronze II into fine spiraliform designs. Meanwhile painted ware begins in the islands, simple dark-on-light designs on jugs, cups, bowls, pyxides and sauceboats. Finally, in the late 3rd millennium, while painted wares and two-handled tankards are found alongside new shapes on the mainland, in the Cyclades there is a return to incision and curious new forms, ring vases and duck vases (called after a slight resemblance).

In Crete the potter's craft flourished brilliantly through the whole Early Bronze Age. Painted wares, red on buff and white on red, are found alongside red and dark mono-chrome on a very wide range of shapes from Early Minoan I onwards. Mottled Vasilike ware and fine gray polished and incised ware are added in Early Minoan II and white-painted patterns on dark surfaces are common in the final Early Bronze period. Some 23 different shapes were in use at Myrtos at the close of Early Minoan II and there are many additional ones from tombs. All this pottery is handmade, on simple hand-turned disks like those found in the potter's workshop at Myrtos.

In Crete other crafts were those of the stone vase maker and seal carver. Hundreds of vessels in pretty marbles, limestones, breccias, serpentines and steatites were carved and drilled out for grave goods, while seal carvers worked in soft stones, ivory and bone to produce exquisite stamp and cylinder seals with geometric or representational designs. The seals also are known largely from tombs, but were probably worn first by their owners when living. At Lerna on the mainland groups of Early Bronze II clay sealings for store jars bore the impression of over 80 different engraved seals. The latter did not survive and were presumably made of wood. The splendid variety of geometric designs, spirals, meanders and quadrants is occasionally enlivened with a spider or rosette. The execution is precise and there is a pleasing relation of pattern to circular surface.

Cycladic craftsmen made wonderful use of their abun-

The underside of a terracotta dish from the Early Cycladic II period (2600–2200 BC); the spiral motifs at the bottom include the stylized outline of a ship.

dant white marbles. They produced scores of bowls and jars for grave offerings and a far greater number of figurines from a few centimeters to a meter in height. Upright figures (intended to lie flat in graves) are usual, female being much commoner than male. But some are more complex creations, a seated figure playing a harp, another standing and playing double pipes and others seated on stools and one on a high-backed chair, found in a grave on Naxos in 1971. The best works suggest much sensibility on the part of their makers, in their understanding of the relation of marble surfaces to simple forms, delicately transformed with the minimum of sculptured detail.

The metallurgists were also remarkably skilled. Shaft-hole axes, daggers, spearheads, chisels, borers, fish hooks, pins, and a harpoon were all produced in bronze for daily use. Bowls and drinking goblets of gold and silver, less commonly of bronze, adorned the houses of the wealthy. Exquisite jewelry in the same precious metals has been found in astonishing quantity in the 16 treasures of Troy II and the great treasure of Poliochni, as well as the lovely naturalistic olive and flower sprays in thin gold sheet found at Mochlos. The goldsmith's techniques of wire-work, thin-sheet-cutting, the joining of thousands of minute links in chains and repoussé decoration were known all over the Aegean, from the Troad to Crete, the Cyclades, the Peloponnese and Lefkas in the west. When one reflects that in the Great Treasure alone at Troy, in addition to dozens of other gold, silver and bronze objects there were 8,700 gold beads of various shapes and sizes, one gains some idea of the specialist knowledge, skill and productive capacity of the workshops of the early Aegean craftsmen.

These products were functional and decorative, intended for religious or burial purposes, or for daily use. Equally though, when we contemplate the figurines and the jewelry, we can scarcely doubt a clear appreciation of skill, design and decoration on the part of both maker and user.

Religion. There is very little indisputable evidence for the religious beliefs and practices of the early farmers and proto-urban peoples of the Aegean. But there need be no doubt that religion did play a fundamental part in life. The earliest Neolithic settlers seem to have arrived from Anatolia, and here, at Çatal Hüyük, the attempt to derive a beneficent and sympathetic response from nature by magic and symbolism is most vividly portrayed in the frescoes and reliefs on the walls of the shrine rooms. At Çatal and Haçilar many female figurines were found in a rich variety of postures and groupings with other figures or animals.

One at least, a female giving birth on a throne flanked by two felines, seems to be divinity, perhaps a prototype of the later Aegean Mistress of Animals and Goddess of childbirth, Artemis Eileithyia.

The most suggestive Aegean Neolithic evidence is the clay (baked and unbaked) and stone figurines, mostly female but sometimes male. These are sometimes close to the Anatolian ones in style and shape, and are certainly concerned with fertility. One seems to represent the act of birth. The maintenance and increase of the population seem to have been strongly desired, but the precise function of the figurines in this respect is not known. Some female examples could have been images of a goddess of childbirth, or votive offerings of women seeking fecundity. Others, with prominent breasts and genital organs, may well have been representations of or votives to a female deity or deities to promote fertility among humans, crops and animals generally. Unfortunately the find spots of these figurines tell us little. No less than 154 have been discovered recently in a small area of excavation at Prodromos in Thessaly, but all are reported to have been in the earth fill of the Neolithic settlement. But at Early Neolithic Nea Nikomedeia five were found in an imposing central building. They may have been votives in a shrine. The Aegean figurine types, and their sometimes close parallels

Above: a seal of the Early Minoan period from the round tomb at Marathokephalo in the plain of Mesara in southern Crete. A fine example of ivory carving, it shows a human figure and a scorpion on each side of a stylized line of cereal grains.

Right: the Keros harpist. This Early Cycladic statuette in white marble suggests much sensibility on the part of its maker in his understanding of the relation of marble surfaces to simple forms.

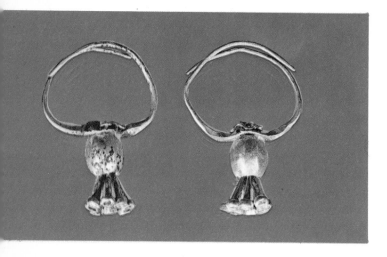

Some of the finest Early Bronze Age jewelry from the Aegean, these pieces were part of a gold treasure from a house at Poliochni on Lemnos. They are about contemporary with the famous Trojan treasure and many of the techniques and shapes are the same.

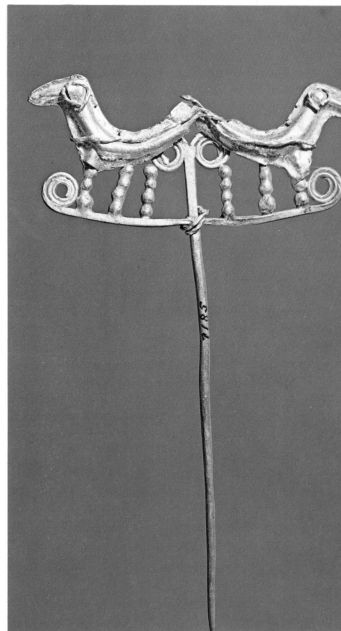

Left: a small gold bead from a necklace found in an Early Minoan round tomb at Kalathiana in Crete. The wire spirals were imitated by potters and makers of green stone vessels.

with the richer and often clearly religious Anatolian pieces, form the best evidence for fertility religion in the Aegean Neolithic period.

In the Early Bronze Age we have evidence for a domestic household shrine at Myrtos in Crete with a female cult figurine on a stone stand. By the end of that period in the island, stone-built sanctuaries were also being set up on mountain summits. Sometimes there had been great bonfires at the sanctuaries, with clay figurines of humans, or parts of humans, animals, and insects such as beetles thrown in. The ritual may have been apotropaic – to turn away plague and disease from humans – just as similar little votives such as eyes, arms and legs are now hung in Greek churches, to seek health or give thanks for its recovery. The animal figurines may be symbolic sacrifices to the Mistress of Animals, who was worshiped on mountain peaks.

The function of the lovely white marble figurines of the Early Bronze Age from the Cyclades is quite unknown. Cycladic figurines seem to derive stylistically from Aegean Neolithic types, but this need not imply similarity of purpose. They were frequently placed in graves, but have occasionally been found in settlements. Most are female, with an incised triangle to denote the pubic area. There is nothing obviously religious about the figurines, but such a function cannot be excluded. The famous seated or standing musicians seem purely secular.

Burial customs. Few Neolithic burials are known, but the practice seems to have been simple inhumation in grave pits. At Prodromos there was a secondary burial of skulls under a house floor, as at Çatal Hüyük. One or two children were buried in clay jars. In the Final Neolithic period (the 4th millennium) there are certain developments. A cemetery with at least seven cremations in black burnished jars was found at Souphli in Thessaly, and another of stone-built cist graves with multiple burials at Kephala on Kea. At these sites, and earlier at Prosymna in the Argolid, the occasional pot had been added as a grave offering.

In the Early Bronze Age, cist tomb cemeteries continued in the Cyclades, sometimes with several hundred graves in one cemetery. At first pots and white marble bowls were included as grave goods; later a rich variety of offerings accompanied burials in the Keros-Syros culture tombs of the second half of the 3rd millennium – marble bowls and cups, figurines and palettes, pottery vessels, metal tools and jewelry, obsidian blades and occasional carved stone seals, amulets or beads. Similar pots, metal tools and jewelry are found in the circular stone platforms with inset graves at Lefkas in the Ionian islands. Little is known of Early Bronze Age tombs on the mainland, but pit graves at Early Bronze II Zygouries contained pottery and a little jewelry. In eastern Attica at Marathon and Aghios Kosmas there were stone cist graves of Cycladic type with multiple burials accompanied by pots.

Crete produces by far the greatest variety of tomb types and richness of grave goods, though burial, whether primary or secondary, is always communal. In the south central area one or more large circular tombs were built of stone. The five discovered by St. Alexiou near Lebena are good examples. The walls were inclined inwards, and rose to form a roughly corbeled roof, or supported one of wooden beams covered with stones. The entrance was a little low doorway, sometimes of two upright slabs with a lintel. A large slab blocked the entrance. In front of this was a pit to give access for burial, or else a whole series of added rectangular chambers.

A tomb might remain in use for several hundred years and contain dozens, if not hundreds of burials. A settle-

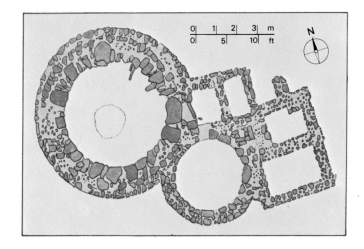

Above: a plan of the Early-Middle Minoan tomb II at Lebena. The burial chambers are circular; the rectangular rooms served for drinking toasts and other rituals. 3000–1700 BC.

Below: a "modern" cheese dairy on mount Ida. This building style, still in use today, shows how the famous round tombs may have been constructed. Note the low doorway and lintel, as in the tombs.

ment could have two or three such tombs in use at the same time, as at Koumasa and Platanos. It has been suggested that these were for separate clans. Grave goods included pots, small stone vessels, metal weapons, toilet tweezers and scrapers, gold jewelry, necklaces of clay and stone and gold beads, engraved stone and ivory seals, amulets and obsidian blades. The external chambers were used as ossuaries for secondary burials, storerooms for grave goods and, most interestingly, as rooms for ritual performances such as the pouring of libations and deposition of food offerings, probably at the time of burial. There is no clear evidence for a continuing cult after death and burial.

Elsewhere in Crete we find burials in caves, in stone-built mortuary houses in the cliffs of Mochlos (with very rich jewelry and stone vessels), in rock-cut tombs with cobbled entrance areas near Siteia in the east, and multiple secondary burials in ossuaries at Palaikastro on the east coast and at Arkhanes south of Knossos. By the end of the

Two Early Minoan I painted vases (3000–2600 BC) from tomb II at Lebena. The little barrel on the left in the red-on-white style is similar to some at Troy, as is the red-on-buff pot shaped like an animal.

Early Minoan period, individual burial in clay pithoi had begun.

The burial practices of the Aegean Early Bronze Age imply a clear belief in some kind of afterlife for which grave goods, often objects of daily use, were needed. But the removal of bones to ossuaries or the retention of only the skulls in a heap, and the general disregard for earlier burials when admitting later ones, all suggest that the grave goods were for a limited time span. Possibly belief in some journey required the provision of the necessities of living; after its arrival in the afterworld the spirit, beyond human control, could be assumed to take care of itself.

Communications and external connections. In a region so endowed with easy coastal and inter-island routes, frequent communication was easy and natural. It is neatly documented for us during the four millennia of the Neolithic period by the distribution of obsidian from Melos. Found in the Franchthi cave from Mesolithic levels, datable to about 7000 BC, it occurs later on most Neolithic and Bronze Age sites. Settlers had come to Crete by sea well before 6000 BC in boats or rafts big enough to transport grain and domestic sheep, goats, cattle and pigs. Our first evidence of actual ships comes in the Early Bronze Age – lead models of long boats from Naxos and clay models from Mochlos and Palaikastro in Crete. Little engravings of ships on Cretan seals datable to around 2000 BC indicate a mast and rigging, and therefore sailing ships.

Another good indication of contact within the region is the wide distribution of similar objects, such as the gold jewelry found in Troy II, Poliochni, the Cycladic graves, Mochlos and the south Cretan round tombs, and Lefkas in the west. Traveling jewelers and goldsmiths clearly communicated ideas, techniques or actual pieces of finished craftsmanship. The export of white marble figurines from the Cyclades to Greece and Crete is another instance of exchange and contact within the region. We may confidently state that by the mid-3rd millennium BC there was a cultural continuum throughout the whole Aegean. Goods and ideas were frequently exchanged, although each major region preserved the basic individuality of its own cultural traditions in settlement buildings, manufactured goods, religious and burial customs. The binding factors were the relatively easy physical routes, a common agricultural economy and shared knowledge of the advantages, in material terms, of urban living.

The extent of the region's external contacts is more difficult to determine. The Aegean clay female figurines, bone belt (or fish) hooks and stone "ear studs" are closely similar to such objects found at Anatolian Çatal Hüyük and Haçilar, so that colonization and the introduction of farming from Anatolia at the beginning of the Aegean Neolithic seem probable. The new colonists at Knossos left a heap of their imported or recently introduced local cereal grains on the floor of their first settlement. Three thousand years later pottery finds in northern Greece and Crete again suggest close contact with and probably some movement from western Anatolia. Early Minoan I shapes have close counterparts in Troy I and immediately preceding northwest Anatolian cultures, even to peculiar barrel-shaped vessels on four feet and little animal vases, again on feet and with a head or spout at one end and a stumpy tail at the other. At the end of the 3rd millennium pottery cups, wheelmade bowls and two-handled drinking goblets used in the Cycladic islands, especially on Kea and Syros, at Manika and Lefkandi in Euboea and in a few instances at Lerna and elsewhere on the mainland, are extremely close to those of Troy III to V. It is as yet unclear whether this represents exchange or further movement from Anatolia. With the new foundation at Lefkandi and a series of burnt destructions in Early Bronze III on the mainland, followed immediately by these new wares, actual new arrivals seem a distinct possibility.

Crete appears to have been untouched by all this, but Early Minoan centers were importing fine stone vessels from Egypt and, late in the millennium, imitating Egyptian stone types in local Cretan rocks. Around 2000 BC they brought back Egyptian scarabs, and may have imported ideas for metal daggers from the Levant, possibly even a few specimens from the workshops of Byblos. Gold for beads and jewelry and ivory for seal carving were also imported, probably from Egypt or the Levant, and some motifs on engraved seals are Anatolian or Egyptian. From about 2600 BC necklaces, consisting of hundreds of tiny faience beads, appear in the south Cretan round tombs and suggest that the knowledge of making faience was learned from Egypt, where just such necklaces had long been in vogue. At the same time two or three silver daggers in Crete may well have come from Italy, while Minoan or Cycladic bronze daggers appear at Lefkas and in Albania.

The pattern seems then to have been one of periodic

One of the finest Early Minoan stone vessels, a shallow spouted bowl of banded tufa, from the tombs of Mochlos. 2600–2200 BC.

movements from Anatolia westwards to the Aegean. In addition Crete developed links with Egypt in the 3rd millennium. These, together with Levantine coastal visits, became more frequent at the close of the Early Bronze Age. Both Crete and the Cyclades seem to have enjoyed some contact with western Greece and may well have been in occasional touch with the 3rd-millennium Villafrancan and Remedello cultures of Italy. The movements from Anatolia and the reception of ideas from Egypt and the Levant clearly played some part in the achievements of the 3rd millennium in the Aegean, although, as we have seen, the development of flourishing little townships by farmers, skilled craftsmen and traders on the threshold of civilization was in the main a locally inspired and created phenomenon.

Society. Now that we have surveyed the major features of this long period we may choose some examples of widely different types of settlement in order to consider how the communities of the time actually lived.

By 7000 BC people had already occupied the Franchthi cave, on the coast near the southern tip of the Argolid peninsula, for 3,000 years. These people knew nothing of the domestication of animals or crops but had evolved a varied range of activities to support themselves. Groups would leave the cave to hunt red deer and, less commonly or with less success, foxes, wild pig, dogs and large wild oxen or bison. They were fishermen too and they left the vertebrae of their catch within the cave. For dealing with the acquired meat, chipped flint and obsidian tools were used. Both materials had to be collected and brought from elsewhere, the flint from some mainland source but the obsidian from across 130 kilometers of open sea, from its source on the island of Melos. Even if a longer route were

used with other islands as stepping stones, much open sea still had to be crossed in some kind of boat or raft of wood, hewn with axes of flint. The only other equipment found seems to have been awls and points of bone from the hunted animals, used for binding and stitching hides to make clothes and containers. One other tradition had been practiced a millennium before 7000 BC, but we do not know if it was continued. A burial was made inside the cave; there was perhaps already an idea of respect for the dead – body or spirit – since the burial was covered with small stones.

A few hundred years after this glimpse of life at Franchthi a site was occupied by newcomers on the fertile plain of Macedon, at modern Nea Nikomedeia near the river Haliakmon. Separate houses were built, up to 11 meters in length. The walls were of wattle and daub on a frame of upright wooden posts. Floors were of mud plaster laid over matting of broad-leaved marsh grass, gathered from near the adjacent river. Inside the house one would find a raised plaster platform into which had been sunk a hearth and storage bin. The house also contained a clay oven. Household equipment consisted of pottery – jars and bowls with ring feet to give them balance. The pots were monochrome, dark gray, beige or reddish brown with a surface coat in pink, light orange or red brown. There were also fine painted pots with designs in red on a creamy ground or a white on red-brown. Other household objects included spinning and weaving equipment (bone needles with eyes, spindle whorls, and loom weights), as well as stone axes, other ground stone tools and chipped obsidian for daily tasks. For ornament a lucky few possessed exquisite little frogs carved in greenstone and there would also be a stamp seal or two of clay with zigzag designs. Mats on the floor left the impressions of their twining and

Early Minoan Vasilike: a view from the west. Note the paved western courtyard. The rooms had red-plastered walls and were filled with fine pottery from the destruction, c. 2200 BC.

twilled manufacture on the bases of wet clay pots put out to get sun-dried before firing in the kiln.

From the long house a villager could go to the large, square central building, 12 meters by 12, divided into three by parallel rows of posts. Here he would find little human statuettes of terracotta a few inches high, made by fitting together separate parts and beautifully modeled to emphasize female fertility. The style, with prominent breasts, buttocks and abdomen, and long neck with slit "coffee bean" eyes, was traditional, brought by ancestors from Anatolia across the Aegean. Five of these figures were found; the imposing central building which housed them may have been a shrine.

Away from their homes the people spent their time in cultivation on the plain; they grew wheat, barley, lentils and peas, and also gathered pistachio nuts and acorns. Flocks of sheep and goats were their chief animals, though cattle and pigs were also bred. The food supply was supplemented by hunting in the adjacent hills; wild cattle, pig, deer and hare were caught. Occasionally the day would be enlivened by the arrival of their own journeymen or foreign traders bringing obsidian from the south for new tools and, more interestingly, news and ideas of what was happening in the world beyond the plain of Macedon.

Approximately 4,000 years later, in the mid-3rd millennium, the Early Bronze Age town of Troy was flourishing. The site covered about 8,000 square meters (six times larger than Myrtos in Crete) and was surrounded by a great stone defense wall pierced by at least two gateways which continued above as defensive towers. Within the citadel were long houses, or megarons, with vestibule, main chamber and sometimes a further room at the rear. The largest hall was over 10 meters in width and at least 26 in length. Others of the same type, but smaller, stood on each side and all opened on to a courtyard which was flanked by a retaining wall with a gateway similar in form to the great city gates. Other megarons or buildings of irregular plan with many small rectangular chambers covered the citadel. Walls were of stone in the lower parts, of mud-brick above, and were roofed with timbers and plaster. Wooden columns supported the large spans and were set on low stone bases. The community as a whole depended on an agricultural economy. Sheep and goats were kept in large numbers, as well as cattle and pigs. Rabbits and deer and wild fowl were caught and fishing provided dolphins, tunny and other varieties to supplement the food supply.

But the Trojans of the mid and later 3rd millennium were also potters and weavers of textiles. Hundreds of large store jars were set in the ground; many pottery shapes with dark monochrome or burnished surfaces, sometimes enlivened by a face modeled below the rim or on the side of a cylindrical lid, were produced for eating and drinking. For spinning, little conical clay whorls were set on wooden spindles. One was found still attached, but many thousands of whorls were simply scattered through the buildings. But beyond doubt a visiting trader would have been chiefly impressed by the vast wealth of metal: ladies wearing necklaces and diadems composed of hundreds upon hundreds of gold and silver beads, pendants and linked chains; men using chisels, knives and hatchets of copper and bronze; men and women eating or drinking from gold, silver, electrum and bronze cups, goblets, bowls and basins. Also delighting the eye were marvelous pieces of craftsmanship in the form of ceremonial axes in valued stones – possibly nephrite and lapis lazuli.

The agricultural and metal wealth of the Trojans, like that of the contemporary people living in fortified Poliochni across the water on Lemnos, or (to a lesser degree) those at Mochlos and the Mesara sites in Crete, or on the Ionian island of Lefkas – or again the wealth suggested by the dozens of impressions on clay for sealing jars and containers in the big house at Lerna in the Argolid – brings us finally to a brief consideration of the structure of society.

Throughout the whole Neolithic period there is little in the material record to suggest differences of social status; we may imagine groups of farming people, possibly clans or extended families with little or no hierarchy, inhabiting the mounds on the plains and the caves in the hills. But in the 3rd millennium, the Early Bronze Age, the development of a type of agriculture requiring much less labor than cereal production alone, and yet highly productive of useful foodstuffs, as well as expansion of metallurgy, must have promoted the acquisition of wealth – presumably personal wealth as exemplified by the jewelry and variation in grave goods – and thus the emergence of a social hierarchy.

That the Trojan and other treasures do not imply a dominant person or class is almost inconceivable. Under the leaders were several forms of specialized craftsmen, potters, metalworkers of all kinds, makers of stone vessels and sculptures, builders and shipwrights making longboats, implying considerable division of labor. Some degree of organization would be needed; agricultural workers had to produce substantial surpluses in order to feed themselves, the craft workers, and the controlling social group. Whether a priestly class or individual rulers had yet emerged we do not know. Soon, however, the social hierarchy was to organize itself for a greater achievement, first in Crete, then on the mainland. The origins of the palatial age nevertheless lie ultimately in Neolithic farming skills and, more immediately, in the achievements of the Early Bronze Age.

Myrtos-a newly excavated Early Bronze Age settlement in Crete

In the mid-3rd millennium BC eastern Crete became populated with stone-built villages on or near the coasts. These communities, along with others in central and south Crete, are the agricultural, economic and possibly architectural forerunners by 700 years of the Minoan palaces. One such settlement was located at Fournou Korifi, a hilltop on the coast east of the modern village of Myrtos. Its complete excavation in 1967 and 1968 revealed a large building complex with nearly a hundred rooms, linking passages and open areas. The site had remained almost undisturbed since its destruction by fire about 2200 BC and the rooms contained a vast store of objects to document the daily life of an Aegean community at its first urban stage, on the threshold of civilization. There were over 700 pottery vessels in use, a variety of stone tools and one or two of copper for agricultural, industrial and household activities. Human and animal figurines were modeled in clay and stone, pottery produced in quantity, seals carved, wine and oil made and cereals grown, wool spun and woven and sheep, goats, cattle and pigs reared. A female divinity was worshiped with a household cult. Obsidian came in from the island of Melos for use as cutting, boring and scraping tools. A few exotic stone vases were imported, perhaps from Mochlos on the north coast of Crete. The living pattern as a whole was probably typical of the Aegean 4,000 years ago.

This aerial view (*below*) shows the hilltop site in its modern environment: hot, dry, limestone scrubland on the south coast of Crete. The landscape was less arid in the 3rd millennium BC. Olive trees were cultivated and vines and cereals grown near the site. The hill has no water supply and this vital commodity came from springs or streams nearby. Note that the settlement is a single, large, cellular unit crowning the summit of the hill.

Left: clues for the archaeologist. The indications that here had been ancient Minoan settlement are revealed in this photograph, taken five years before excavation: an abundance of scattered stones from house walls, large bushes indicating some depth of earth and thus the possibility of undisturbed finds, and a dark, ashy level below the stones, which suggested burning within the ruins. *Below*: the excavators' good fortune. Many rooms had been burnt in the final destruction around 2200 BC and afterwards abandoned. Excavation in Room 82 revealed here 44 vessels of all shapes and sizes from big store jars for wine, oil, grain and water to brilliantly painted jugs and bowls for eating, drinking and pouring "at the table."

Right: in the southwest corner of the settlement a room of great importance is seen here just coming to light. At the top a strange, unique female figurine in terracotta is emerging. This was to become the Goddess of Myrtos (page 66). Just to the left in the picture are traces of her stone altar, not yet revealed by the excavation. Over the floor of the room are broken vessels for offerings and, all around, dark marks of the fire which brought an end to the settlement.

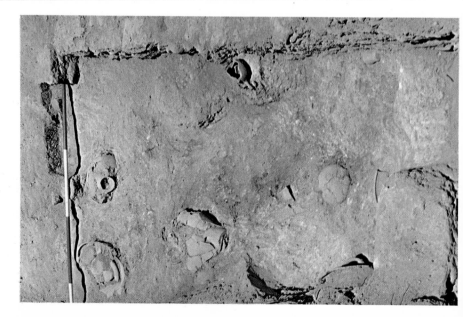

Above: the main group of rooms on the south front, just after excavation. Note the well-built stone walls, neat openings for doorways, and fairly small spans (the measuring pole is two meters long).

Right: a moment of discovery. The excavation foreman, Andonis Zidhianakis of Knossos, holds a jug which he has just cleaned and removed from the ground. It was only a few inches below the modern surface, yet had remained complete and unbroken for over four thousand years.

Left: Room 54. It was full of pithoi or big storage jars, forerunners by some 800 years of the great storage magazines in the palace of Knossos. *Below left*: the buildings were preserved best in the southern area, seen here immediately after excavation in 1968. In the bottom right corner is the shrine with its little stone altar against the wall. Here too were living rooms with stores of household pottery, kitchens and workrooms with large jars and tubs for making wine and olive oil. Beyond is the Libyan Sea with easy access to the north African shore. *Below right*: a large jar, found unbroken in Room 54 (*left* it is seen during excavation), being carried by one of the workmen to the workshop for cleaning, recording and photography. *Opposite*: a schematic plan of the site. The first period of occupation ran c. 2600 to 2400 BC. Later the settlement was greatly expanded and new rooms added in all directions over the hilltop. Passages linked the different parts of the complex, which covered about 1,250 square meters of the summit by the time of the destruction around 2200 BC. *Opposite, below left*: a plan of Room 80, the largest in the settlement, a living and working area. In the northwest corner (top left) was a cupboard; within were fine painted jugs, a censer for burning aromatic seeds, and cowrie shells. Along the south wall was a line of store jars. The central structure of the room was a stone-built support for the roof. *Opposite, below right*: a skilled technician has a vital role to play in the excavation team. Here Petros Petrakis fits a large broken amphora together, piece by piece, with glue and wire clamps. A single vessel can be found broken in 300 fragments and require 40 hours of jigsaw-like work.

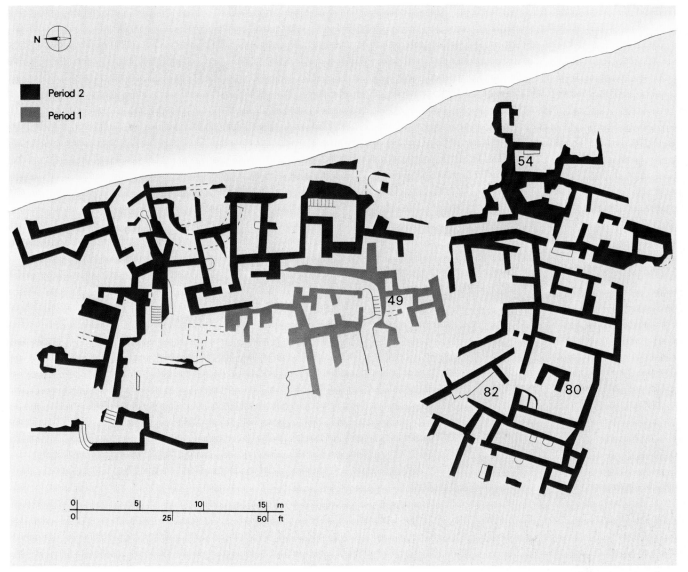

Period 2

Period 1

N

54

49

82   80

0   5   10   15   m
0   25   50   ft

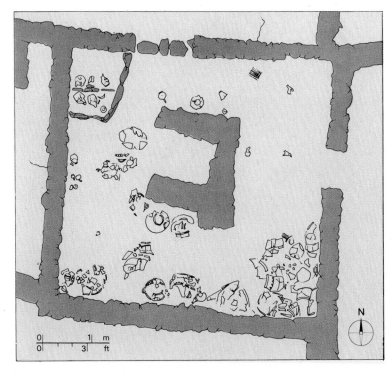

0   1   m
0   3   ft

N

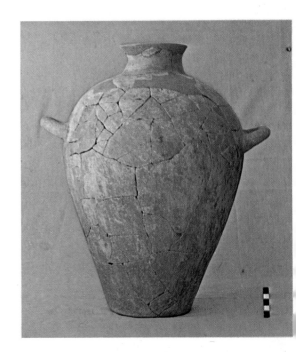

Left: the Goddess of Myrtos, 21.1 centimeters in height. She is painted with hatched panels which must represent dress. She has a non-human, stalk neck and holds in the crook of her arm a miniature jug painted in the commonest Myrtos style.

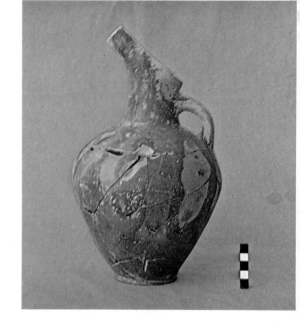

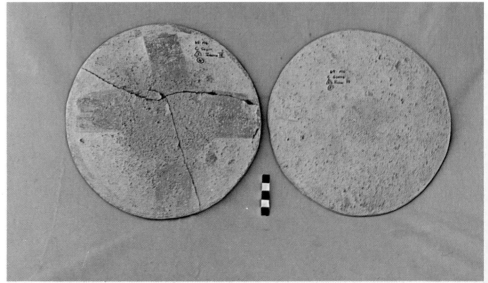

Top right: Myrtos produced over 700 complete vessels of many types. The jar, 45.8 centimeters tall, is of a shape that held wine since a similar one contained grape remains from wine-making. All the Myrtos pottery was hand-made on turntables (*bottom right*) and these jars, with walls only four millimeters thick, represent the finest technical achievement of the Myrtos Early Bronze Age potters. *Center*: the brilliantly mottled jug, height 29.15 centimeters, was for pouring water, wine or oil. The mottled style is called Vasilike Ware after the site where it was first found, a day's walk from Myrtos. *Below right*: Room 49, dating from the earliest period of occupation, proved to be a potter's workshop, the oldest known in the Aegean world. On the floor were eight circular disks, flat on one face, convex on the other. Here are two convex faces, their centers rubbed away by turning. All the pottery of Myrtos was made on such disks, the potter himself supplying the energy by turning the disk with his hands. They thus provide unique evidence for the technology of the ceramic craft before the introduction of the spindle-mounted, freely rotating or fast wheel.

4. The First Palaces of Crete and Urban Life in the Aegean 2000-1600 BC

A votive figure in clay of a worshiper, one of many discovered in the mountain peak sanctuary at Petsophas in eastern Crete. c. 2100–1800 BC. Ht. 17.5 cm.

A stone figurine of a male worshiper from either the end of the Pre-Palace period or the start of the Old Palace period (2200-1800 BC), found in a round tomb at Porti in the plain of Mesara. Note the fine detail of the carving and the hands held to the breast, a standard attitude of worship in Minoan Crete. Ht. 6. 3 cm.

In the Early Bronze Age the beginnings of urban life created considerable regional diversity for the first time in the Aegean. After the basic sameness of Neolithic life we are confronted with the contrasts between the great House of the Tiles at Lerna, the Mesara sites in Crete with their wealth of stone vessels, metalwork and engraved seals, the long megarons within fortified Troy, or the marble figurine workshops of the Cyclades. Nevertheless, the wide distribution of objects, techniques and ideas produced a degree of cultural unity and understanding among the diverse settlements. Developing together, these two aspects – regional diversity and cultural connections – form the basic pattern of Aegean life in the Middle Bronze Age.

Though the period has approximate dating boundaries, our chronological discussion must proceed from the best dated area, which is Crete in the time of the first palaces. These were founded in the 20th century, probably around 1930 BC. The evidence is complicated, but the pottery phase which immediately precedes the palaces, Middle Minoan I A, is roughly datable to the 21st and 20th centuries by associated Egyptian scarabs. The first pottery phase within the palace period, Middle Minoan I B, is reflected in Minoan metal types in the Töd treasure of silver vessels, buried with the Egyptian pharaoh Amenemhet III, who died in 1903 or 1895 BC. Thus the Middle Minoan I B or initial phase of the palaces had begun by this date, so that with the MM I A evidence a foundation date around 1930 BC will not be far wrong.

Within wider limits, the Middle Bronze Age (Middle Minoan I to II in Crete, Middle Helladic in Greece, Middle Cycladic in the islands) is chronologically fixed between the Early Bronze Age, clearly dated to the 3rd millennium by radiocarbon dates from Eutresis, Lerna and Myrtos, and the Late Bronze Age which, as we shall see in later chapters, runs parallel with the 18th and 19th Dynasties of New Kingdom Egypt.

The subdivisions of the period are based on changing styles of pottery. In Crete we can define Middle Minoan I A, I B and II. But MM II is a palatial style, the brilliant polychrome wares of Knossos and Phaistos. While it developed out of MM I and flourished in the palaces, with a few deposits elsewhere, the MM I styles continued in use on town sites and in tombs. Both the MM I provincial and MM II palace styles ended around 1700 BC with the destruction of the first palaces.

On the mainland we cannot yet subdivide the Middle Helladic period so closely, since the stylistic and stratigraphical evidence of pottery is not so sensitive as in Crete. But this should be possible when the material from Lerna and Lefkandi is fully published and can be studied alongside that of Eutresis and other well-published Middle Helladic sites. There is, however, a clear difference between early and late Middle Helladic, both in the increasingly rich repertoire of gray Minyan Ware shapes and the development to polychromy on the matt painted wares. Both these categories developed without interruption and reached their fullest expression in the 17th century BC, by which time the Second Palace Period had begun in Crete.

In the Cyclades, Middle Bronze Age development is even harder to define within the period from about 2000 to 1700, but we shall discuss below the pottery of Phylakopi, almost the only excavated town site. At Troy the Sixth City with its majestic walls is dated by Professor Blegen from 1800 to 1300 BC. It may have begun a little earlier but certainly continued with successive building phases down into the Late Bronze Age period of Mycenaean expansion.

The major features of the Aegean Middle Bronze Age are the strong differences between the mainland and Crete, occasioned by the wave of destructions on mainland sites

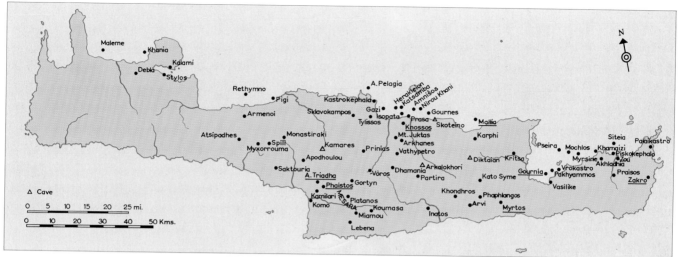

at the end of Early Bronze II or in Early Bronze III, and the probable arrival of new population groups. In Crete, the Middle Bronze Age evolved as a palatial civilization out of the early period without any interruption. Thus in Crete we have to do with palaces, flourishing towns, brilliant artifacts and wide overseas connections; on the mainland with rather humdrum towns, often fortified and having an occasional link with the Cyclades or Crete. The Aegean as a whole, including Troy, is now at an urban stage, with many towns greatly increased in size beyond their Early Bronze Age predecessors. Troy, Eutresis and Knossos are good examples of this. But the basis of life is still mixed farming. The fullest development in terms of production, organization and cultural richness was in Crete.

The First Palace period in Crete. A palace – that is a large building with many rooms grouped round the four sides of a rectangular central court, with another court on the western side – was built at Knossos, and others at Phaistos and probably Mallia. At Zakro Middle Minoan occupation has been found below the Late Minoan palace, but we are not certain that there was a palatial building in the earlier period, though the surviving central court apparently had a predecessor.

The Second Palace of Phaistos with its Grand Staircase overlay the First Palace of Middle Minoan I–II (2200–1700 BC). The little shrine rooms of the First Palace can be seen here at the lower level, below the staircase.

At Knossos the old mound was deliberately leveled to the top of the Neolithic stratum, with the removal of most Early Bronze Age remains except below the west court and south front. The new building was at first a series of separate architectural blocks placed around the central court. The blocks may in fact have been intentionally the same idea as the large individual houses which begin in Middle Minoan I. Before the destruction of the first palace in MM II they had been linked and united into a single great building. During MM II the palace was in fact given all the main lines which are visible today. The west facade and west magazines were built, as were the south terraces and north entrance. Pottery stores were put up in the northeast area and a great cutting was made in the southeast where all the main exterior walls of what was later remodeled into the domestic quarter were built now, before 1700 BC. This was a huge architectural achievement, as was the mighty viaduct and approach road to the palace on the south side. Within the building an elaborate drainage system, brilliantly engineered, ran everywhere, using terracotta pipes tapered at one end to fit into the next pipe in order to give a greater head of water to clear any obstruction.

At Phaistos the destruction debris of the first palace was used as a foundation for the second, and therefore many of the original rooms have been preserved below, showing up to three major building phases. Moreover on the west side the great facade of the second palace was set much further in, with a consequent increase in the size of the west court. This covered and preserved the superbly built old facade behind which lay an interconnected group of shrine rooms at the north end and living rooms with rich deposits of polychrome pottery to the south. Here, in the middle of the west side, a great entrance corridor ran through from the paved west court to the central court, which was flanked by a columned portico. South of the corridor were many small rooms, again filled with fine pottery. These rooms had very thick walls and presumably supported an upper story.

Tests below the later palace revealed substantial walls of the older building and, below the top of the later grand staircase, magazines full of pithoi for storing large quantities of wine, oil and grain. The block plan of Knossos does not appear to have been used at Phaistos. The many interconnected small rooms are more like the Early Minoan settlement plans. But the palace plan as a whole, based on the central court, and the great west facade facing the west court are new. Doro Levi's excavations have also revealed circular stone granaries and a paved and stepped road ascending up the Phaistos hill towards them from the south. There was also, as at Knossos, a flourishing town with houses and paved streets in the First Palace period.

At Mallia the position is not so clear. The central court seems to have existed, with rooms on its west side containing important metal finds under those of the later palace. But recently a large building covering at least 1700 square meters, with over 60 rooms and open areas, has been discovered to the west of the later palace. It has no great court (at least none has been found) but it dates to the First Palace period and is, with its shallow staircases, ritual chamber below ground, plastered walls and benches, the best preserved building of that age yet found in Crete. The finds include beautiful specimens of Middle Minoan II polychrome pottery. Moreover, the discovery of storerooms filled with clay jars and pithoi and the occurrence of hieroglyphic inscriptions on vases, seals and clay sealings suggest an administrative function for the building.

All these buildings exhibit great skill in construction. Well-dressed stone facades and wooden columns accompany the older techniques, which utilized mud-brick and selected but undressed stone construction. But perhaps the best surviving stonework is shown in two places outside the palaces. The Khrysolakkos tomb at Mallia may have been a royal burial place, on the evidence of its elaborate plan and rooms for rites as well as burials. Its exterior facade is constructed with upright slabs (orthostats) on a foundation course, all of finely dressed stone. At Knossos meanwhile a carefully planned system of paved roads was

Pithoi at Phaistos. A section of the magazine buried under the landing at the head of the grand staircase of the later palace. 1700 BC. Note the storage capacity for wine, oil and cereals here in the First Palace period.

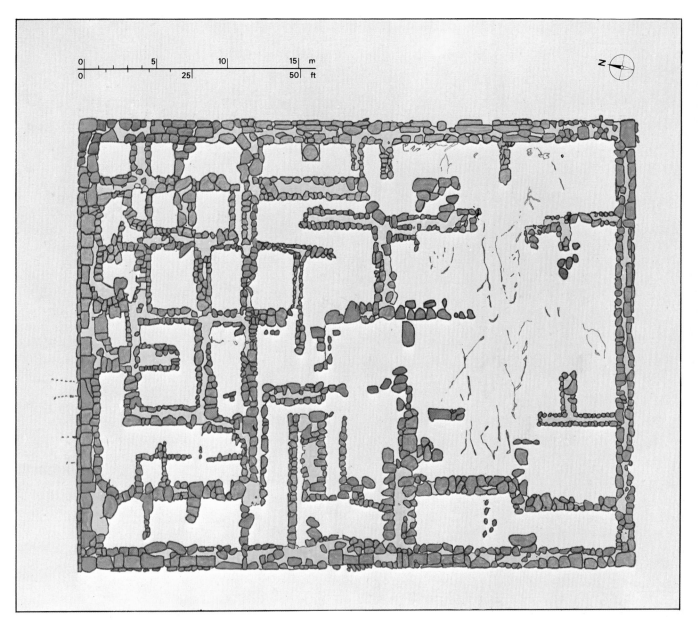

A plan of the Khrysolakkos tomb at Mallia. It has an exterior wall of very fine masonry and may have been a royal burial place. c. 1900–1700 BC. The famous gold pendant of the two wasps (shown above in chapter 2) came from here.

constructed north and west of the palace. The Royal Road and one newly found on the west, making a T junction with it, were constructed with two lines of slabs giving a constant width of 1.40 meters; the paving was raised just above flanking drains and side pavements of cobbles.

What can be said about the origins of the first palaces of Crete? The palace plan in itself, based on a large central court, was a bold innovation. It may have been formed with some knowledge in mind of contemporary palaces like those at Beycesultan in Anatolia and Mari on the Euphrates, which Minoan travelers could have visited. But it is now becoming clear that the plan also owes something, perhaps a great deal, to the layout of Early Minoan settlements. Vasilike and Myrtos were cellular building complexes with many rooms; the former had a paved western court, while at Myrtos there was an unpaved open area at the center of the settlement. It seems possible therefore that the basic architectural idea developed out of Early Minoan planning, possibly with additional, externally derived knowledge of the courtyard palaces of Anatolia and the Near East. Within the palaces characteristic Early Minoan features are repeated – plastered walls, benches and low tables against walls, cupboards of upright slabs in corners of rooms – but the column appears to be new. Finally we must stress the economic organization implied by the palaces. Here, as we shall see, there is direct development from the Early Bronze Age.

Towns and villas. Towns and large individual houses also flourished. Our evidence for the former comes mainly

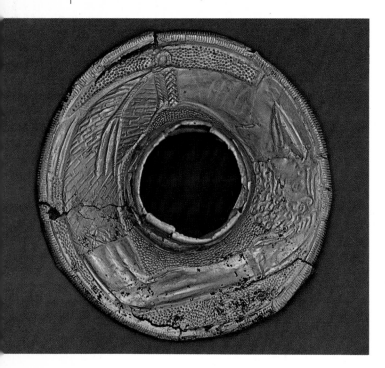

Above: the gilt pommel of a sword from Mallia. It depicts an acrobat brilliantly rendered in repoussé technique. Note his hairstyle and short kilt. c. 1700 BC.

Opposite: faience town mosaic from Knossos. A group of polychrome plaques represent houses with flat roofs, windows, several stories and a little room on the roof. 17th century BC.

from tests under buildings of the Late Bronze Age. Such tests have shown that all the great sites like Aghia Triadha, Gournia, Palaikastro and Tylissos were substantially occupied in the Middle Minoan period, as most had been, on a smaller scale, in the 3rd millennium. One site, Monastiraki in the Amari valley west of mount Ida, consisted of settlement buildings on a low hill around a more important construction with storage rooms, pithoi and lumps of clay bearing seal impressions used for closing the great jars. There appears therefore to have been a small palace or chief's house in Middle Minoan I–II dominating the town buildings, a precursor of the arrangement at Late Minoan Gournia and Myrtos Pyrgos and a contemporary parallel for the great sites, since towns also existed around the palaces. Drainage channels ran between houses at Knossos, and the paved roads of Late Minoan settlements probably originated in the First Palace period.

A new development, at the palace sites and elsewhere, was the individual villa or mansion of several rooms, including some for storage and workshops. Two were excavated at Vasilike, but the best series is at Mallia. Here several of the Late Minoan houses are rebuildings of Middle Minoan ones, while the large, newly excavated building referred to above is either a very large house or a palace. We shall consider the social implications of these houses shortly.

One other Middle Minoan individual building is note-

worthy. On a hilltop near Khamaizi in east Crete there is a single-storied house which is almost oval in plan. Over a dozen rooms lead off a central area which was partly a court, partly a cistern with a huge stone surround. One room contained pithoi, another was a household shrine with figurines. There were two entrances, one with an overflow channel from the cistern. Just outside the building another, earlier, room contained a hoard of bronze tools, double axes, an axe-adze and a chisel, perhaps belonging to a carpenter. The oval house was the final outcome, perhaps for a local leader, of at least three Early Minoan building periods, during which some of the houses also had deliberately curved walls.

Crafts. The artifacts of Middle Minoan Crete display a richness and sophistication which, with the palaces, towns and villas, provide sufficient evidence that we are concerned not just with a culture, but with civilization. The pottery continued many shapes evolved in Early Minoan times, particularly the one-handled cup and the jar with a short spout on the shoulder, bridged over by the rim. But the development of a fast potter's wheel, revolving on a spindle, enabled the palace workshops to create many refinements of shape with thin, sometimes almost eggshell-thin walls, carinations and flutings of profile, probably in imitation of metal forms. On the black lustrous surface was painted a variety of abstract, particularly spiraliform designs in several colors, white, red, orange, purple, which show an astonishing understanding of design in relation to surface area and curvature. At the same time myriads of humbler pots were made, from big storage jars to cooking pots, standing lamps and offering tables (often highly burnished red or brown).

The metalsmiths were producing tin bronze, shaft-hole tools like those of Khamaizi, as well as long daggers and knives. The achievements of the Mallia goldsmiths were quite outstanding. The delicate and elaborate pendant of two conjoined wasps is well known; a gold-handled dagger with cut-out designs on the hilt comes from the large building west of the palace, which itself produced the magnificent long swords, one of which had a pommel covered with gold sheet, picturing an acrobat rendered in repoussé technique. A famous collection of gold objects, the Aigina Treasure in the British Museum, may originally have come in part at least from Mallia.

Stone vase makers were everywhere developing their craft. Large bowls, buckets, jars and lamps were now carved in dark blue serpentine for the palaces and houses, and hard, exotic stones like white speckled obsidian from Yiali in the Dodecanese and rosso antico from the southern Peloponnese were now tackled. A stone vase maker's workshop at Mallia belongs to this First Palace period. Seal carvers also began to experiment with hard stones like amethyst and carnelian, along with the traditional steatites, bone and ivory. Faience, used already in the Early Minoan period for beads, is now mastered for a wider range of objects; a little pot from Knossos has added gold sheet while a group of polychrome plaques represent houses with flat roofs, windows and several stories.

Another lively craft was that of the terracotta figurine maker. The human form was now well understood, male with short skirt or loincloth and dagger at the waist, female with long, bell-shaped skirt, bodice, high hat (known before the palaces, around 2100 BC at Petsophas near Palaikastro) and sometimes amazingly elaborate coiffures skillfully modeled in the clay. Animal figurines – bulls, deer, sheep and goats – continued as in Early Minoan, though the horned beetles of Piskokephalo in east Crete are newcomers.

Writing. There is one other important development. Pictographic or hieroglyphic writing was used on three- and four-sided prism seals and on clay bars, labels and roundels in the First Palace period. There may have been several functions for the signs and sign groups, administrative or identificatory information on the clay objects, amuletic or magical or religious formulas on the stones, which were probably also used as seals on containers and documents, indicating the owner's personal identity. But at Phaistos, in the destruction material of the first palace, there were also found a few clay tablets in the Minoan Linear A script, a syllabic form of writing probably derived from the hieroglyphic. The importance of the find is twofold: the Minoan written script, widely used in the Second Palace period, is already known in the First and thus points to strong continuity between the periods; second, the script must have been invented to promote easier and faster administrative recording and thus more efficient economic organization.

Economy. This last involved a full development of Early Minoan agriculture and incipient craft specialization. In that earlier period each village had produced its own subsistence requirements. The palaces and their contents imply organization on a larger scale. We do not know if a quota system like that of the later palaces was yet in operation, but Phaistos, for example, will have needed to control much land in order to fill the many store jars of its palace magazines with oil, wine and grain. The same must hold for the large buildings at Mallia, though towns like Gournia and Palaikastro presumably organized their own agriculture on a scale necessary for their increased size. Craft specialization was practiced in workshops at palace sites and the finest pottery traveled far, in and outside Crete. But there must have been many local craft centers of metallurgy, stone vase making and for pottery and

figurines, especially in the Mesara plain and other south Cretan sites whose tombs held so many artifacts.

Burial customs. The burial customs of the First Palace period show continuity as well as innovation. The old circular communal tombs continue in use and new ones are built, such as the great tomb at Kamilari, and that on Gypsadhes at Knossos, or are added to existing cemeteries as at Platanos. Additional rectangular chambers are built outside the tombs to store bones or offerings from earlier burials. The rectangular ossuaries at Arkhanes and Palaikastro also continue to be used without interruption, as do the stone mortuary houses at Mochlos. At the same time two new customs come in, burial in pithoi and in oval clay chests (larnakes). Sometimes these are in new cemeteries such as at Pakhyammos near Gournia or Mavro Spelio at Knossos, or are added within existing tombs like the circular one at Voros north of the Mesara, or in the Arkhanes ossuaries. Grave goods develop stylistically from earlier types. The clay and stone vases have lost something of the variety and liveliness of Early Minoan, but none of the quantity. Scores of plain buff, red or black monochrome clay cups, jugs and bowls and little pots of dark serpentine accompany burials, along with a few sealstones, ornaments, figurines and bronze daggers.

Religion. Several kinds of sanctuary now give expression to religion. The domestic shrine for household cults, first seen at Myrtos, continues in a shrine room just inside the west wall of the palace of Phaistos. The room, 3.62 × 2.57 meters, had low, plastered benches around the walls, while set in the floor lay a large clay offering table with a central hollow. The rim of the table was impressed with a repeated pattern of cattle, perhaps symbolic of their offered blood. The shrine also contained a beautiful, inlaid stone offering table and a triton shell. We know from an engraved seal that these were blown as

The communal round tomb of Kamilari, near Phaistos. Built c. 2000 BC, it was used for several hundred years.

ritual trumpets. A pit, interpreted as sacrificial, lay near the shrine and other little rooms were connected with it. These contained clay cups, stone offering tables and a fine circular table, red-burnished like the rectangular table in the main room.

At Khamaizi there was a cult room with human figurines in the house. At Mallia a Middle Minoan II shrine has recently been found about 100 meters west of the palace. It consisted of three rooms. The central one was a vestibule approached from a paved area; to the west was a storeroom for jars of offerings; to the east stood the shrine proper with a clay offering table bearing the imprint of a double axe on its underside. In the center of the room on the floor was a low terracotta slab with a hole for pouring in libations, presumably to a deity of the underworld. Around the slab were grouped flat stones for other offerings or possibly for participants to stand on. A clay shell, animal figurines, stone vessels and pottery jars, lamps and fine Middle Minoan II polychrome ware made up the equipment of the shrine.

Caves were now used as sacred places; the Kamares cave high on mount Ida gave its name to the beautiful Middle Minoan polychrome pottery, offered here together with grain (unless this was to feed pilgrims), probably by the people of Phaistos who could see the cave from their palace. The famous Diktaian cave at Psykhro, traditional birthplace of Zeus, also began to receive offerings in the First Palace period. Lastly, there are the stone-built mountain summit shrines. These began at the end of the 3rd millennium, before the palaces were built. Petsofa above Palaikastro started in Early Minoan III (c. 2100 BC) and is the best known (being the best published, by Sir John Myres in 1903). But there are many more on summits all over the island, including the western Rethymno province. Offerings took the form of pottery, animal bones (presumably therefore sacrificed animals) and in particular human and animal terracotta figurines. It was noted in chapter 3 that the great bonfires with the offerings represented rites for healing and protection from disease.

Whether religion was monotheistic, with a great female deity who took various distinct forms, or whether these represent separately conceived divinities is not easily decided for this period. But the very different circumstances, places and ritual apparatus of cults suggest some form of polytheism; a household goddess is indicated at Myrtos and in later shrines, and thus by implication in Middle Minoan domestic ones also. The peak sanctuaries and their offerings, as well as a Late Minoan impression of a gold ring, suggest a mistress of animals, worshiped on mountain summits. A third divinity may have been worshiped in the sacred caves. But later stone vessels inscribed with very similar Linear A sign groups come from both caves and peak sanctuaries (especially Petsofa in east Crete).

Trade. The first palace civilization of Crete developed

wide overseas connections. There was an actual settlement on the island of Kythera (which seems to have started in Early Minoan II) and exports of stone and clay vases to mainland Argos, Lerna, Mycenae, Aigina, Kea, Pefkakia on the east Thessalian coast, and to Miletos and to several Cycladic islands, especially Phylakopi on Melos. Fine clay vases also went to Byblos in Syria, Cyprus and Egypt. In return the palace workshops imported copper, tin, gold, ivory and fine stones for seals, and occasionally vases. Middle Kingdom scarabs came from Egypt and one or two haematite Babylonian cylinders were imported, probably coming from the intermediate Levant. The pattern of foreign connections established in the First Palace period is an expansion of late 3rd-millennium activity, and in turn is the basis for wider maritime commerce, known from tradition as the thalassocracy (rule of the sea) of Minos, which characterizes the Second Palace period, from about 1700 to 1400 BC.

Society. Society in Middle Minoan I to II Crete had clearly become hierarchical, with rulers, priests, scribes, craftsmen of many kinds, farmers and traders. But although the Khrysolakkos building at Mallia would seem to have been a royal burial place, interment is still essentially communal, which suggests no great distinctions of class. Even individual burials in pithoi or clay larnakes (chests) are placed indiscriminately in caves, communal tombs or simple earth pit cemeteries. Probably the major social structure was still that of the clan or extended family. The context in which society developed seems to have been entirely peaceful. There is no sign of violent destruction in settlements, no fortifications, and cemeteries were gradually abandoned or continued into the Second Palace period. Knossos, Phaistos and possibly Mallia suffered destruction in Middle Minoan II, around 1700 BC, but direct continuity of culture thereafter suggests that earthquakes rather than human agency were the cause.

A uniformity of culture is found throughout the island, elegantly documented by the palaces and wide distribution of basically similar mountain peak sanctuaries. At the important settlement of Khania in the west pottery forms are closely akin to those of the Mesara. The central areas have close ceramic links with east Crete. We have seen that there is no evidence for newcomers to the population in the First Palace period, so many are the continuities from Early Minoan times. We may therefore speak archaeologically of a homogeneous population, the Minoans. Evidence of skull and skeletal size is not great, but the remains from the Mavro Spelio tombs at Knossos and from Palaikastro, though with varied skull forms, do not suggest any wide differences of physical type which would imply radically different population groups.

The Aegean islands in the Middle Bronze Age. Most of the Aegean islands were occupied in the Middle Bronze Age. Important settlements have been excavated at Aghia

A terracotta model shrine from the Middle-Late Minoan round tomb at Kamilari, near Phaistos. It shows two worshipers and four seated divinities with altars before them. 2000–1700 BC.

Eirene on Kea and at the second city of Phylakopi on Melos. Graves attest occupation on Syros and Amorgos and there are traces of settlement on Delos, Paros and Tenos. On Thera there are indications of occupation below the great town of Late Minoan I A, while Kythera was populated with Minoans at the coastal site of Kastri.

However, the contrast with the richness of the Early Bronze Age communities of the Cyclades is marked. Gone is the wonderful sculptural tradition of stone vessels and figurines; metal tools and weapons are far fewer in quantity, though a spearhead and daggers were placed in a grave on Amorgos. But the chances of preservation and excavation tell us more of settlements than in Early Cycladic times.

A Middle Minoan II cup with walls of eggshell thinness. The delicate designs may reflect dress patterns and the shape as a whole probably copies metal originals.

The flying fish fresco from the town of Phylakopi on Melos. The style is entirely Minoan, and similar fish were found in faience in the contemporary temple repositories at Knossos. 16th century BC.

At Aghia Eirene on Kea there are clear Anatolian connections in the Early Bronze III pottery, and new people may have moved in. New buildings were constructed over the Early Bronze Age houses and a fortification wall with a gateway and projecting tower enclosed rooms on the northern part of the site, giving access to a spring outside. Towards the end of the Middle Bronze Age this wall was replaced by a major fortification further out, which extended all around the landward side of the peninsula and enclosed an area up to 125 by 100 meters in the widest parts. Middle Bronze Age graves, mainly for children and probably outside the old fortification, were found to contain a plain inhumation as well as pithos and cist burials. There was clearly a reasonably prosperous urban settlement with its own fine red-burnished ware and imports of gray Minyan pottery from the mainland and a few Middle Minoan I and II pieces from Crete.

On Melos the second city of Phylakopi was more fully revealed by excavation. A rambling complex of many-roomed houses, separated by narrow streets, was exposed over an area of about 80 by 50 meters, but the settlement was probably much larger since a long stretch of a big fortification wall was uncovered 50 meters to the south-west. This wall, built at the beginning of the Middle Cycladic, was strengthened and enlarged in Late Cycladic I to enclose the Late Bronze Age town, which was built over the destroyed second city. Middle Bronze Age Phylakopi produced attractive local pottery, especially bowls, cups and jugs with turned-back spouts, all with sparse, matt-painted decoration on the light surface. One jug was exported to Knossos while, as at Kea, fine Middle Minoan and gray Minyan pottery came in. From one room in the second city came fragments of a lovely flying fish fresco in blue and yellow against a buff ground. The style is entirely Minoan, and similar fish were found in faience in the contemporary temple repositories at Knossos. The fresco was probably painted by a Minoan artist. On the

other hand Melian jars, boldly decorated with birds, were exported to Knossos at this time, near the end of the Middle Bronze Age. Graves in this period were intramural for children with chamber tombs outside the town for adults.

The city was violently destroyed, by what cause we do not know, at a time corresponding to the end of Middle Minoan III in Crete, probably early in the 16th century BC. The loss of all ceramic originality and total dependence on Cretan shapes and styles in the next period, Late Cycladic I, was taken by the great Swedish scholar Arne Furumark to mean that Phylakopi, while not becoming a colony of Minoans, passed under Minoan political control.

A cultural break thus coincides with the end of the Middle Bronze Age at Phylakopi. At about the same time the big fortification wall was built at Aghia Eirene. Whatever its purpose (to keep Minoans out or protect a settlement under Cretan domination) the Kean site became, like Phylakopi, heavily influenced by Minoan Crete in the early part of the Late Bronze Age. By this time the destruction of the first palaces of Crete had taken place about a hundred years before and the island had already entered on its most flourishing epoch.

The mainland. At many of the big mainland sites severe destruction took place at the end of Early Bronze II or during EB III. We have noted the appearance of completely new features, mainly long houses with curved or straight ends and Anatolian ceramic forms, in the archaeological record in the wake of these destructions. One or more of these features, especially drinking cups, jugs and plates, appear at Manika and Lefkandi on the west coast of Euboea, at Lerna and on Aigina and Kea. There can be little doubt that new people were arriving, probably from Anatolia, during a period that may have lasted up to 300 years (2200 to 1900 BC). Anthropological research on their skulls and bones suggests a very mixed stock. This then is the inception of the mainland Middle Bronze Age and it was a crucial historical stage.

Since it is generally accepted that the Mycenaean Linear B tablets are written in an early form of Greek and since it is now clear that there was no cultural break between the Middle and Late Bronze (Mycenaean) Ages on the mainland, it follows that the new people of Early Helladic III and Middle Helladic I are the ancestors of the later Greeks and that they spoke some sort of Greek. This language was to develop considerably (Mycenaean Greek is a good deal different from Homeric Greek), but it must already have been recognizable as the Greek language.

It has also been pointed out that one of the most distinctive Middle Helladic pottery styles, matt-painted ware, is uniform in eastern Thessaly, Boeotia, the Argolid and Lakonia, and again uniform, but different from that of the former area, in Aitolia, western Thessaly and the Sperkheios valley of central Greece, and that these two areas correspond roughly to the areas posited for the first differentiation of the East and West Greek dialects.

Settlements of the period are known all over Greece and there are many similarities in the material culture. R. J. Buck has shown that at least 140 sites had matt-painted ware. A number of major towns were given a strong fortification wall, a practice which is continued in Mycenaean times. Molyvopyrgos in the Chalcidice peninsula, the settlement on Aigina, possibly Lefkandi on Euboea, Asea, the Aspis hill at Argos, Malthi and possibly Pylos in the Peloponnese were walled towns, as were Phylakopi and Aghia Eirene in the Cyclades. But many sites appear to have been unprotected by fortifications. Coastal Lerna and possibly Aghios Stephanos in the southern Peloponnese are examples.

Houses often take the form of free-standing, long megarons with porch, main room and back room with a rounded or straight end. Mud-brick and stone foundations are usual for walls. Hearths and sometimes low benches are found in the main room, while the back room was often for storage. Activity must have been mainly out of doors. Roofs were made of reeds, clay and timber and must have been gabled on the apsidal houses at least, but could have been flat, supported by wooden posts, on the rectangular buildings. In general accommodation seems to have been primitive, but the House of the Tiles at Lerna in the Early Bronze Age is exceptional and most of the people throughout the Bronze Age on the mainland lived in houses similar to those of Middle Helladic Eutresis.

Food was provided by the cereal crops of wheat, barley and oats; peas, chick peas, lentils, beans and olives were also grown and almost certainly figs and grapes were too, though these are attested only for Early and Late Helladic times. Sheep, goats, pigs, cattle and dogs were kept and red deer was hunted to supplement the supply of meat. The careful study of the fauna at Lerna was referred to in chapter 3, brown bear and lynx being added in the Middle Helladic to the long list of animals caught or kept in earlier

times. A newcomer in Middle Helladic is the horse, *equus caballus*, whose bones appear during this period at Lerna. The status of the animal is not known, but from Late Helladic representations and sacrificial skeletons we may reasonably infer that it was a prestige animal in the Middle Bronze Age also.

Graves in the earlier and middle parts of the period were as unpretentious as the houses. Simple earth pits or stone slab-lined and covered graves are typical, with a layer of small pebbles to make a clean floor for the single or occasionally multiple inhumations. Accompanying goods were non-existent or poor, a pot or two, rarely a bronze tool or weapon; a gold diadem at Corinth and another at Asine are exceptional. Burials also took place in pithoi or smaller jars, particularly of children. Sometimes these were grouped in round, earth-covered tumuli which were of course outside the settlements. Intramural burial was, however, common, near or under the houses in pits, stone cist graves or pithoi. There seems to have been a simple funeral rite involving a toast to the dead, the cup broken afterwards and left at the grave.

Towards the end of the period, around 1600 BC, there is a clear rise in the standard of funerary architecture, which must mirror increasing prosperity among the living. At Eleusis the cist graves become larger and better built, with a side door for introducing the body. At Marathon two carefully built circular stone tumuli have recently been found. Rectangular cist graves are inset into the circular platform and one grave imitates an apsidal house in its plan. One late Middle Helladic burial in tumulus I had with it 11 fine clay vases; another contained simply a sacrificed horse. At this time also the first grave circle was built at Mycenae. Late Middle Helladic cist graves within its circular perimeter wall contain rich burials with pottery, weapons and jewelry far exceeding the offerings of earlier MH tombs. Sets of stone arrowheads were placed in later

The so-called Tomb of Thrasymedes, son of Nestor, at Koryphasion near Pylos. The architectural idea of the tholos may have been taken from Crete to Messenia at the end of the Middle Bronze Age. The earliest tholos on the mainland, dating from c. 1600 BC, is nearby. The one pictured here is only a little later. It had been set into a preexisting burial tumulus. A whole ox had been sacrificed inside the tomb.

Gray pottery called Minyan Ware because it was first found in Boeotia, home of the legendary King Minyas. The style is a mainland Middle Bronze Age creation.

MH male graves, while beads, rings and pins were probably for females.

In Messenia tumuli with pithos burials are found and so is a completely new type of tomb, the great vaulted, beehive-shaped tholos. The oldest is at Koryphasion near Pylos, with pottery of the late Middle Bronze Age. The architectural idea of the tholos may have been taken from Crete, where roughly corbeled circular tombs were in use at Knossos and Arkhanes. But the people of the mainland, as we have seen, transformed it socially to take only the burials of leading families. Further north, on the island of Lefkas, Middle Helladic communal family graves are found with gray Minyan pottery, fine metal daggers and a slotted spearhead (another came from Sesklo).

Metal objects are rare before the later Middle Bronze Age. They were too valuable to put in graves, save occasionally, and this must indicate relative poverty when one recalls the rich metal grave goods of earlier and later periods. Daggers, spearheads, knives, sickles, chisels, pins of bronze are found infrequently on settlement sites. Many tools were of stone, particularly shaft-hole axes, arrowheads and arrow polishers and straighteners. The bow seems to have been much the commonest offensive weapon, though swords appear at the end of the period, made in or learned from Crete.

Pottery. By contrast, pottery of several attractive and distinct classes is found abundantly in settlements and was often placed in graves. The best known is the polished gray pottery known as Minyan ware after its finding in quan-

tity at Orchomenos in Boeotia, legendary home of King Minyas. Much has been written about this pottery in the past. On the basis of its sudden appearance at the beginning of Middle Helladic and in Troy VI at the same time, it was thought to be the hallmark of a newly arrived population in each area. Continuing discoveries make the matter less clearcut. At Lerna the pottery appears in Early Helladic III (level IV at Lerna), after the big EH II destruction of the House of the Tiles. At Lefkandi a limited test trench to bedrock showed poorer gray and brown wares of phase 2 emerging as true gray Minyan ware in phase 3. It may therefore be that the pottery was not introduced from outside, but developed within Greece. But it would still have been the product of newcomers who may have been skilled in a tradition of gray wares. We have seen that newcomers seem to have arrived from western Anatolia, but on present evidence the chronological priority of Minyan ware lies with Early Helladic III Greece, which is earlier than Troy VI.

The pottery itself, wheelmade and attractive, has two main shapes, a carinated bowl with two high-swung handles and a similar bowl without handles but set on a tall foot, turning it into a drinking goblet. Sharp, metallic profiles are favored, with carinations, horizontal flutings and ribbing. Similar shapes appear in other burnished fabrics beside gray, namely black, red, brown and yellow. Decoration is added by incision, except on yellow Minyan, which is left plain. Yellow Minyan is in fact the direct ancestor of lustrous buff early Mycenaean ware.

The matt-painted ware we have also mentioned is in a completely different style. It appears later than Minyan ware and may have its origin in the Cyclades. Dark matt (non-lustrous) paint is used for geometrical patterns on large storage jars and on small domestic shapes. Sometimes the shapes and decorative patterns are copied from Middle Minoan Crete, which exported actual pieces to Middle Helladic sites. But the style as a whole is a mainland creation and it reaches a pleasing elaboration on some of the large jars. Late in the period it develops into a bichrome style with red and black patterns on the buff ground. The influence here is probably Cycladic, for a rich bichrome style had developed in the islands of Melos and Thera. Alongside these fine wares, coarse pottery was abundant everywhere for cooking and storage vessels. An incised variety was popular in the western Peloponnese.

Society. Middle Helladic society cannot be reconstructed in detail, but we know of farmers, potters, builders and a few metallurgists. There was some exchange of goods, especially at coastal sites like Lerna, Aigina and Pefkakia on the coast of Thessaly. These imported pottery from Crete while Minyan ware went to Phylakopi and matt-painted ware apparently reached the Lipari islands in the central Mediterranean. There is no doubt, though, that the period from about 2100 to 1700 BC was decidedly poor in comparison with the First Palace period of Crete or even with

A kantharos or drinking cup from Lerna.
1900–1700 BC. The second major style of mainland
Greece in the Middle Bronze Age, matt-painted
decoration on a buff surface.

Phylakopi in Melos. Writing was unknown, unless one includes potters' marks – no less than 147 of which are recorded from Middle Helladic Lerna. They are not known in Early Helladic but were common at that time in the Cyclades. Hence the Middle Helladic people of Lerna may have learned from the island tradition.

In the 17th century BC there was a marked rise in prosperity. The late Middle Helladic graves in Circle B at Mycenae and in the Marathon tumulus clearly document this in the contrast between their richer grave goods and those of earlier Middle Helladic graves. Tholos tombs began to appear in Messenia and Cycladic vases were imported at Lerna, Mycenae and at Samikon in the western Peloponnese. Tumuli at Aghios Ioannis near Pylos and the walled precinct of graves at Aphidna in Attica probably date, as Marathon does, to this late Middle Bronze period. All these richer burials probably imply development in society, the emergence of richer groups or families who were soon to wax richer still. Within a hundred years of these developments, by 1550 BC, the wealth of the Circle B graves at Mycenae had been outclassed by the incomparable riches of the Shaft Graves in Circle A.

Troy in the Middle Bronze Age. The excavations of Dörpfeld and Blegen established a clear break in the history of Troy between the fifth and sixth settlements. Troy V is the last stage of the Early Bronze Age and was replaced and built over by a completely new town, Troy VI, at the start of the Middle Bronze Age, around 2000 BC. Two features now appear for the first time. These are a distinct gray ware and the horse, commonly found at Troy thereafter. Moreover, of 98 pottery shapes classified by Blegen's expedition, 90 are new and unconnected with the Trojan Early Bronze Age. Given these major innovations it seems clear that, just as in Greece, so at Troy new people had arrived and had taken over the site. Possible relationships between these people and newcomers in Greece are considered below.

Troy VI, with its magnificent fortifications and fine houses, is much the most important known Middle Bronze Age settlement in the east Aegean and west Anatolian region. There was occupation in the citadel of Poliochni on Lemnos, at the site of the later Heraion on Samos, and at Emborio on Chios. At least one Middle Minoan II pot reached Miletos, while Larissa, Old Smyrna and other sites had pottery like that of Troy VI. But it cannot be only because of the chances of excavation or survival that these places have nothing comparable with the splendid remains of Troy.

The sixth city had eight major phases of life, lasting down well into the Late Bronze Age, to the time of transition between Late Helladic III A and B pottery in the second half of the 14th century BC. Its most potent remains are the fortification walls and towers, but these were mostly built, in Aegean terms, in the Late Bronze Age, around 1400 BC. Well over half the circuit has survived, about 350 meters in length. It was built in sections terminated by gateways. The latter are formed either by one section of wall overlapping another and producing a narrow passage, or by a direct passage through the wall with a protecting tower on the outside. Another tower was added to the middle of a section and a vast third one formed the northeast angle. The masonry was magnificent, great blocks of hard limestone carefully fitted and with attention to the vertical joints so that they were staggered over those of the course below. The face was not vertical but had an inward inclination or batter. Vertical offsets marked off each straight section of the polygonal walls. The stonework was crowned with a crude brick superstructure, with the intention of providing the surest possible defense against attackers.

These great fortifications of the Late Bronze Age replaced an earlier system of less powerful construction but with the distinctive vertical offsets. One section of this earlier wall was left and incorporated into the new one. But the earlier wall, built apparently in the early part of the Aegean Late Bronze Age, replaced a still older one, a section of which survived directly behind it in one place. This oldest fortification, again with offsets and batter on the outward face, dated back to early Troy VI. It was thus built at about the same time as the Middle Helladic fortification walls of mainland Greece.

The expeditions of Dörpfeld and Blegen were able to uncover the remains of many fine houses of Troy VI, close to the interior edge of the city wall. Those on the higher terraces had been removed in the construction of large buildings in Hellenistic and Roman times, or by Schliemann. The houses were built with a remarkable orientation and city plan in mind. It was Dörpfeld who first showed that some houses did not have the usual rectangular plan, but a slightly trapezoidal one. The reason for thus making the innermost wall somewhat shorter than the outer one, nearest the city wall, was to allow the radiating streets to run in converging lines straight up to the center of the citadel without the joggle which the projecting corners of strictly rectangular houses would have caused. It is therefore inferred that a strong central authority or ruler controlled the citadel at this time and determined the whole town plan.

The houses themselves were carefully built of stone in the lower part, with the usual mud-brick superstructure, or

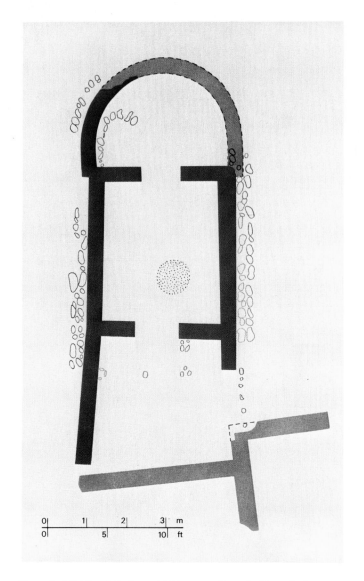

Plan of a Middle Helladic apsidal house at Eutresis. Note the long hall plan to be taken over in the Mycenaean palaces.

else with walls entirely of stone. Timber frame roofs were flat or gabled and supported by one or more rows of wooden columns set on stone bases. Few houses had the strict megaron plan of a rectangular room entered from a porch at one of the short ends. There were sometimes back rooms or small compartments for storage, while entrances were often on one of the long sides over a high sill. In size the houses ranged from over 13 meters by over 10, to about 25 meters by 16. A smaller house, about 11.20 by 6.30 meters, dates from the early or middle part of the Middle Bronze Age. Blegen showed that with its neat rectangular construction and its compartments, it was a clear forerunner of the later, more substantial buildings.

The houses contained storage jars, fine "table" pottery, loom weights for weaving and other domestic equipment such as the occasional bronze knife, pins, awls and arrowheads, as well as stone spindle whorls and whetstones. Most of the houses that survive were built in Late Troy VI,

Troy VI. Its most potent remains are the fortification walls with their inward slope and vertical offsets.

Beside the walls were built large fortification towers of which this is the finest.

the time of the Aegean Late Bronze Age. This was proved by the imported Mycenaean pots. For example, over 20 were found on the earliest floor of house VI F and they are dated to around 1400 BC. But throughout all the phases of the sixth city polished gray ware was used in elegant shapes – drinking and food bowls and goblets with carinated profiles, swung high above the rim and with a short or tall pedestal foot. Jugs for pouring wine or water were also made. In the early phase at least 21 shapes were in use at Troy and the range expanded as time went on. So tenacious was the tradition that gray ware copies of imported Mycenaean pots were made and added to the repertoire. Pottery in the second major Middle Helladic style, matt-painted ware, was also imported into the sixth city, probably from central Greece or the Peloponnese.

The sixth city of Troy continued through eight main phases until it was overwhelmed somewhere between 1350 and 1300 BC. The dating evidence was imported Mycenaean pottery, mainly of Late Helladic III A, but with some III B. The magnificent fortifications tumbled down, but there was no evidence of burning and looting. The city was in fact rebuilt, the fortifications repaired and the houses reinhabited by the previous occupants, since no sign of new cultural features appears in Troy VII A. Blegen therefore considered the cause of the destruction to have been a severe earthquake.

Troy at this time has claimed our attention for a number of reasons. It has an uninterrupted cultural life throughout the Aegean Middle and Late Bronze Ages, with continuity in pottery styles and building techniques, the latter culminating in the magnificent walls and structures of the 14th century. Throughout all this time its people had intimate links with the Aegean region to the west. What was the nature of the relationship? Carl Blegen stressed the newness of Troy VI pottery and its close connection with Middle Helladic gray Minyan ware. He thought the newcomers to each region were one and the same people and since, as we have seen, the people in Greece were in all probability the area's first Greek speakers, he was able to see the people who founded Troy VI as Greeks also, "the earliest of their race to gain a foothold in Asia Minor." The introduction of the horse at the start of Troy VI and during the Middle Helladic period in Greece supports this view of the first arrival of one branch of Indo-Europeans in Greece and west Anatolia. Recent excavations and studies, however, show the question to be more complex. Movement of people from west Anatolia across the Aegean at a slightly earlier date, in Early Bronze III (late 3rd millennium), was noted above, while gray Minyan ware appears to have evolved in Greece itself. However, in its earliest phases at Lefkandi in Euboea it may be connected with the Anatolian red-brown wares, while the full gray Minyan of Middle Helladic has many links with the gray ware of Troy VI.

In summary, then, the problem of Minyan pottery in Greece must, at the start of our thinking, be kept distinct from the arrival of the first Greek-speaking peoples. But it is now beginning to look as though a very close relationship between west Anatolia and the newcomers to Greece still holds good, at a slightly earlier date, a century or so before 2000 BC. Within Greece the newcomers at once develop their gray Minyan pottery, while their Early Bronze III Anatolian relatives, with David French, develop their gray ware into that of Troy VI, or, with Blegen, are replaced by horse-bringing newcomers whose gray pottery also suggests a close relationship with contemporary Middle Bronze Age Greece.

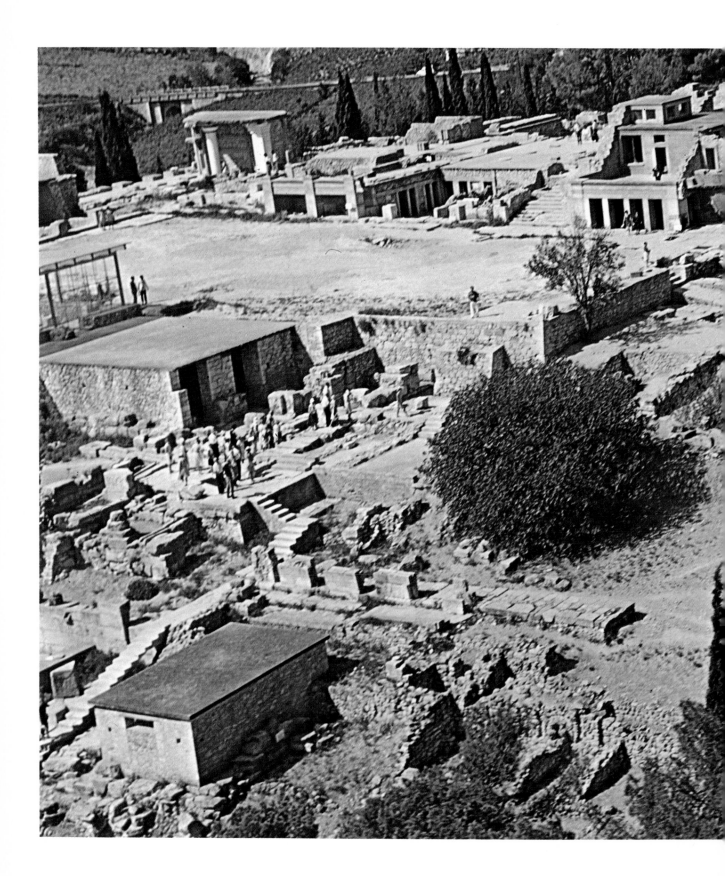

The Palace of Minos

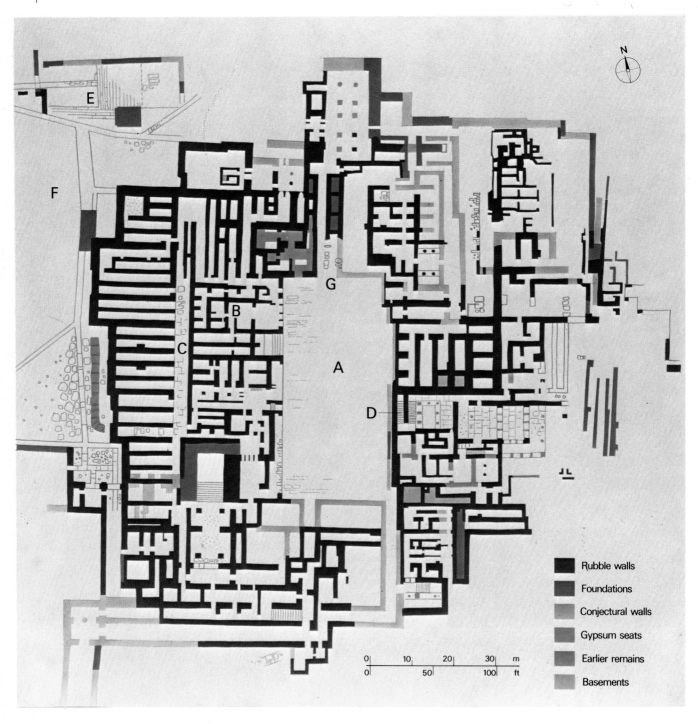

Rubble walls
Foundations
Conjectural walls
Gypsum seats
Earlier remains
Basements

Set on a low hill some five kilometers south of modern Herakleion, the great palace of Knossos was the focal point of the Bronze Age town. The low hill is in fact man-made, consisting of the accumulation of building levels and occupation debris extending back some 4,000 years before the palace was laid out, c. 1900 BC. At this time the surrounding town houses were given a well-planned system of paved stone roads, the oldest in Europe. The palace seems to have consisted at first of separate blocks of rooms, but these were joined into a single great complex during the First or Old Palace period (c. 1900–1700 BC). The building we see today was constructed, in its main lines, by 1700 BC, but after a destruction, probably by earthquake, around that date many modifications were made. The building then remained in use as a palace until c. 1400 BC, being occupied by Mycenaean rulers from the Greek mainland in its final phase.

Opposite: a groundplan of the palace of Knossos, carefully designed round a Central Court (A). Notice the functionally well-defined areas, storage chambers, cult rooms and shrines, workshops, residential apartments, all on the ground floors and given easy access by long corridors and entrance passages, or easily reached from the central courtyard. *Above left*: Sir Arthur John Evans (1851–1941), seen here among the walls of the palace he excavated. *Above right*: one of the most dramatic moments in the history of archaeology – the throne and Throne Room (B) of the palace which came into view on April 13, 1900 for the first time in 2,300 years. *Center right*: the careful excavation and marvelous preservation of the architecture and fragmentary paintings on the walls of the Throne Room enabled Evans to restore it as it was on the day when religious rites in the room failed to save the palace from destruction. *Below right*: some of the pithoi in the western magazines (C) used for storage of oil, wine, grain and other products.

Above: the Grand Staircase (D) off the Central Court in the eastern wing of the palace is perhaps the greatest marvel of Minoan architectural engineering. Here it is seen (*left*) partially restored and (*right*) as today with restoration complete. Five flights of elegant, shallow, stone steps, from which paved landings lead off to stately halls and corridors, continued up to at least one story, and probably more, above the level of the Central Court. Note the figure-of-eight shield frescoes. *Below*: the Minoan town west of the palace was served by this splendid road. It was lined on each side with fine houses and, apparently, with platforms or grandstands for watching great processions along it, since on the east the road ends in the elegant Theatral Area (E), probably designed for religious dances, and on the west leads off to the so-called Little Palace.

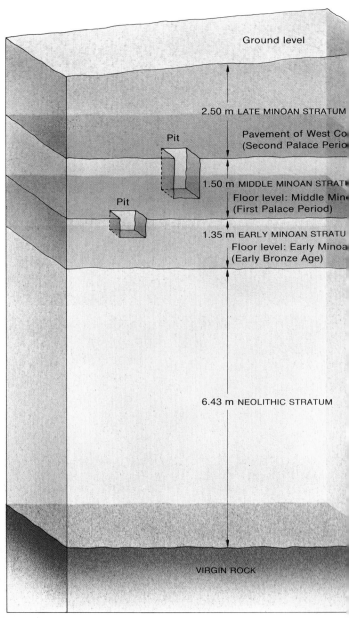

Ground level

2.50 m LATE MINOAN STRATUM

Pit

Pavement of West Co (Second Palace Perio

1.50 m MIDDLE MINOAN STRATU

Pit

Floor level: Middle Min (First Palace Period)

1.35 m EARLY MINOAN STRATU

Floor level: Early Minoa (Early Bronze Age)

6.43 m NEOLITHIC STRATUM

VIRGIN ROCK

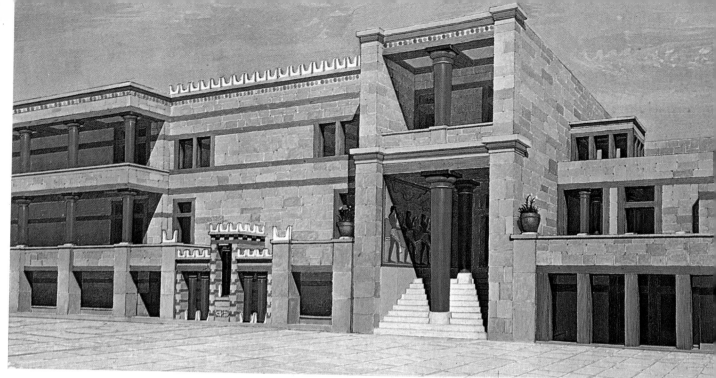

Opposite: below the present West Court (F) of the palace
lie four and a half millennia of history, partly
represented in this section. Neolithic people first built
their houses here and the accumulation of debris gradually
raised the ground level. Over the remains came stone
buildings of the Early Bronze Age (3000–1900 BC) and
over these in turn houses of the period of the First Palace
(1900–1700 BC); the paved court was laid alongside them.
Before 1700 BC this was extended over the razed houses
and great pits were dug and lined with stones, to receive
rubbish from the Old Palace. These pits in turn were
covered by the surviving paved court and raised stone
paths of the later palace. *Above*: this gaily colored and
accurate reconstruction of the West Wing of the palace,
seen from the Central Court, was executed by the late
Piet de Jong, Evans' draughtsman. The remains
preserved today give the ground-floor plans, while the
splendid staircase with its central column must have led to
major rooms above. To the left of the staircase were small
shrines, one with a cult pillar, and chests let into the floor
to store ritual equipment, such as the faience snake goddess
and her companions who came from here. To the right is
the entrance to the antechamber of the Throne Room.
Center right: the northern entrance passage to the palace
(G), leading straight into the Central Court. Note the huge
plaster relief of a charging bull on the restored west wall.
A bull cult was much practiced by the Minoans, as were
bull-leaping sports by specialist teams of men and women.
Below right: the most elaborate tomb among the many on
the hillsides of the Knossos area, and architecturally one of
the finest, is the so-called Temple Tomb built into sloping
ground not far to the south of the palace. It was probably
made for the burial of one of the rulers of Knossos, being
first built in 1700–1600 BC. It consisted of a columned
portico opening on to a paved court; this led through a
stone doorway and paved inner hall into a crypt with
walls and two pillars of superb ashlar masonry.

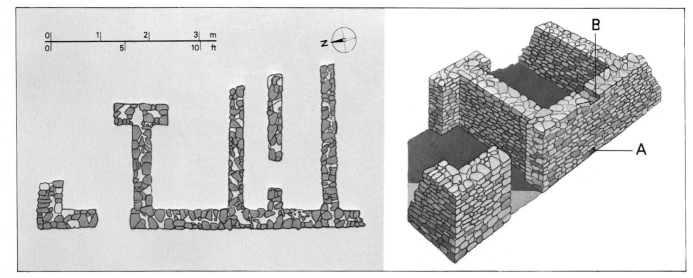

Above: reconstruction of a house at Knossos built 500 years before the palace. Note the drain (A) and roof beam slot (B).
Left: faience plaque showing what Minoan buildings looked like in elevation.
Below: an amphora from the Old Palace depicting the native Cretan palm tree. *Right*: the famous Cupbearer fresco from the southwestern part of the palace.

Above left: "la Parisienne," the most famous of all Minoan womens' heads. She was in fact a priestess in a long robe, her hair fastened in a special kind of sacred knot. *Above right*: the Prince of the Lilies fresco from the south entrance to the Central Court of the palace. *Below right*: this fragment of a fresco shows us what a Minoan column looked like (no real ones have survived). Unlike Greek columns it tapered downwards; the wooden shaft, painted red, stood on a separate base, here shown black to represent the originals in dark stone, and supported an elaborate capital like a two-tier cushion.

5. The Great Age of Minoan Crete 1700-1100 BC

The Second Palace period (1700–1450 BC). The Minoan culture was in no way diminished by the destructions of the palaces at Knossos and Phaistos around 1700 BC. There are no indications of newcomers in the archaeological record and the rebuilding of the palaces into essentially the sophisticated structures whose remains we see today ushers in the greatest period of the island's civilization. The settlement pattern, like the huge range of artifacts, is an expansion of that in the First Palace period: communities flourished all over the island, including the western parts; coastal towns like Gournia, Mochlos and Palaikastro continued on a larger scale, and the palaces at Knossos, Mallia, Phaistos and Zakro were still the social and economic centers of their districts.

Meanwhile a new type of habitation appears, the country mansion – architecturally akin to the great houses adjacent to the palaces, economically the local expression of the extensive agricultural development of the fertile parts of the island. The other major change is that the great circular communal tombs of the Mesara plain and Asterousia mountains are for the most part no longer in use. This does not necessarily mean that their settlements had ceased to be inhabited; Aghia Triadha, the only relevant site substantially excavated, certainly flourished. But there may have been some movement of people to town sites in the region, like Phaistos or Komo on the south coast.

The chronological limits of this great age are roughly 1700 to 1450 BC, with possibly a margin of two or three decades either way at the beginning and one or two at the end. For absolute dating we depend on links with Egypt. The First Palace period is contemporary with the 12th and 13th Dynasties, on the evidence of an imported Egyptian scarab found at Knossos and Middle Minoan I and II pottery in Egypt. From an early phase (Middle Minoan III) of the Second Palace period at Knossos comes an alabaster lid with the inscribed name of the Hyksos pharaoh Khyan (17th century). Late Minoan I B and contemporary Late Helladic II A pots are found in Egypt and the Near East in the time of Tuthmosis III, about 1500–1450 BC, while during Late Minoan I B there are several representations of Minoans in Egyptian tombs dating from the reign of the same pharaoh.

In a period limited to two and a half centuries and in an earthquake-prone area, one might well expect stratified evidence of destructions, rebuilding and new building, with developing pottery styles. Thus at Knossos there was an earthquake around or soon after 1600 BC which destroyed one or two large town houses, after which new buildings like a mansion west of the Little Palace were begun. In the east Cretan towns there are also buildings with contents from this Late Minoan I A phase (c. 1550 to 1500 BC), to which also belongs the whole amazingly preserved settlement at Akrotiri on Thera, with its scores of imported Late Minoan I A vases. Subsequently the palaces, towns and houses, built in Middle Minoan III, Late Minoan I A or I B, were all destroyed around 1450 BC.

The palaces. In the 20th century BC the palaces had been carefully laid out around a great central court. The stairways of the surviving remains, rebuilt and modified in the Second Palace period, show the palaces to have possessed at least one upper story. In the most ambitious construction of all, the east side of the Palace of Minos at Knossos, there were two stories below the level of the central court, reached from the grand staircase with five stone flights, one story at the same level as the court and at least one above. On all these floors were majestic rooms supported by columns and pillars, long corridors and linking stairways. Construction was in stone, either smoothly dressed ashlar masonry or rougher blocks, carefully plastered, both types secured against earthquake with huge wooden framing beams. Ceilings were of beams overlaid by stone slabs.

Knossos occupied about 19,000 square meters, while the other palaces were smaller. Functionally they were divided into fairly distinct units. In all four palaces the western part of the west wing consisted, on the ground floor, of storage magazines with great pithoi originally filled with oil, wine and grain. At Knossos the magazines also had rectangular stone cists let into their floors and into that of the long corridor outside them. The cists were covered with stone slabs and also lined with lead sheeting; they must have been intended for the safe-keeping of many valuables. Between the western storage area and the central court were ground-floor rooms for cult and ritual activities. The Zakro shrine and its adjacent treasury of stone vessels, the great libation table at Mallia, the temple repositories and shrines at Knossos, including the throne room opposite its underground lustral chamber, all show this. The throne room and anteroom in their present form, however, seem to have been built in the final, Mycenaean period of occupation, after 1450 BC.

On the opposite side of the central court at Knossos, Zakro and probably Phaistos were the domestic quarters and royal apartments. At Mallia there were further rooms for making and storing oil and wine on the ground floor of the east side; domestic quarters might have stood above these, as well as have been associated with a banqueting hall (as J. Walter Graham has argued) north of the court. Domestic quarters lay north of the central court at Phaistos, while in that palace and at Knossos and Zakro workshops for metallurgy (Phaistos), pottery and stonework were situated in the northeastern unit.

Towns and mansions. The Minoan towns and villages seem to follow the irregular street plans of the First Palace period, though there was expansion and new buildings were constructed on the old remains in the 17th and 16th centuries BC. The settlements are mostly on or near the coast, to exploit easy sea routes and adjacent fertile land. There are several types of site. Palaikastro and Pseira are exacavated examples of dozens of small towns (Palaikastro, covering certainly about 22,000 and very possibly about 45,000 square meters, is the largest known) with

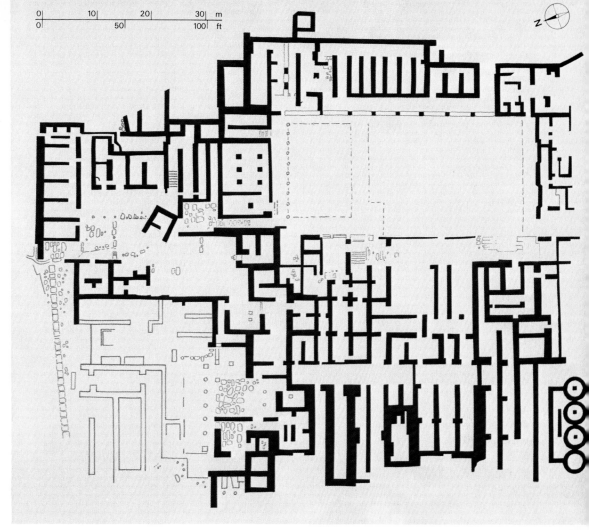

Previous page: the palace of Knossos: view from the south wing to Juktas on the horizon, where a mountain peak sanctuary served the palace community.

Right: a plan of the palace of Mallia. In the 20th century BC the palaces had been carefully laid out around a great central court. Cult rooms and store rooms made up the west wing and the circular structures in the southwest corner were probably granaries rather than cisterns.

blocks of living units defined by the cobbled streets. There were 20 or more ground-floor rooms in each block, some at least being for storage, cooking and other work, with stairways leading to living and sleeping rooms upstairs. A ground floor and an upper floor and possibly a small room on the roof were probably normal, as the faience plaques from Knossos and the Arkhanes house model indicate. Within the town blocks there would be well-defined houses like one recently excavated at Palaikastro.

Knossos, Mallia and Zakro form a second type, sites with palaces surrounded by large houses, those of Zakro bounded by cobbled streets over the rising ground. Late Minoan Mochlos seemed to consist of such houses alone on the waterfront and hillside. Some were elegant, with storage rooms, small courts and living apartments divisible by doors into smaller rooms, as in the palaces and in the Santorini houses. Phaistos, Gournia and, on a smaller scale, Myrtos Pyrgos form a fourth type of settlement, with an important main building on the summit of the hill and a town quarter of small buildings (not grand like those of Zakro) on the lower slopes. Aghia Triadha, within the limits of the present excavation and its reporting, seems to be a large single complex, though something less than a palace, unless the flat area south and east of the main constructions could be shown to be a central court. Tylissos, near Herakleion, is yet another kind of settlement, consist-

ing of three large, conjoined mansions each with its storage and living areas and upper floor. It introduces us directly to the villa or mansion type of the Second Palace period.

Large freestanding houses were constructed in the First Palace period at Khamaizi, Mallia and Vasilike. They now spring up around palatial settlements and in other settlements, as we have just seen; they also spread into the Minoan countryside. Examples are Sklavokampos in the main valley west of Tylissos, perhaps placed to facilitate the transport of blocks of serpentine from quarries to the west down through Tylissos to Knossos; Vathypetro, a large establishment controlling the fertile, undulating country south of Arkhanes, with rooms for grape-pressing and olive oil manufacture; Nirou Khani on the coast east of Herakleion, storing large double axes of bronze sheet for ritual use, mounted on poles (perhaps intended for export to Aegean centers); and fourth, a whole group of villas in the fertile valley running south from Siteia in east Crete. These country mansions are also known from surface surveys in the valleys of west central Crete. Here they seem related to larger settlements a few kilometers distant. Mixorrouma near the settlement at Spili, and a small villa or farm near that at Saktouria are examples. But such buildings have not yet been found in the far west of the island, the province of Khania; they will surely come to light there too, as the region is increasingly explored.

Architecture and wall painting. The architecture of this Second Palace period has been excellently described by J. W. Graham. Large, smoothly dressed blocks of limestone were used not only in the palaces but in country mansions like that at Myrtos Pyrgos. Usually, however, the provincial buildings were made of unworked, gray limestone blocks, plastered over. Refinements are found everywhere: an elaborate drainage system of terracotta pipes at Knossos and Zakro; a fine stone drain down the main street at Palaikastro; stone-built, circular swimming pools entered down a flight of steps at Arkhanes and Zakro; walls faced with thin sheets of gypsum or colorful banded calcite at Aghia Triadha, Knossos, Myrtos Pyrgos and Phaistos; well-designed courtyards and main rooms everywhere. The terracotta model recently found at Arkhanes gives a marvelous idea of what a Minoan villa looked like in full elevation, with its deliberately unimposing entrance, little passages, stairway and columns, as in the well-preserved South House at Knossos.

The most attractive architectural refinement was the decoration of the walls with brilliantly colored scenes of Minoan life, religion and natural environment. Fragments of paintings have survived from many rooms of the palace and from the House of the Frescoes at Knossos. There were large-scale compositions of acrobatic bull-leaping, swimming dolphins, a pack of monkeys in a flowery landscape, griffins heraldically flanking the throne, richly dressed court ladies, some dancing, others watching a spectacle from a grandstand, as well as processions of men bearing precious vases, and even scenes with chariots, recently reconstructed by Mark Cameron. Small-scale or miniature compositions show crowds of spectators on grandstands,

Above: a terracotta house model found at Arkhanes. It gives a marvelous idea of what a Minoan villa looked like in full elevation. Note the balcony in front resting on rounded beam ends. A staircase leads to the upper floor with its columned roof. Ht. 23.5 cm.

Below: the famous bull-leaping fresco from the East Wing of the palace of Knossos. Men, shown red, and women took part in these dangerous sports. 1600–1400 BC.

Opposite left: a gold and ivory figurine of a bull-leaper in midair. Comparison with the fresco below helps us to understand his acrobatics. Note the ivory carver's detailed rendering of the veins and finger nails on the outstretched hands.

Opposite right: equipment for making wine and heating olives for oil, found in the domestic quarters of the mansion of Vathypetro. Note the collecting tub in front, the storage jar behind and the channel for oil. 1550–1450 BC.

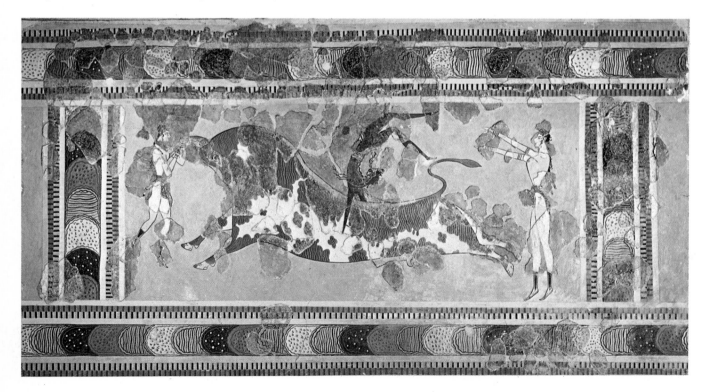

The Great Age of Minoan Crete | 95

obviously watching bull-sports or similar activities, since behind the delicate court ladies are cheering men with arms outstretched. In addition to these flat painted murals, plaster relief frescoes of large size were also mounted on the palace walls, like the famous charging bull guarding the north entrance passage at Knossos and the "Priest-King" with his lily headdress in a corresponding position in the southern entrance of the central court.

Equally colorful frescoes of all kinds, large, miniature and relief, are found all over the island, though, alas, only preserved in fragments. A beautiful composition of white lilies on a red ground was found at the villa at Amnisos, small-scale scenes with priestesses and large compositions with cats and birds in grassy landscapes at Aghia Triadha, miniature frescoes of helmeted men at Tylissos, a large relief fresco of a richly dressed goddess at Pseira, and flowers and plants in the villa at Epano Zakro. The brilliant discoveries of well-preserved wall paintings in room after room at Thera enable us to visualize how the Minoan centers must have looked in their own time.

Skilled craftsmen. The Minoan craftsmen were now producing their finest objects at a level of artistic sensibility, religious inspiration and technical ability which secures them a firm place among humanity's most attractive achievements. Individual pieces in pottery, stone, metal, ivory and faience have been described, and the work of the builders and fresco painters has been indicated in chapter I. We note now some general aspects of the production of artifacts, before considering briefly the nature of Minoan art.

A wide variety of types was produced. Pottery ranged from hundreds of storage pithoi about five feet high, through tubs for wine and oil-making to smaller storage vessels, three-legged cooking pots, lamps and clay stands, incense burners and a huge variety of bowls, cups, jugs and plates for table ware, and ritual vessels for pouring or holding offerings during cult ceremonies. These fine wares were decorated with red or black paint, and sometimes white as well in Late Minoan I A, in several distinct styles. Early in the period (Middle Minoan III) purplish and dark surfaces survived from First Palace times, with white spirals or little dots, while a vertical rippled decoration was popular in red on buff, especially on cups.

Then in Late Minoan I A (1550 to 1500 BC) the light ground style became general, with spirals and reed motifs used as well as rippling. In the final phase, Late Minoan I B (1500 to 1450 BC), a few workshops at Knossos were producing beautiful cups and jugs with patterns of papyrus, ivy, olive sprays and other plants, as well as abstract designs, while perhaps a single atelier made vases in a rich marine style, covering them with fishes, nautiluses, shells, seaweed and octopuses.

The range of metalwork and stone vase carving was equally wide. A set of silver vessels lay in the South House at Knossos, and cauldrons, bowls, ewers, hydrias and lamps of bronze were found in hoards all around the palace and at Mochlos, with occasional pieces elsewhere. At Tylissos there were several enormous bronze cauldrons made of separate sheets riveted together. In gold, there are the famous Late Minoan I cups from the Vapheio tomb near Sparta. Naturalistic statuettes of male and female worshipers, one arm raised to the head in salute, were made in bronze. Perhaps the finest of these, a man with hair in long

ringlets, armbands and tiny dagger at his side, came to light in 1973 in the sanctuary of Kato Syme. Equally splendid is the statuette of a bull and leaper in the British Museum.

Bronze tools and weapons were made by the score: double axes, adzes, chisels, hammers, and saws for carpentry and stonework, or for ritual use, socketed spearheads engraved with running spirals, daggers with bronze, silver or gold rivets for attaching the haft, and swords a meter long for hunting and fighting (best known from those deposited as offerings, along with gold miniature double axes, in a sacred cave at Arkalokhori), knives and sickles for agriculture, pins, rings, bracelets for adornment, as well as delicate gold rings with human and divine figures in elaborate ritual scenes.

In stone hundreds of vases were carved. A blue-black mottled serpentine was most popular, but alabaster, breccias, gypsum, limestones, marbles and very hard rocks like the porphyry, lapis Lacedaemonius, obsidian and rock crystal were cut, drilled, carved and polished into bowls, cups, jars, lamps, tall stands and sacred rhytons of conical and animal head shape. The most revealing class, of which about 30 pieces survive, mostly as fragments, is the serpentine and chlorite rhytons with relief scenes such as the mountain peak sanctuary guarded by heraldic agrimia (Cretan wild goats) from Zakro, the "Harvester Vase," Chieftain Cup and Boxer Rhyton from Aghia Triadha and fragments from Knossos with shrine buildings and figures in procession, or of a bull captured in a net, as on the Vapheio cup. Still in stonework, we have the hundreds of engraved sealstones, the finest achievement of the Minoan craftsmen. Agates, carnelian, chalcedony, haematite, jaspers, lapis lazuli, lapis Lacedaemonius, obsidian and rock

crystal were all cut, usually in lentoid, amygdaloid (almond-shape) or flattened cylinder form and carved with schematic buildings and ships, abstract motifs, brilliantly naturalistic animals (especially bulls), birds and fishes, or with exquisitely done human figures or divinities in ritual scenes.

Craftsmen in faience, ivory and plaster were equally active. Huge ivory tusks were found imported at Zakro, to be carved into products like the ivory acrobats, model birds and animals and decorated plaques found at Knossos and elsewhere. Faience was fired into polychrome vessels, bull's-head rhytons and a large sea nautilus (at Zakro), or into the famous Snake Goddess and companions from Knossos. Plaster was used for relief frescoes and for low offering tables, of which examples with brilliant paintings of dolphins in a marine setting have been found at Thera – either Minoan or locally imitated.

Although separate workshops existed for the materials described above – for instance there was one for ivory north of the Royal Road at Knossos, and others for stone vases at Knossos, Mallia and Zakro – it is clear that there was a close sharing and appreciation of decorative motifs and shapes between craftsmen in different media. Potters imitated metallic and occasionally stone shapes, lapidaries imitated pottery and metal vases, while shapes like animal rhytons and Vapheio cups were common to all three. The rendering of the male and female form is the same in metal, ivory, faience, on frescoes, on relief stone vases and even on small sealstones and gold rings. These interrelations of representation demonstrate the artistic unity of the Minoan craftsmen.

Another aspect is the confidence of these craftsmen in

Left: a painting of bronze vessels as they were found in the Tomb of the Tripod Hearth to the north of the palace of Knossos. The hearth itself is made of plaster and is shown in the foreground. c. 1400 BC.

Opposite left: a sardonyx sealstone of lentoid shape from Knossos. The Minoan Mistress of Animals goddess stands between two attendant griffins. 16th–15th centuries BC.

Opposite right: a faience plaque from the temple repositories at Knossos. It shows a beautiful, naturalistic rendering of a goat or an antelope feeding its young. c. 1550 BC.

their technical ability. The skills and knowledge required to fuse silver rivets to a bronze dagger by heat and pressure alone (as in Sheffield plate), or to produce swords a meter long, or to turn a block of brittle and hard obsidian into a large and highly naturalistic shell rhyton, or to combine colors, glazes, shape and firing skills in a faience statuette are considerable, even by modern standards.

The quality of Minoan art, its combination of color, technical skill in execution and feeling for shape, whether three-dimensional, abstract, human or from the world of nature, is readily appreciated. But to understand its nature is for us difficult, if not impossible. The function of the products was often religious: many of the finest stone vessels were apparatus for shrines; many sealstones and some wall paintings depict cult scenes, while metal figures, miniature or huge axes and sometimes swords were deposited as offerings to the gods. Thus the craftsman's motivation was probably at least in part religious, like that of a medieval painter or builder. But purely secular products in pottery, bronze, faience, ivory, stone or fresco were made with equal skill and sensitivity. There was an intense delight in the natural world, its animals, birds, plants and sea creatures.

This delight is a constantly apparent inspiration in Minoan art, what Myres and Forsdyke have so aptly called "the desire to interpret nature in terms of its underlying character and life." The delight rested on a proper appreciation of the natural environment and its potential and recurrent use for all levels of civilization. Along with these artistic motivations runs a strong decorative sense, a love, indeed sometimes over-exuberant, of complex and attractive patterns. Finally the craftsmen-artists and their viewers sought to capture the fleeting moment, as in a photograph;

to savor the present by rendering a particular point of activity on a fresco or stone or metal relief vase. Yet this rendering was always generalized. There was no sense whatever of the particular individual, simply the expression of the Minoan physical type, athletic for men, full-breasted for women, and a few rare variants among the men.

Writing. Another achievement of the Second Palace period was the development and wide use of the Minoan writing system. The Linear A script, as it is called to distinguish it from Mycenaean Greek Linear B, had been developed by scribes in the First Palace period at Phaistos. Now it is known from 27 Minoan sites, but the quantity of inscriptions (about 400) is as yet too few to permit decipherment. There are small archives of tablets from Aghia Triadha, Arkhanes, Khania (recently found) and Zakro and single tablets from sites like Myrtos Pyrgos, Palaikastro and Tylissos. These obviously record allocations and quantities of produce like grain, wine and oil, much as on Linear B tablets.

But the script has a wider use than Linear B and appears on clay bars, labels and roundels, probably for identification of owner or product, on a pithos from Epano Zakro in a quite long inscription, and in an even longer one of 37 signs on a silver pin from a burial in a tomb on the Ailias hillside at Knossos. This inscription, brilliantly revealed by recent cleaning in Herakleion Museum, may be religious, as may at least two separate formulas found inscribed on a series of stone offering tables and other stone vessels. The formulas perhaps indicate the names of two divinities. Several of the vessels come from the mountain peak sanctuary of Petsofa, above Palaikastro in east Crete, while another is from the famous Diktaian cave above the Lasithi plain and others from near Arkhanes, Knossos, Prasa east of Herakleion and from a settlement at Apodhoulou in west central Crete. It seems that religious officers and perhaps ordinary donors of sacred gifts could read, perhaps even write in this period, while scribes worked at several places.

A unique inscribed object dated to about 1600 BC is the famous terracotta disk found, with a Linear A tablet, in a house on the north edge of the palace at Phaistos. Each side is inscribed with a long text running spirally from the edge to the center. The signs, which are often repeated, have been impressed with stamps, thus indicating the world's earliest "printing press." The inscriptions are undeciphered, but recent research has shown, contrary to former views, that several of the individual signs are paralleled on Minoan objects and, in the case of the crested heads, in Minoan clay figurines. The disk may therefore turn out to be Minoan too, the hieroglyphs perhaps conserved for a religious purpose into the time of the Linear A script.

Burial customs. In marked contrast to all these rich indications of the buildings of the living, there is a mysterious lack of evidence for contemporary tombs. But we do know that different types were in use. The stone circular tombs built in the First Palace period continued at Kamilari off the west end of the Mesara plain, at Arkhanes, and on the Gypsadhes hill at Knossos. Another may have been built on the Kephala ridge north of Knossos around 1600 BC. It has a stone entrance passage with Minoan signs (Linear A script) carved on one block. Chamber tombs, sometimes with several compartments, were used in the Ailias hillside at Knossos; but the best example of this type and date comes from the Minoan site near Kastri on Kythera. A large rock-cut chamber tomb, supported by a pillar left in the center, was made at Poros outside Herakleion and contained richly endowed burials of Middle Minoan III to Late Minoan I A date, with pottery cups, engraved seals (including a cylinder imported from Syria) and decorated and inlaid gold rings. Rich Late Minoan I burials have also been found at Myrtos Pyrgos by Gerald Cadogan, with bronze tools, fine stone vases and pottery accompanying the skeletons, which were laid on the ground floor of a two-story tomb building. Yet these and other contemporary graves are extremely few in number when one considers the dense settlement pattern and wealth of the period.

Religion. From the wealth of relevant artifacts and from the many and varied cult places it is clear that religion played a dominant part in Minoan life. Evans, Nilsson, Banti, Rutkowski and others have described its external characteristics from these remains. There were distinct types of cult place: stone-built sanctuaries with one or more rooms stood on mountain summits all over the island. Representations on stone relief vases from Knossos

The enigmatic Phaistos disk. A unique inscribed object of terracotta dated to about 1600 BC but as yet undeciphered. Some of the stamped signs have close links with other Minoan objects. The disk may therefore turn out to be Minoan, the hieroglyphs perhaps conserved for a religious purpose.

and Zakro give an idea of the elevations of the buildings. At these shrines ash levels indicate that great bonfires were lit, into which were deliberately thrown little clay figurines of human beings and animals, or separately made parts of each. Burnt animal bones suggest that sacrifices were also offered. As we have noted, inscribed stone offering tables, apparently with formulas to a goddess, sometimes form part of the cult apparatus.

Second, certain caves were clearly sacred places. The Diktaian cave above Lasithi and those of Eileithyia at Amnisos and at Skoteino a little to the east have prominent stalactites which may, especially at Amnisos, have been held sacred. Within the caves bronze figurines, miniature double axes or everyday swords might be offered and inscribed, and decorated or plain stone offering tables used.

Third, rooms within palaces and mansions were clearly shrines. In a ground floor room of the palace at Knossos the roof-supporting pillar of squared blocks had engraved double axes, and channels round its base, perhaps for liquid offerings. Another pillar in a house on Gypsadhes hill south of the palace had dozens of little conical cups carefully placed upside down around its base, with carbonized vegetable remains under some. At Myrtos Pyrgos a shrine stood on an upper floor of the mansion, with decorated clay tubes forming part of the cult objects, while in a house at Knossos a shrine contained a series of clay vases connected with worship of the household snake. Self-contained rural shrines also existed. One at Rousses near Khondhros had several rooms with many pottery vessels and stone offering tables, while at Kato Syme a mountain (but not mountain summit) shrine had cult vessels and libation tables, with a bronze figurine and swords being found elsewhere on the site.

Shrines are also portrayed on seals, gold rings, on their clay impressions (sealings) which have survived and on stone relief vases. Worship of a tree within a fenced or built enclosure or sprouting up between ritual horns of consecration is also shown on these objects. Worship of pillars and boulders is clearly represented in scenes on gold rings. The two main symbols of Minoan religion are bronze double axes mounted on poles, which are set in pyramidal stands, and horns of consecration (a stylized form of a pair of bull's horns), both represented on frescoes, rings and seals and existing *in corpore*. Stone altars had incurved sides and conch shells were used as ritual trumpets.

The evidence thus consists of different types of shrine, a wide range of cult objects, especially rhytons (conical and animal-shaped vessels with holes for pouring liquid offer-

around 1400 BC, and though some of these might have been introduced by the incoming Mycenaeans, others seem purely local.

The material remains clearly indicate a mountain goddess, who was worshiped at peak sanctuaries, was a Mistress of Animals (the latter aspect being represented on sealstones and both aspects on the clay impressions of a gold ring at Knossos) and may have been associated with a male god who is shown as a Master of Animals on seals. The powerful goddess has much in common with the later Artemis, and may even have been known as such. The name occurs on the tablets. The corresponding male god of animals has similarities with the later Apollo-Paian, among whose functions were those of hunter, and healer or averter of pestilence. The burning of clay animal figurines in the mountain peak bonfires was perhaps an expression of the cult of both the Mistress of Animals (the later cult of Artemis also involved such mountain bonfires) and the Master of Animals, to avert human disease and the destruction of crops by rodents and other animals who are

A sealstone of chalcedony set in gold. The engraved scene shows a huge lion or dog with a knobbled collar and two men, probably the animal's attendants or tamers.

A gold ring with a cult scene in relief, a new find from Arkhanes. A Minoan goddess stands in the center with smaller human figures on each side. c. 1500 BC.

ings through) and fascinating pictures on gold rings, sealstones and stone relief vases of cult activities in progress. Interpretation is naturally hypothetical, but several aspects stand out. Minoan religion was dominated by female divinity intimately connected with the natural world and was evolved to promote the fertility and annual renewal of the fruits of the earth. Whether the female divinity was a single great goddess worshiped under different aspects, as Evans thought, or whether there were separately conceived goddesses (and gods) has been much discussed. The evidence above seems to point to a developed polytheism. The Knossos tablets list several distinct deities in the period

represented among the figurines.

The Mistress of Animals may have been identical with or distinct from a goddess of fertility with whom there was intimately associated a young god as son or consort. This is a vegetation cult, the yearly death and resurrection of the young god (known from later religion and inferred for Minoan) having the purpose of promoting the annual renewal and fertility of crops. Similarly in Greek religion Artemis has her young consort Hippolytos.

A domestic cult also flourished, involving the worship of a household goddess whose chief attribute was the snake. Snakes are found as guardians of the house in some societies,

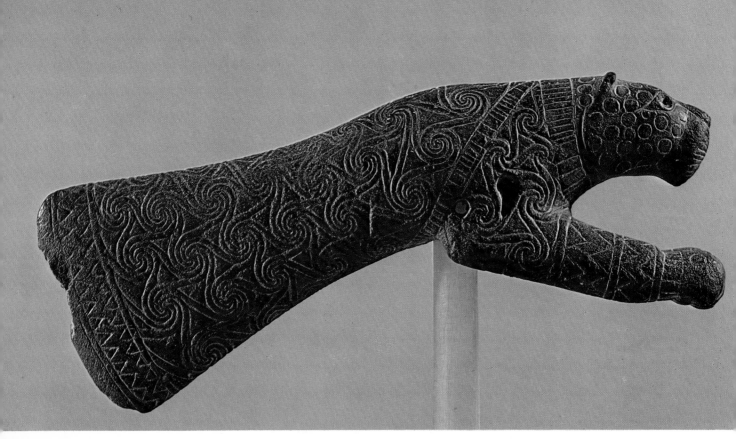

among them the Minoan. The household divinity as Snake Goddess is known from as far back as an Early Minoan statuette from Koumasa and later from the famous faience statuettes of Knossos and from Gournia, where terracotta figures with snakes were actually found in a shrine. The household goddess without her snake attributes is represented chiefly by figurines earlier and later than our present period. She has points in common with the later Athena, protectress of domestic crafts, whose name is in fact pre-Greek and appears on the tablets.

Eileithyia, later goddess of childbirth, is known from the tablets, where she receives a pot of honey, and she had Minoan sacred caves at Amnisos (referred to in the *Odyssey*) and at Inatos, on the south coast. In Greek religion Eileithyia was sometimes identified with Artemis, but often remained a distinct goddess, and this she may have been for the Minoans, being worshiped in her caves presumably as goddess of childbirth. But the recent find (1974) of a cave directly associated with the peak sanctuary of Juktas, south of Knossos, when added to the fact that the same inscription formula is sometimes found on stone tables in both sacred caves and peak sanctuaries, suggests that the mountain peak and cave goddess may have been one, Artemis-Eileithyia, in Minoan cult.

A dove goddess is mentioned on the tablets and clay doves occur on ritual objects. They are later found associated with Aphrodite. The Minoan bull sacrifices may have been to Poseidon, known in the tablets and intimately associated with bulls in later religion. The name of Hermes also occurs on the tablets, and the recently found and richly endowed shrine at Kato Syme was dedicated to this god in

The figure of a panther in the form of a stone axe-head which terminated the royal scepter-head, found in the palace at Mallia. c. 1700 BC.

Greek and Roman times. Since there appears from the finds to be cult continuity right back into the Late Minoan period, it is very possible that there was also a Minoan cult of Hermes.

The evidence is thus sufficient to make polytheism likely. We should add lesser gods and goddesses, worshiped locally and known from epithets like Velkhanos, Brito-martis and Diktynna long given to Greek national divinities (in these cases Zeus and Artemis) who had once been assimilated with them. Cult scenes on gold rings also involve a goddess or goddesses with orgiastic dancing female votaries, or votaries offering flowers, including opium poppies (a goddess of death?), or in association with tree and boulder or pillar worship, or in attitudes of mourning. There was, too, a large class of demons and spirits often connected with the watering of vegetation and known from representations chiefly on sealstones and clay impressions of these.

Society. Reasonable inferences can also be made about the structure of Minoan society. The palaces and the elaborate economic organization which they imply suggest a ruler at the top, and tradition tells of the brother kings, Minos, Rhadamanthys and Sarpedon, who are associated respectively with Knossos, Phaistos and Mallia. Society was evidently hierarchical. The country mansions suggest local rulers, probably under economic obligation to the palaces; documents were sealed with the same gold ring at different sites or sent sealed to those sites, which implies some kind of central bureaucracy. The many specialist craftsmen formed another group or class, and traders or merchants supplied them with imported raw materials like ivory, fine stones and metals, possibly under palace direction. There was a class of scribes, probably one or more at each main center. Priestesses and priests flourished abundantly.

We may also certainly infer a large class of agricultural producers who filled the storage jars with oil, wine, grain and meat. Their precise status is unknown but they must have been under the control of local or palace rulers. Officials of many kinds must have controlled and organized the work of the craftsmen, scribes and traders. These officials were perhaps members of the royal family or nobility living in the great houses around the palaces. The bull-leaping teams were exotic specialists forming a distinct group of their own, though perhaps within the sphere of religious control.

But while these broad economic or occupational groups may be defined, the exact status of any one group in relation to another – those interwoven relationships which produce distinct social fabrics – remains unknown. Kinship structure is likewise extremely shadowy; communal burial suggests that a clan or extended family pattern was still strong, although single burials in pithoi or chests, with their own grave goods, imply recognition of personal wealth and individual status. Social hierarchies created by economic specialization also suggest some lessening of clan influence.

The Minoans abroad. By the 5th century BC, when Bacchylides, Herodotus and Thucydides recorded it, one well-known story in the Greek tradition spoke of a first rule of the Aegean sea and islands by King Minos of Crete. Later writers like Aristotle and the geographer Strabo accepted this and the discoveries in the prehistoric Aegean enable us to see how much validity the tradition had. Another indication is the distribution of the place name Minoa at several places in the Aegean and at one or two in the central and east Mediterranean. The name seems to make most sense as a survival of Bronze Age influence from Crete. Its bestowal would have been pointless later.

It is during the Second Palace period that we find most evidence of Minoan activity outside Crete. We saw in chapter 4 that during the First Palace period, c. 1900 to 1700 BC, and even earlier, Minoan pottery and stone vessels reached Aegean, Near Eastern and Egyptian centers. The great expansion of this trade in the present period enables us to speak of three classes of evidence for external activity: actual settlements of Minoans overseas, exported products, and artistic and other cultural influences. To balance this, the island received necessary and luxury imports. On the other hand, with her cypress forests in the mountains, Crete had no need to import timber and in foodstuffs she was self-sufficient.

The criteria for a Minoan settlement outside the island may be posited as a coastal location, preferably on a small and easy promontory, like so many sites on the island itself; a plan of rather irregular streets and house blocks like Gournia or Palaikastro; Minoan architectural features such as rooms with pillars of square stone blocks, or a row of incut door jambs to enable doors to close off the room into smaller areas; the Minoan tomb type with several chambers opening off a central one; local pottery in Minoan shapes with scores of typically Minoan little conical cups (but not imports of Late Minoan I fine decorated ware, which could be exported anywhere and whose presence need not imply an actual Minoan settlement); evidence of Linear A writing; and, perhaps less persuasively, local stone vase manufacture (there being no evidence of specifically Cycladic or Mycenaean types at this period); and finally, evidence of Minoan religious ritual. The presence of all or a majority of these features, especially the quantities of cheap but uniquely Minoan conical cups, should indicate a Minoan settlement.

Accordingly, excavations on Aegean Late Bronze Age sites make it clear that there were settlements of Minoans at the coastal sites of Kastri on Kythera and Triandha on

The circular libation table at Mallia (1500–1450 BC), probably for multiple offerings of seeds and fruits. A focal point of palace religion, it stands near the great staircase.

Rhodes which satisfy most of our criteria. At Iasos on the Anatolian coast, where Italian excavations are in progress, and the local pottery, including many conical cups, is mixed with quantities of imported ware, and on Naxos and Karpathos with their unexcavated, surface pottery, settlements are highly probable. At Aghia Eirene on Kea, so fully excavated by John L. Caskey in recent years, local pottery, including hundreds of conical cups, a local stone vase industry, evidence of Linear A, the female statues of goddesses from the temple with Minoan dress and figures (the breasts are even molded over conical cups) and obvious Minoan religious derivation all suggest that at least some Minoans joined the population in the 17th or 16th centuries BC. In connection with Aghia Eirene we may recall Bacchylides' poem telling of a settlement placed on the island by Minos.

There remain two of the most important sites, which are among the nearest to Crete. Phylakopi on Melos had been inhabited since the Early Bronze Age, but we saw in chapter 4, following Arne Furumark, that its "Minoanization" at the start of the Late Bronze Age was so complete

as to suggest direct control from Crete, if not an actual settlement from the greater island. The site has most of the criteria set out above and the forthcoming new excavations may clarify its status.

Although the excavator, Spyridon Marinatos, rightly emphasized the Cycladic character of the Akrotiri settlement of Thera, there are very many features among the superabundantly rich finds which are Minoan. The coastal location is typical; the plan is emerging as akin to the mansions of Tylissos or the mansions and streeets of Zakro; divisible rooms with door jambs occur and there is a sunken chamber for religious ritual, certainly taken from the Minoan type; much of the local pottery is in Minoan shapes (and there are many dozens of imported clay vases, along with other fine Minoan stone and metal vessels); and Linear A is known. The settlement seems to have been a new foundation in Late Minoan I A, and it is, I think, likely that it was a Minoan foundation which soon developed its own independent artistic spirit, fusing it with the Cycladic tradition of painted vases, but always remaining in close touch with Crete. The excavator believed, and was surely

This cover was found with ritual objects, including figurines of dancers, in a shrine room at Palaikastro. The decorative style dates it to the 13th century BC. It probably covered a lamp in the shrine, a lamp handle protruding through the opening. Ht. 12 cm.

right, that the frescoes were painted by local artists. Many of the scenes appear to owe little or nothing to surviving Cretan frescoes, while others, like the pack of monkeys and the exquisite red lilies (though not the composition as a whole) show close awareness of the same metropolitan animals and flowers.

Exported Minoan products of this period consisted mainly of fine decorated pottery and vessels, and lamps of serpentine and other stones. Some other luxuries also went out: lead figurines (Kambos in Lakonia), bronze figurines (Aghia Eirene on Kea, Phylakopi on Melos), the gold cups with bull scenes (Vapheio in Lakonia), vessels of gold, silver and bronze (Mycenae, Vapheio, Thera and elsewhere), sealstones and gold rings (Mycenae, Vapheio), ostrich eggs with faience mountings (Mycenae, Thera) and probably swords (Mycenae). In the distribution of exports there are dense concentrations in the Argolid, the Aegean islands and Dodecanese, and not insignificant amounts in Messenia (pottery, one or two stone vases, Linear A signs and very possibly the tholos tomb), Lakonia (Kambos, Vapheio and perhaps pottery at Aghios Stephanos near Skala) and, increasingly, in Cyprus, where Late Minoan I pottery is at last coming to light. Finally there was an outer fringe of places receiving, to our present knowledge, only a few pieces: the Lipari islands in the west, Delphi, Troy, Samos, Chios (though M. S. F. Hood reported conical cups, which might indicate more than "fringe" status), Miletos and one or two Syro-Palestinian and Egyptian sites.

Minoan artistic influence is discernible in Late Helladic I to II A pottery (1550 to 1450 BC) and Minoan craftsmen may have been producing Minoan products in the Argolid and Messenia to adorn the contemporary shaft graves and tholos tombs, or even building such a tomb near Moira in Messenia. Minoans also made visits to the courts of Hatshepsut and Tuthmosis III in Egypt and are represented as "Keftiu" bearing precious gifts on the wall paintings of several contemporary Egyptian tombs of nobles.

All this external activity forms one side of the economic pattern of exchange. What were the Minoans receiving in return? For some areas we can affirm, with more or less confidence, the nature of the exchanges. Minoan activity in the west may have been to secure Etruscan or Sardinian copper, but this is highly speculative, with only the Aeolian evidence available. A little amber came from Britain or northwest Europe; a gold-mounted amber disk at Knossos could have come from the Wessex culture of southern England. Nearer home interest in Messenia cannot be explained in terms of Minoan requirements, unless there was a route up the coast to Epirote metal sources, which the Mycenaeans seem to have used at this time. From Lakonia, however, the two fine stones, lapis Lacedaemonius and rosso antico, were obtained, with Kythera as an intermediate station. Contact with the Argolid seems to have been social or political (there are very few imported Mycenaean objects of this period in Crete), with Mycenae

building up its power. There are surprisingly few links with Attica, but Minoan finds at Thorikos hint at the acquisition of silver from the local ores, which were being worked already at this date. On this route Kea would have been another intermediate post, while Siphnos, which had a town called Minoa, may, like Thorikos, have been yielding its metals. Emery was used in Late Minoan stone drilling and presumably explains a route to Naxos, one of the sources of emery. White-spotted obsidian, a prized stone for vases, came from Yiali in the Dodecanese, perhaps exploited from Minoan Triandha on Rhodes. Black Anatolian obsidian must have come through coastal sites like Iasos. Copper was obtained in ox-hide shaped ingots from Cyprus, tin perhaps from Anatolia or, like ivory and lapis lazuli, through Syro-Palestinian areas of contact. Certainly alabaster and probably gold, amethyst and carnelian came from Egypt.

Such, in brief, is the economic pattern of Minoan external exchange known to us. How is it to be explained? First, there is no trace of a spirit of conquest or of naval supremacy, which Thucydides was perhaps consciously seeking as a parallel to the 5th-century exploits of Athens. Explanation in purely economic and social terms is probable. The evidence can be grouped into three geographical bands whose strength diminishes in proportion to their distance from Crete. Within the southern Aegean, from Kythera in the west to Iasos on the Anatolian coast, were actual settlements of Minoans. Then comes a band of important contacts, but without settlement: Messenia, Lakonia, the Argolid, Cyprus (exporting its copper) and Egypt. Finally there is an outer area of vestigial contact, at Lipari in the central Mediterranean, Delphi, Attica, Troy, Miletos, Kos and the Syro-Palestinian littoral. Samos and Chios have stronger evidence of finds, and the sites at Tigani and Emborio may turn out to have been actual Minoan settlements, or fall at least within the second band of activity. This pattern, decreasing by distance, seems to represent a natural expansion in terms of production and population from a civilization in its most developed state, both economically and socially, as happened later with the Mycenaeans in the 14th and 13th centuries. The Minoans were so far in advance of their Aegean neighbors artistically and technically that their products were sought everywhere, even beyond the Aegean.

The social implications of this expansion may also be expressed. In the Aegean, sites on Kythera, Melos and Thera, Karpathos and Rhodes, were near to Crete. Expansion of population from Crete seems possible for their settlements, and very likely played a part in the foundation of others. As in 8th and 7th-century Greece, there may even have been a land shortage in Crete at the time. All fertile areas seem to have been occupied and there are concentrations of new sites in districts with little or no previous population, such as the Zou valley south of Siteia and the region from Arvi to Myrtos on the south coast, which had at least five Late Minoan I settlements.

The so-called Chieftain's Cup of serpentine stone from Aghia Triadha (16th–15th centuries BC). The prince stands proudly on the right with his staff of office, kilt and necklace. On the left an officer leads a line of long-haired Minoans apparently covered in large hides.

Minoan destructions, Mycenaean Knossos and its fall (1450 to 1380 BC). After some 15 centuries of peaceful rise to civilization and enjoyment of its fruits, Minoan Crete suffered an enormous disaster around the mid-15th century BC, after which the island never again rose to its former splendor (save perhaps in the 17th century AD). Every major site on the island was destroyed, although at Knossos the damage seems to have been only partial. The event or events took place at a time when the finest Late Minoan I B marine style pottery was in use. The immediate agent of destruction was intense fire, but what was its cause? There are two possibilities – attack and conquest from outside, which means in effect by the Mycenaeans; or a natural catastrophe caused by the stupendous explosion of the Santorini volcano.

This took place at some point after Late Minoan I A, the settlement on Thera having been destroyed during that period, and buried in places under an accumulated natural earth level before the great explosion occurred. Vulcanologists and others have described the drastic effects of much smaller eruptions and explosions than that of Santorini; tidal waves, violent accompanying earthquakes and poisonous ash fallout rendering land unusable for a time. From seabed ash cores of varying thickness recovered by marine scientists north and south of Crete, we know that such an ash level, at least 10 centimeters thick, covered the whole center and east of Crete.

While a human cause of the Minoan destructions cannot be excluded, it seems unlikely for at least three reasons: first, the magnitude and thoroughness of the disaster, including the collapse of great stone walls at the palace at Zakro; second, the fact that Mycenaean occupiers would have had little to gain by the total destruction of centers they would have needed for agricultural and economic control of the island; and third, the fact that the sites remained unoccupied by Mycenaeans or Minoans for at least a generation after the disaster. The natural explanation is also open to objections (tidal waves must be ruled out, given the fire destructions and relatively high, south Cretan location of some of the destroyed settlements) but in the form of accompanying earthquakes, poisonous ash, fallout and possibly blast waves, seems to the author more probable than the alternative. The correlation of two events – the vast eruption after Late Minoan I A, and the greatest destruction horizon ever documented in Crete and on several Aegean islands – seems reasonable.

Although they may not have caused the destructions, the next thing we know is that the Mycenaeans are present at Knossos. As the recent, highly successful excavation by Mervyn Popham of a mansion beside the Little Palace has shown, the newcomers arrived by or during the period of Late Minoan II pottery which exhibits a fusion of immediately preceding Late Minoan I B and contemporary Mycenaean decoration and shapes, notably the Palace Style amphoras (found also in the palace and rich tombs nearby and decorated with formally arranged patterns with Mycenaean influence or derivation), the stemmed goblet and flat alabastron (a low, round vessel, closed, with only a small mouth). This mansion was burnt and destroyed by about 1400 BC, shortly before the next major horizon, which is the destruction of the Palace of Minos at a time when Late Minoan III A 1 styles were giving way to Late Minoan III A 2 types, not later than about 1380 BC. Apart from its wealth of treasures in stone, terracotta, metal and fresco the palace also contained hundreds of Linear B tablets written in Mycenaean Greek. They list some 85 Cretan place names and show that by 1380 BC the Mycenaeans of Knossos were in contact with the whole island and in control of at least part of it.

The point is neatly confirmed by archaeology, since the earliest pottery on many provincial sites subsequent to the Late Minoan I B disasters is contemporary with or only slightly earlier than the early 14th-century Knossos palace destruction pottery. Early Late Minoan III vases are found at Aghia Triadha, Gournia, Mallia, Palaikastro, Phaistos and Tylissos. Confirmatory evidence of the actual presence of the newcomers in the Knossos region (apparently resident only there) is found in new types of chamber tombs approached down a long passage with insloping sides, burials of tall warriors with daggers, spearheads, swords and helmets beside their pottery, gold cups and wonderful sealstones, and in new types of frescoes with chariot scenes and painted copies of huge figure-of-eight shields or of griffins like those flanking the throne later on at Mycenaean Pylos. The Linear B tablets remain, however, the clearest evidence for Mycenaeans, though the pottery of the newly excavated mansion is also crucial.

Apart from the Knossian warrior graves just referred to

and apparently built for Mycenaean conquerors, other tombs of the period about 1450 to 1380 BC have produced many rich and spectacular finds bearing witness to the high degree of prosperity enjoyed by most, if not all, of the contemporary Minoan population. At Katsamba, the port of Minoan Knossos in the eastern suburbs of modern Herakleion, a cemetery of large chamber tombs contained fine pottery and Egyptian stone vessels, including one with a cartouche of the Pharaoh Tuthmosis III. A little further inland, in the valley leading to Knossos, were more rich burials. Particularly fine was the large, keel-vaulted tomb of dressed stone blocks at Isopata. Even though the burials had long been plundered, a rich collection of imported Egyptian alabaster vases remained for Sir Arthur Evans to discover. Other cemeteries in the district included graves with swords, gold jewelry, Egyptian scarabs, a hoard of bronze vessels, as well as pottery and a few beautiful stone vases. At Arkhanes to the south a beehive tholos tomb recently found contained in its side chamber an unplundered burial, perhaps of a princess, with magnificent jewelry, gold rings, stone vessels and another hoard in bronze. A horse and a bull had also been sacrificed in this tomb.

Across the island, chamber tombs near Phaistos with long entrance passages like those of Sellopoulo near Knossos contained burials of local nobility, again with fine gold jewelry, sealstones and pottery. From nearby Aghia Triadha a contemporary grave, dated to around 1400 BC, held the remarkable painted limestone sarcophagus exhibited in Herakleion Museum. It is covered with detailed scenes in many colors showing sacrifices and rites at the tomb of a dead man of considerable importance. All the burials we have cited, in chamber tombs, pit graves and tholoi, were those of local nobility or royalty, at Katsamba and Isopata probably of merchant princes who had many connections with Egypt. Poorer people buried in the Zapher Papoura cemetery just north of the palace of Knossos had simpler offerings of pottery, ivory and metal. Kings had been earlier and were now also buried in elaborate tombs like the Temple Tomb south of Knossos.

The position in the Aegean islands and former Minoan settlements around 1400 BC is complicated. Kea, Kythera and possibly Phylakopi on Melos and Triandha on Rhodes seem to have been abandoned during Late Minoan II, although the major destruction at Aghia Eirene on Kea may have taken place a little after those of Late Minoan I B in Crete. But around or soon after 1400 BC Mycenaean pottery appears on all the main island sites and there is a rich burial on little Skopelos. The Aegean then rapidly becomes part of the expanding Mycenaean culture.

If one looks at Knossos from an Aegean or Mycenaean point of view it is clear again that a major disaster must have occurred around or soon after 1400 BC, since it is up to this time precisely, as we have seen, that rich objects, Cretan and particularly Egyptian, appear in Knossian and nearby tombs, and precisely from this time onwards that

Above: the painted limestone sarcophagus from Aghia Triadha (c. 1400 BC). It is covered with detailed scenes in many colors showing sacrifices and rites at the tomb of a dead man.

Opposite: a Late Minoan I bull rhyton found on Pseira. The bull, an obvious source of fertility in an agricultural community, was a cult animal for the Minoans. 1550–1450 BC.

Crete becomes nothing more than of marginal significance externally, while the Mycenaeans now begin, suddenly, to dominate the Aegean and spread their products from Sicily to Carchemish on the Orontes. The fall and burning of Knossos, caused either by rebellious Cretans or by earthquake or by other Mycenaeans (and tradition speaks of Theseus' expedition from Athens), was therefore a pivotal point in Aegean history.

The post-palatial age (1400 to 1200 BC). Although recent excavations and studies have greatly improved our knowledge of these two centuries, they still remain among the least known in the Cretan Bronze Age. We are particularly short of excavated settlement evidence; yet finds in tombs make it clear that the period was a flourishing one all over the island, though without the brilliant range of artifacts which typify the palace age. Kydonia (modern Khania), with its substantial buildings, abundant and beautiful locally made pottery, well-endowed chamber tomb cemeteries and plentiful imports of vases from Cyprus, was the dominant site of the west, though tombs at Kalami, Armenoi, Pigi and Rethymno (all apparently

new foundations in Late Minoan III) have such good pottery that thriving western communities must have existed there too. In central Crete the traditional settlements, Amnisos, Knossos, Tylissos, Phaistos, Aghia Triadha, Mallia and others, were all inhabited and new ones were founded, such as Aghia Pelaghia on the northwest corner of the bay of Herakleion, Gournes to the east, Dhamania in the center, with a fine, square-chambered tholos tomb, and probably Prinias. In the central parts of southern Crete new settlements appear at Kephali Khondhrou and Phaphlangos and in the east of the island at Kritsa and Myrsine, to judge by the fine vases from their tombs.

There is some change in the settlement pattern. In the Second Palace period there was, as we have seen, much emphasis on coastal sites. Some of these, such as Amnisos, continue. Khania seems to expand considerably in Late Minoan III A and some of the new sites, Aghia Pelaghia and Gournes, are on or near the coast. But at formerly major coastal settlements like Mochlos, Palaikastro and Zakro habitation is greatly reduced or non-existent. At the same time most of the new sites listed above are inland

or well clear of the coast. This may reflect Crete's greatly reduced role in international affairs, her more internal existence.

On the other hand, the little that we know of settlement plans and buildings indicates a firm continuity from Late Minoan I. Kephali Khondhrou, a new foundation in Late Minoan III A, was a village occupying at least 1,400 square meters with over 70 rooms excavated, forming about ten house blocks with paved floors and courts. Besides rooms with decorated and plain household pottery of all kinds, there was a domestic shrine with a rhyton for pouring libations, a conch shell (presumably used as a ritual trumpet) and a tube for the sacred snake. The site, which lies on a low hill without defenses, was destroyed by fire in Late Minoan III B in the 13th century. It was probably typical for the period, though much less rich than Khania or Knossos.

At the latter site extensive cemeteries of this period indicate a flourishing community. Evidence of occupation has come to light along the Royal Road west of the palace and there was a little domestic shrine with a pair of sacred horns west of the newly excavated mansion. Certain

rooms of this building were reoccupied after the Late Minoan II destruction, as were parts of its neighbor, the Little Palace. The status of the main palace building is problematical. Some areas of it (and only some) were used in the 13th century and contained extensive numbers of vessels, notably stirrup jars for storing oil. These are globular or inverted pear-shaped pots with a spout on the shoulder, and two little handles closing over the tiny neck. In another room was the Shrine of the Double Axes, with goddess figurines and other sacred objects on a bench in front of which stood vessels of offerings.

Leonard R. Palmer has argued that not only this pottery but all the famous destruction debris of the palace, including stone vessels, frescoes and Linear B tablets, belongs to this date. But in the main the tablets and other rich finds (the latter, including decorated clay vases, datable stylistically to around 1400 BC) are in quite separate areas from those where the Late Minoan III B, 13th-century pottery lay. The position was clearly one of reoccupation of limited areas of the old palace, exactly as has been found to be the case in the newly excavated mansion. But the number of vessels in use indicates that the reoccupation, even if non-palatial in nature, was that of a thriving community. It does not, however, seem to have been on the same scale as at Kydonia, either with regard to international contacts or the manufacture of local artifacts.

The tombs of the 14th and 13th centuries are, first, the beehive tholoi, found all over the island from Stylos in the west (with a variant further west, at Maleme) to Akhladhia near Siteia in the east. They may well have been reserved for leaders or leading families of the local communities, while others were buried in chamber tombs in the soft limestone hillsides. Some of these, as in the newly excavated cemetery at Armenoi near Rethymno, are reached from long passages (dromoi) with insloping sides, which is a Mycenaean type. Within all types of tombs burial was usually made in or beside a large clay chest on four feet, with a gabled lid. Offerings of pottery, jewelry and occasionally bronze swords, or daggers, or older stone vessels, were placed beside the chest. The chests clearly imitate wooden prototypes and were richly, if somewhat crudely decorated with painted scenes. These usually have

a religious context, with pairs of sacred horns and double axes, and show hunting, bulls, octopuses, a ship (probably the voyage to the afterworld), the Minoan goddess with raised arms. The Armenoi tombs have produced magnificent new examples with polychrome hunting and religious scenes in red, blue and black on the buff surface.

The 14th and 13th centuries seem, then, to have been prosperous and peaceful. The pottery is of high quality, with octopuses decorating stirrup jars and kraters and stylized flowers and abstract patterns appearing on other shapes. A pyxis from the Kalami tomb east of Khania shows a man playing a seven-stringed lyre in a religious setting, with attendant birds. This may well be the first mythological representation of the god Apollo as Lyre-Player, or of Orpheus.

The degree of Mycenaean penetration or influence, after the fall of Mycenaean Knossos at the beginning of the period, appears to have been slight. Both Linear A and Linear B seem to have been known in the Khania region, the former on tablets, the latter painted on stirrup jars.

Above: a clay figurine of a poppy goddess from Gazi near Herakleion. 13th–12th centuries BC. Ht. 79 cm.

Opposite: sarcophagus from Episkope (Hierapetra). Such chests were used for burial in the Late Minoan III period. 13th century BC.

There is a little influence on pottery styles and tomb types, and a few imports. But the culture of Late Minoan III A and B Crete is still thoroughly Minoan, quite distinct in artifacts, settlements and burial customs from that of the mainland.

The end of the Bronze Age in Crete. Around 1200 BC this peaceful scene is disturbed. Many sites are abandoned; some, like Kephali Khondhrou, burnt. The character of life in the final century of the Minoan Bronze Age shows many changes, and in this parallels the wider Aegean scene des-cribed in chapter 6. After the destructions and abandon-ments there are sudden appearances of Mycenaean influ-ences in the pottery of the early 12th century (Late Minoan III C) and a few Mycenaean clay figurines are found. It is probable that Mycenaean refugees came to Crete, as they did in some number to Cyprus, after the destruction of the mainland centers around 1200 BC.

Then during the 12th century the settlement pattern changes dramatically. The abandoned, low-lying sites are replaced by new foundations on high hills, difficult of access. Karphi above the Lasithi plain is the best known of these refuge cities, being the fullest excavated site of the period in the Aegean. It occupied at least 4,000 square meters on the saddle top of its mountain, with blocks of houses and irregular streets of the old Minoan type. A domestic shrine contained remarkable statuettes of god-desses with raised arms, while similar ones came from the high shrine of Prinias and from Gazi on the coast west of Herakleion. Imaginative potters decorated their wares with elaborate fringed patterns and animals appeared on kraters. Bronze tools, arched fibulae and long dress pins were in use and iron, though scarce, was known. The people cultivated the olive, kept the customary animals, sheep, goats, cattle, as well as horses, and hunted wild boar and deer. The dead were buried in tholos tombs lower down the mountain. Karphi presumably replaced older and more congenially located settlements down on the Lasithi plain. In this it was not unique.

Other sites are found on high hills in the 12th century, Vrokastro above the Gulf of Mirabello, Kastri above Palaikastro, Atsipadhes (not certainly so early) and Arvi (perhaps beginning already in Late Minoan III B, the 13th century), high above the coastal Late Minoan I site, in south Crete and the large and important site of Kastro-kephala, with a vast and well-preserved circuit wall per-haps of this date, high above the west coast of the bay of Herakleion. Although coastal occupation did not end (Khania, Gazi and Myrsine for instance seem to have con-tinued into the 12th century), the move to sites in such high, inhospitable positions must indicate disturbed times, though the cause of the trouble is not yet known.

From about 1150 to 1100 BC there is no lack of cultural liveliness or of external contacts on the part of Crete. More Mycenaeans seem to have arrived, Minoan potters pro-duced the arresting Fringe Style and originated an Octopus Style in the Aegean, with ornate octopuses covering the surfaces of stirrup jars. Around 1100 BC, as Vincent R. d'A. Desborough has shown in his detailed monographs on this age, Cretans went to Cyprus, introducing their pottery pyxides and their goddess with raised arms, while Cypriot flasks and bird-shaped vases appear in Crete. Then in the 11th century, the sub-Minoan period, although there is a decline in pottery styles, we find that the old tombs are still in use, while various features new to the mainland and Aegean also continue to appear in Crete, having first occurred in the later 12th century – iron objects and tech-

The "Abbott Jug," thought to have come from Egypt or the Levant, perhaps a Minoan export to one of those areas. The Marine Style predominated from c. 1500 to 1450 BC.

nology from Cyprus, bronze stands from the same source imitated locally in clay, amber beads, long bronze dress pins, arched fibulae, an Italian or Sicilian type of fibula, and swords of the European Naue II type. Possibly by 1000 BC, Desborough suggests, Crete first felt the new Athenian Protogeometric style of pottery which had been developing in renascent Athens for some 50 years.

What, finally, can we say of the population in this complex and ill-documented period, from about 1200 to 1000 BC? Archaeologically several aspects stand out. First, there are impressive continuities of things traditionally Minoan; settlement plans, tomb types, artifacts and above all religion. From the new excavations by Giovanni Rizza of the rich and widely connected tombs at Prinias, and from sanctuary sites like the cave of Eileithyia at Inatos, the Diktaian cave above Psykhro and the shrine of Hermes at Kato Syme, there appears to be longer continuity, through to the Geometric and Archaic periods, by which time Crete was under the control of Dorian aristocracies. Second, into these continuities come new features, Mycenaean styles and probably Mycenaean Greeks in the 12th century, iron objects and technology from Cyprus, pins and fibulae which have northern and western origins. The fibula of Karphi, like the amber beads, presumably came directly from the west, while the pins and arched fibulae perhaps came from the sub-Mycenaean mainland. Mercenaries may have acquired swords of European type, like that in a 12th-century tomb at Mouliana in eastern Crete. Third, Desborough and Ingo Pini have pointed to an interesting divergence of tomb types after 1200 BC. In the center of the island we find chamber tombs in use, from Lasithi eastwards the tholos, whereas both had occurred all over the island earlier.

In a famous passage in the *Odyssey* (XIX, 175ff) Crete is said to be populated (not later than the 8th century) by Achaeans, Dorians, Eteocretans, Kydonians and Pelasgians. The last remain unknown to us, but the remainder could fit into the archaeological evidence of the period 1200 to 800 BC. The Achaeans in Homer are the Mycenaeans, who made some impact on Crete in their dispersion from the mainland in the 12th century. The Kydonians would be the Minoan people of western Crete whose center, modern Khania (ancient Kydonia), has been shown by the excavations of J. Tzedhakis and a Swedish team to have been exceptionally flourishing in the 14th and 13th centuries, and as such worthy of separate mention. The Eteocretans have long been considered the remnants of the old Minoan population who survived with their language in eastern Crete to the 4th century BC, their capital being at Praisos. It is therefore an obvious suggestion, as yet far from confirmation, that the preference noted above for tholos tombs in eastern Crete in this period represents the survival, continuing for some centuries, of one of the oldest, most distinctive and socially important burial modes and corresponds to the tradition of the Eteocretan area.

Finally, with the Dorian Greeks we come to the borders of historical Crete. When they first reached the island it is impossible to say. The Gortyn Law Code of about 450 BC implies that they had been there a long time. If new features in the archaeological record of southern Greece in the later 12th century are associated with incoming northwestern Greeks, including Dorians, then the arrival of Dorians in Crete, as part of their subsequent spreading across the southern Aegean, might have been in the 11th century.

Strictly, therefore, the Dorians do not concern us here. But what they found in Crete when they did arrive, and which they took into their social system, religion and legal codes, was a mixture: elements from the Achaean Greeks (who had come first in the 15th century, then again in the 12th) intermingled with the indigenous culture. The intermingling, as we have seen, may rather have been coexistence, since the indigenous Minoan culture was scarcely affected by the Achaean Mycenaeans, whose typical megaron buildings are exceedingly ill documented in Crete.

That mixed culture, found by the Dorians in Crete – Kydonian, Eteocretan and perhaps Pelasgian – was essentially the ancient Minoan way of life, which passed on to later Greeks an agricultural tradition of diversified and highly productive land use, as well as crafts like the manufacture of the great storage pithoi which Archaic Crete was to develop so richly in later years. Above all, through its sanctuaries and cave shrines, it bequeathed a mythological and religious heritage which lent diversity, expression and focus to the aspirations of later Greece.

Thera-a Bronze Age city beneath a volcano

Thera, the nearest island of the Cyclades to Crete, is an active volcano. At least two town sites were established c. 1550 BC. They were destroyed by an eruption c. 1500 BC, but the volcanic ash and pumice effectively sealed the ruins. Some excavation was carried out in the 1860s, but it is only in the last eight years, under the late Professor Marinatos' direction, that a series of unbelievably complete houses, their brilliant wall paintings still in the rooms, has shown us just what an Aegean Late Bronze Age site was like – a Pompeii, but almost twice as old. A second, greater explosion may have destroyed the Minoan civilization of Crete.

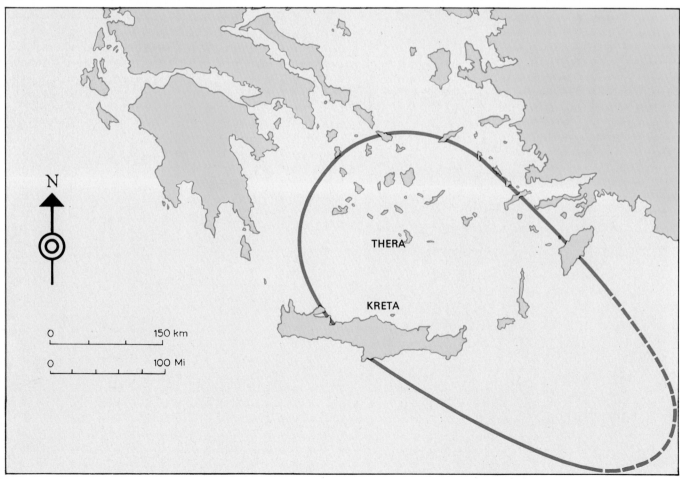

0   150 km

0   100 Mi

THERA

KRETA

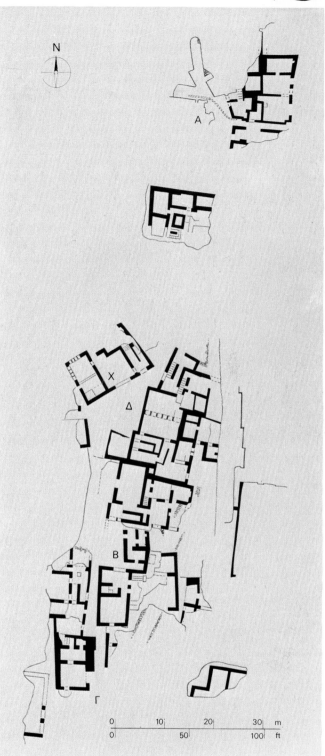

Opposite above: the volcano of Thera has erupted many times since the cataclysmic explosion of c. 1500 BC. Here we see a phase in the eruption of 1926 on the central islands of Thera, Nea Kamene, the active part of the volcano today. *Opposite below*: the great eruptions of Thera have blown volcanic ash and dust high into the atmosphere. The material is conveyed by the winds prevailing at the time and eventually settles in the seabed. By plotting its distribution and depth on the seabed scientists have shown that the highly poisonous fallout covered the whole of central and eastern Crete to a depth of at least 10 centimeters, thus greatly damaging the agricultural economy of the Minoan civilization for a time. *Above*: a view of Phira. The dramatic, highly colored cliffs of Thera are in fact the interior walls of the top part of the crater.

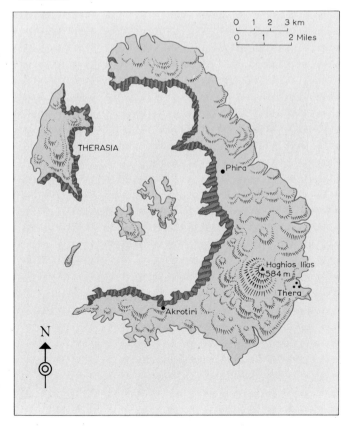

Left: the map of Thera today shows how the enormous central caldera was formed by the great explosion c. 1500 BC. Rich Bronze Age houses lie on Therasia, while the new excavations have been at the Akrotiri site on the south coast. *Above*: the emerging town plan at Akrotiri. The plan as a whole is reminiscent of Minoan towns like Palaikastro or Zakro. The houses themselves are finely built; no two are the same, but all are of Minoan type in their endless variety of individual room shapes within a general block plan.

Opposite: this enchanting fresco, the best preserved from the prehistoric Aegean, occupied three walls of a small room in House Delta. The artist gives us a moment in springtime, when the Aegean's brilliant flora makes its brief appearance. *Above*: in House Beta three walls of one room were painted with antelopes. *Below*: one prominent house (X) seems to have belonged to the Admiral of the Fleet. One room was decorated with an amazing frieze over seven meters long but only about 0.40 m high, depicting scenes of worship, war and navigation including these unique ships.

Left: the south wall of the same room in House Beta was painted with this fascinating panel of two young children boxing. The subject could scarcely be more different from the antelopes, yet the scene is linked by the same panel continuing at ground level and by the wavy red band above, while a frieze of ivy leaves ran all round the room above the door level. The two children, whose sagging stomachs indicate their youth, each wear one glove and a girdle.

Opposite: towards the center of the excavated area stands a house with staircases and many rooms, one of which was probably a house shrine. The walls were decorated with a group of three female figures, brilliantly drawn and dressed in elaborate, colored robes. The woman seen here, with long, black hair, huge gold earring, red lips and painted cheek, advances towards a central group which appears to figure a seated goddess being presented with a robe.

The fresco of the Blue Monkeys, from a room in House Beta, is one of the most dramatic of the Theran series. A whole pack of these African apes leaps about in a stylized rocky landscape spread over two walls in a large, continuous band which denies one corner of the room as it sweeps round. One animal is shown full face, others appear to be stealing food and all are intensely agile. The reconstruction of the fresco is a triumph of patience, skill and understanding on the part of the Greek team of restorers. The monkeys are of the same date (c. 1500 BC) and are closely comparable in style to those of a famous fresco from Knossos, although there they are quietly gathering flowers in a verdant landscape. Both artists (or perhaps there was just one) must have seen such monkeys to portray them with this vivid realism.

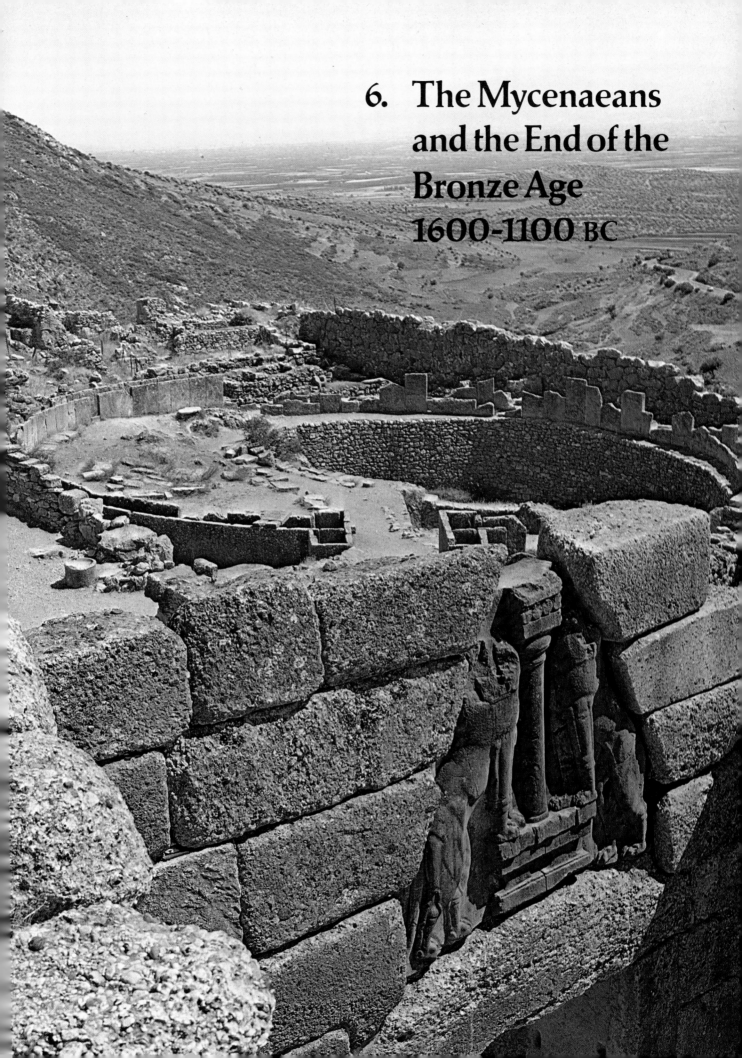

6. The Mycenaeans and the End of the Bronze Age 1600-1100 BC

The Early Mycenaean Period; the Shaft Graves. On the mainland there was a marked increase in prosperity and wealth towards the end of the Middle Bronze Age. This is documented by innovation and elaboration of funerary architecture – the beehive or tholos tombs in Messenia, cist tombs at Eleusis, tumuli at Marathon, and by the artifacts placed with the burials. The greatest expansion took place at Mycenae, which was the leading city of Greece from about 1600 to 1200 BC. On the west side of its acropolis lay a cemetery of the Middle and early Late Bronze Age. Within this cemetery were two special areas. The most famous is that found by Schliemann, Circle A, containing six shaft graves. This circle is now within the walls of Mycenae, but its inclusion therein and the fine ring of parallel slabs around the graves were later work, done when the citadel ramparts were built in the 13th century BC. The inclusion can only mean that the grave circle was regarded with special veneration by the later Mycenaeans, presumably as the burial place of earlier kings of Mycenae.

The other circle was found and excavated by the Greek Archaeological Service in the 1950s. It is therefore called Circle B, though it is in fact slightly older than A. Circle B contained 24 graves, dated within the period 1650 to 1550 BC. Some of the graves had been surrounded by a still earlier circle, of which traces survived. There were 14 shaft graves, the remainder being simple earth pit graves, with one elaborate stone, keel-vaulted tomb. A shaft grave was carefully constructed: a deep rectangular shaft was dug and the lower part of its sides lined with stone walls; a layer of clean pebbles was put in to make the floor. On this was placed the inhumation burial, lowered down on a hide or wooden board, with the grave goods all around. Wooden beams, bronze-cased at their ends, were set across the tops of the walls to form the roof. Stone slabs covered them and the rest of the shaft was filled up with earth. Special graves received an upright stone marker or stele, which in a few cases bore sculptured decoration of spirals and a hunting or fighting scene with men and a chariot.

Grave goods within Circle B consisted of pottery – mainly drinking goblets and jugs – gold and silver vessels, bronze swords, knives, daggers and spearheads, gold ornaments, obsidian blades and stone arrowheads. Three outstanding objects were a death mask made of electrum, a tiny amethyst bead with a lively rendering of a bearded head, perhaps a portrait of a Mycenaean prince, and a wonderful bowl of rock crystal (probably Minoan work) with a handle in the shape of a reversed duck's head.

Circle A was begun about 1600 to 1550 BC with the first burial in grave VI. Then from about 1550 to 1500 (Late Helladic or Mycenaean I period) came a second burial in grave VI, two burials in I and those in II, III, IV and V. Finally there was a third burial in I within the period 1500

to 1450 (Late Helladic II A), the time of the stone keel-vaulted grave in Circle B. The development in grave goods corresponds with the dates of burial. The first burial in VI has weapons and a gold diadem; grave II has weapons, a gold cup and a faience jar from Crete; III, IV and V held incomparable treasures.

In III there were eight gold vessels and one of silver, in IV 11 gold vessels and five of silver including a rhyton in the shape of a stag and another rhyton showing in relief the defense of a walled city. These three graves also contained 20 bronze vessels, several of pottery and an enormous quantity of ornaments, diadems, armbands and legbands in gold, exotic vessels of stone from Crete, ostrich eggs which had come from Africa first to Crete and had there been mounted in gold, gold rings with engraved scenes of combat, boars' tusks from helmets. In addition to all this were gold masks which, with their varied physiognomies, must have been intended as reasonably lifelike portraits of those buried. Finally, there were the weapons, many great bronze swords a meter long, of thrusting and slashing types, and the brilliant daggers, their bronze blades inlaid with a darker strip of bronze, in which were human figures, animals, birds and plants in scenes of combat and hunting, all again inlaid in gold, silver and black niello.

The shaft graves of Mycenae open the Late Bronze Age or Mycenaean period and in their stupendous richness establish some fundamental characteristics of early Mycenaean civilization. First, continuity and enrichment: The tomb type, elaborate in itself, is a direct development from the Middle Helladic stone cist grave (such as II and VI, the earliest in Circle A); the personal wealth of the contents of A is a great advance on that of B, itself a notable enrichment of earlier Middle Helladic wealth. Second, a clearly stratified society with selected, dominant groups and multivariate craftsmen. The skeletons of those buried show tall, strong figures, up to nearly six feet in height; these giants of their age are a dominant group emerging from Middle Helladic society. Their many weapons show that they were warrior rulers. They had in their service highly skilled workers in many crafts; their foreign relations were wide – with Crete, the Near East (knowledge of chariots), the Adriatic, Italy, the Aeolian islands and maybe Sardinia (possibly copper, silver and tin) and with central and northern Europe (large numbers of amber beads). Third, a rich, highly complicated, experimental mixture in art, including exquisite, skilled Minoan work in stone, metal and faience; also products of the rulers' own mainland craftsmen which vary from the marvelous technology and beauty of the inlaid daggers, and the countless spiraliform designs on the gold roundels, to the experimental, less sure copying of Minoan subjects and patterns; and finally, an admixture of exotic foreign products.

Mycenaean expansion; the 15th century. The 100 years after about 1500 BC witnessed the full formation of Mycenaean civilization so that by 1400 BC the mainland

---

Previous page: the famous Lion Gate, entrance to the acropolis of Mycenae. 13th century BC. Behind are the Shaft Graves of Circle A.

A battle scene, depicted in relief on a silver rhyton from Shaft Grave IV at Mycenae. 1550–1500 BC.

peoples were ready to build palaces, dominate the Aegean and enjoy recognition by the Hittite kings in Anatolia. The course of this formative period is therefore crucial, but it is also complex, and must be followed through the material record of monuments and products of art.

Early settlements have left little architectural evidence, and this is often obscured by later Mycenaean buildings; nevertheless the pottery shows that occupation was widespread. Korakou in Corinthia, Nikhoria and Pylos in Messenia, Tiryns, Eleusis, Thermon in Aitolia and Iolkos and its port Neleia in Thessaly are examples of major sites. The dearth of settlement architecture is compensated for by notable funerary monuments – which also imply adjacent settlements of importance. Tholos tombs had first appeared at the end of the Middle Bronze Age, around 1600 BC. At Mycenae several of the great group of nine were built in the 15th century, while both shaft grave circles received their last burials in the first half of the period. At Vapheio, south of Sparta, a local prince was richly buried in his tholos tomb with weapons, bronze and stone vessels, pottery and an exquisite collection of Minoan and Mycenaean sealstones on each wrist. Another untouched burial was found in one of two tholoi at Myrsinokhori near Pylos, a warrior prince with ten swords and daggers, fine sealstones and a necklace of amber beads. At Kakovatos further north there were three tholos tombs with

amphoras painted in the finest Palace style marine patterns derived from Cretan pottery. These rich western tholoi succeeded the burials of earlier local princes of the Shaft Grave period, as at Peristeria, where the gold cups could have come from the same workshop as those of the Mycenae graves. Meanwhile the less wealthy were buried in chamber tombs cut in the rock.

Our reconstruction of 15th-century mainland history is largely determined from its works of art. In the first half, as in the 16th century, many fine objects were imported from Crete and the designs on mainland vases are often strongly influenced by those of the Late Minoan I B style. As we saw in chapter 5, this period was the culmination of Minoan civilization and of its overseas influence before the disasters around 1450 BC. By contrast, the pottery, metalwork and ivory carving of the second half of the century show a complex fusion of Mycenaean and Minoan styles. The kylix or drinking goblet with a deep bowl curving into a small foot was now popular, decorated with a rosette or other single motif. The shape and style were adopted in Crete, and shallow cups with a band of "sponge print" decoration are found in both areas, as are jugs with vertical wavy bands of paint.

At the same time the fine swords of mainland burials, like those in the royal tholos and chamber tombs at Dendra, would have looked quite in place (and perhaps actually were in place) in the Knossian Late Minoan II warrior graves. So too might the gold and silver vases of the same tombs be interchanged, or carved stone friezes with split rosette patterns at Mycenae and Knossos. Necklaces of gold rosettes from contemporary burials in the Dendra tholos and at Arkhanes, or carved ivory boxes with attached miniature figure-of-eight shields from a 1400 BC tomb below the agora of Athens could again be exchanged with those from Arkhanes and the Tomb of the Tripod Hearth near Knossos.

All this comparability of styles and types in the decade or so around 1400 BC is to be seen as an expression of Mycenaean expansion in the later 15th century. We observed in the previous chapter that – momentously from the point of view of Cretan history – the Mycenaeans took over Knossos in the wake of the great destructions in Crete around 1450 BC. In terms of the steady rise of the Mycenaeans this event should occasion no great surprise. They developed rapidly in wealth through the 16th century and enjoyed links as far west as Albania and the Lipari islands, but were probably contained by the Minoans at their acme in the first half of the 15th century; nevertheless they enjoyed the full advantages of Minoan technological knowledge and artistic brilliance. They then expanded further to control Crete by 1400 BC and thus were poised to develop their own civilization still further, at home and abroad. Control of Crete taught them how to organize a great palatial system based on written records, and gave them any artistic and technical knowledge they did not already possess. Then after the fall of Knossos early in the

A reconstruction of the throne room at Pylos by Piet de Jong. Pylos is the best-preserved Mycenaean palace site, and a master architect must have been responsible for the careful axial planning of the whole. 13th century BC.

14th century they rapidly came to dominate the art and commerce of the Aegean for the next 200 years.

The Mycenaean Palace Age; the 14th and 13th centuries. The major Mycenaean sites were crowned by the palace of the local ruler. These buildings have been found and excavated at Mycenae, Pylos and Tiryns, traced on the acropolis of Athens and partly investigated beneath the modern city of Thebes, while others probably existed on the huge walled hill of Gla in Boeotia, at Iolkos on the coast of Thessaly and at the Menelaion site near Sparta. The plan is quite different from that of the Cretan palace. It is based on the old Middle Helladic megaron, a main room with a throne at one side, preceded by an antechamber and porch. At Pylos and Tiryns the latter opened on to a courtyard. Pylos is the best-preserved Mycenaean palace site, and a master architect must have been responsible for the careful axial planning of the whole. The central column on each side of the entrance gateway is aligned with the left-hand column of the porch and with the pair on the left side of the great hearth in the megaron, while the other pair in the megaron are in line with the right-hand column of the porch. The central hall or throne room is surrounded by corridors and smaller rooms, with staircases leading to an upper story.

The ground-floor rooms at Pylos served the daily requirements of the palace. These included the archives room where the state records were kept on clay tablets, store-rooms of various kinds, such as the pantry with 6,400 plain cups, bowls and drinking goblets kept on shelves, and the olive oil store (behind the throne room) with rows of pithoi set in a plaster bench and tablets – recording elaion (olive oil) – found scattered about. Bedrooms would have occupied the upper floor. There seem to have been separate apartments for women – smaller megarons beside the main one at Tiryns, a group of rooms beside the entrance gateway at Pylos.

Each palace was adapted to the shape of its site. At Pylos, apart from the palace, there was a notable series of separate, free-standing buildings, a large, rectangular wine store, a group of rooms with columned halls (built slightly before the main palace), and another unit, possibly an armory, at the east corner of the hilltop. At Mycenae the acropolis held the palace and many large houses, while Tiryns was a huge single complex with the main megaron block and courtyard at its center and galleries within the great walls which probably provided stabling for horses and storage for chariots.

Careful attention was paid to the water supply. Passages and tunnels were cut from within the acropolises at Athens, Mycenae and Tiryns, down through or under the walls to underground springs. At Pylos water was brought by a wooden aqueduct from a spring a kilometer distant and conducted through the palace and industrial areas in terracotta pipes. Bathrooms were found at Tiryns and Pylos. At the latter the bath was set in plaster, there was a little platform in front to assist getting in and out, water pithoi were placed in one corner, the drain hole in another and there was a pottery goblet for a drink or to hold a sponge. Shall we ever approach nearer to a Homeric scene? It was in King Nestor's palace at Pylos that the lovely Polykaste bathed Telemachos, the son of Odysseus, when he was journeying to Sparta to seek news of his father.

Palaces, houses and shrines had their walls covered with brightly colored paintings. At Thebes and Tiryns there were court ladies in procession, wearing richly decorated dresses and bearing caskets before them. Tiryns also had hunting scenes and pictures of the old Minoan bull-leaping sports, perhaps copies from the ruined walls at Knossos or learned originally from the painters of Knossos and maintained on Mycenaean walls. At Pylos, fragments of many scenes have survived, including in the older buildings beside the main palace a sack of a city with falling warriors and, in the main palace, painted griffins guarding the royal throne, as at Knossos, and a beautiful scene with a long-robed minstrel seated on a rock playing a lyre, with a dove flying by. Perhaps this was a court bard whose sung stories were continued and developed down to the Homeric epics.

Hunting scenes were also portrayed at Pylos, and at Mycenae, with grooms controlling the horses. Mycenae, however, has recently produced the most brilliant examples of Mycenaean frescoes yet known. On the walls of a cult room on the acropolis were female figures, priestesses or goddesses, one holding what seem to be sprays of grain, while in a private house Professor George Mylonas has uncovered a painted figure-of-eight shield (like those of

Knossos again) and a female figure with richly embroidered dress, delicate jewelry and exquisitely rendered hands touching the jewels. In this masterpiece the face, as usual, is expressionless and not intended to represent any particular person, but there is a rare delicacy of feeling in the detail of the woman's gesture. Pylos and Tiryns also preserved traces of beautiful painted floors divided into squares, with octopuses and other motifs in each.

Fortifications. Palaces and town sites were sometimes fortified with massive walls, like the later Greek acropolis towns. The Mycenaeans were master builders in unworked, megalithic masonry. The fortifications of Mycenae and Tiryns seem to have been started in the 14th century and expanded in the next, when the steep site of Dendra, the huge hill of Gla, Mycenaean Argos and the acropolis of Athens also had mighty defensive circuits erected around them. Thebes, Eutresis, Krisa near Delphi and Teikhos Dymaion west of Patras were also fortified, and a great defensive wall was built across the isthmus of Corinth. Its purpose can only have been to keep out intruders from the north. The circuit walls were pierced by small, corbeled posterns and huge imposing gateways of which there are mighty examples at Gla and Tiryns. The finest is the Lion Gate at Mycenae, with its massive trilithon uprights and lintel, surmounted by the great triangular slab with its sculptured lions flanking a column, their forepaws resting on stone altars with incurved sides. Such altars are known from actual examples at Arkhanes in Crete and from gold models and representation on a stone rhyton from Zakro. The whole Lion Gate relief expresses

Above: a bathtub at Pylos. It recalls Homer's famous description of Polykaste bathing Telemachus in Nestor's palace at Pylos.

Right: a fresco of a court lady recently discovered in a private house on the acropolis of Mycenae. 13th century BC.

A painted figure-of-eight shield from Mycenae. These shields were painted on walls where real ones would be hung when the warriors were at home. 13th century BC.

symbolically the spiritual and temporal power of the rulers of Mycenae.

Towns and houses. While these fortified centers dominated their respective regions, most Mycenaean settlements were unwalled. The palace hill of Pylos, Korakou on the coast west of Corinth and sites in Attica like Spata and Eleusis or Lerna and Nauplion in the Argolid are examples.

Whether fortified or not, Mycenaean towns exhibit a variety of plans. The governing factor was the terrain, though a low hill site was usually chosen. But very few sites were newly inhabited in the Late Bronze Age. The Mycenaeans simply continued, expanded and enriched the occupation of their Middle and Early Helladic predecessors. Houses might have a megaron plan with anteroom leading to the main room, as in the chief's dwelling at Mouriatadha and at Nikhoria, both in Messenia. More often they consisted of several linked rooms. The buildings themselves might be joined one to another to form a continuous complex, as at Tiryns and Zygouries, or were large, essentially free-standing structures such as the big houses at Mycenae. The last covered the upper citadel around the palace block and extended outside the great walls, as did the town of Tiryns.

The finds within the houses at Mycenae indicate an opulent class of traders and landowners. The House of the Oil Merchant, some 27 by 18 meters, with a dozen rooms on the lowest floor alone, was so named from a store of jars filled with oil and sealed ready for dispatch. The House of the Sphinxes and that of the Shields contained remains of carved ivories which had been used as inlays for furniture or boxes; these, with fragments of frescoes, fine pottery, vases of serpentine and other fine stones, Linear B tablets recording a variety of spices for scenting the oils and, architecturally, staircases evidencing upper floors, all hint at the wealth and elegance of the town of Mycenae in the 14th and 13th centuries.

Elsewhere dwellings were humbler, but not without interest. At Zygouries, on the route from Corinth to Mycenae, a building nearly 15 meters by 11 with five rooms, corridor and threshold preserved (it was much larger originally) clearly belonged to a person of importance. Over 1,000 clay vases were found in it, many in new, unused condition. In one room there were over 500 deep cooking bowls, 75 small saucers to eat or drink from, jars, stirrup vases, basins, ladles and cups, often packed one inside the other. Many large kraters (wine mixing bowls) stood in rows against the wall in another room. Open drains and water channels served other rooms on the ground floor. The living rooms were on the second floor; fragments of painted wall plaster had fallen from them into the pottery stores below. This substantial house at Zygouries offers a good example of Mycenaean provincial town architecture and domestic activity, much less rich than the great houses of Mycenae, but full of urban industry.

Fortifications at Mycenae. The circuit walls of massive Cyclopean masonry were pierced by small, corbeled posterns. 13th century BC.

Tombs. An equally clear indication of social hierarchy is given by Mycenaean tombs. The ruling family or leading families all over Mycenaean Greece were buried in the monumental tholos tombs. These are particularly common in the western Peloponnese and the Argolid, where the group of nine at Mycenae is best known. But the distribution ranges through Attica and central Greece to Karditsa and Volos in Thessaly. The tholos was a stone corbeled vault, beehive-shaped, set mostly below ground level and approached by a long passage (dromos) cut into the hill slope, a great cylindrical shaft having first been dug out for the vault to be built within it and supported by the earth fill. In the finest tombs, like those of Mycenae, the dromos was lined with ashlar masonry and there was a monumental doorway. Within, a small side chamber might open off the dome-shaped vault. The best surviving example is the side chamber of the great tholos at Orchomenos, with its ceiling of beautifully carved slabs.

The side chambers must have been used for interments, as one of the tholoi at Arkhanes in Crete has shown with its rich, unplundered burial, dated to the early 14th century. Usually, however, the dead were laid on the floor of the vault or in shallow pits cut in it. Very few tholos burials have survived undisturbed since antiquity; those in the tombs of Dendra and Vapheio belonged, as we saw, to the 15th century. We can only guess at the original splendor surrounding those laid to rest in the great 14th-century tholoi of Mycenae. The so-called Treasury of Atreus seems to have been decorated with metal rosettes fixed all over the interior walls. Meanwhile, one other aspect of the original importance and monumentality of Mycenaean tombs has recently been discovered at Thebes, where the entrance and walls of a tholos-scale chamber tomb (over ten meters by six) had been covered with painted scenes, including human figures, as in the tombs of New Kingdom pharaohs.

While the rulers of Mycenaean society were interred in their tholoi the remainder of the population, whatever their degree of wealth, had smaller burial places. These were single chambers cut into sloping hillsides and approached, like the tholoi, down a long dromos whose sides in the 14th and 13th centuries sloped inwards as they rose to the ground surface. The entrance to the tomb had a blocking wall of stones, dismantled each time a new burial was made in the family grave. Because they are smaller and contained less rich finds than tholoi, many chamber tombs, even whole cemeteries, have survived intact and can tell us much about ordinary Mycenaean society and burial customs. Re-use of tombs is a case in point; over 20 interments were made in a single tomb at Mycenae, the older skeletons being pushed aside and their more valuable offerings perhaps removed when new burials were made in the central area. Such, too, we may infer, was the practice in the great tholoi. At the moment of a new burial necessary fumigation was made with aromatic substances laid on live charcoals in braziers, which are regularly found. With the

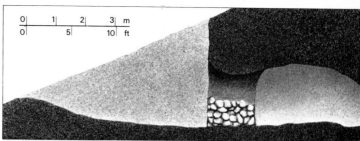
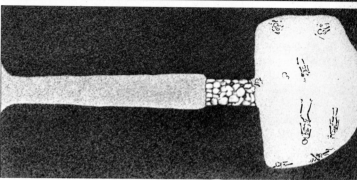

Plan and section of a Mycenaean chamber tomb. Because they are smaller and contained less rich finds than tholoi, many chamber tombs have survived intact.

dead were placed objects of daily life, jewelry, weapons and pots, thought necessary for use in or on the way to the afterworld, as well as the distinctive little clay figurines, brightly painted and usually female.

Chamber tombs vary greatly in the wealth of offerings, even within the same family, and this probably reflects differences in social status. The tombs at Spata in central Attica contained fine ivories and stone vessels and may well have belonged to the leaders of the settlement. On the level of a whole community the most interesting deductions were those of Tsountas and Wace, based on their great experience at Mycenae. Here the chamber tombs were in distinct groups or small cemeteries of up to about 20 graves. These probably represented separate communities or clans (with several families in each, according to the number of tombs), living in small hamlets and in dependence upon the rulers and nobility in the palaces and great houses up on the citadel. Elsewhere large cemeteries of chamber tombs, sometimes with a few earth-cut pit graves or stone-lined cists, will have belonged to whole villages.

At Tanagra in Boeotia a recently found cemetery has many terracotta chests within the tombs, with scenes painted on them giving important evidence of ritual mourning and other funerary rites. But the Boeotian finds are of even greater interest in that burial in clay chests (larnakes) is the standard Late Minoan mode, otherwise almost unexampled on the mainland. Dr. Ruth Edwards has, however, drawn attention to links between Crete and Boeotia in cult and mythology: Apollodorus has an account that Rhadamanthys, king of Cretan Phaistos, lived in Boeotia, while Kadmos was the brother of Europa, King Minos' mother.

Written records. The leaders of Mycenaean society organized their agriculture, industries, land tenure, storage arrangements and to some extent their religious practices through a meticulous system of written records. Inscribed clay tablets have so far been found chiefly at Pylos and Knossos (from the Mycenaean occupation which ended with the fall of the Palace about 1380 BC) and in much smaller numbers at Mycenae, Thebes and Tiryns. Thebes has also produced stirrup vases with painted Linear B inscriptions, and one or two other such vessels have turned up elsewhere.

The tablets list persons according to occupation (bakers, bronze-workers, carpenters, fullers, heralds, masons, messengers, potters, shepherds, unguent boilers); or quotas of goods required or distributed through the area ruled (corn, bronze, livestock, oil, wine, wool), often in quantities involving minute fractions and elaborate weights and measures; or possessions kept within the palace (chariots, chariot wheels, furniture with ivory inlays, gold and silver vessels, swords, textiles, tripods). The documents also hint at the structure of Mycenaean society, discussed below, and at types of land held, precautions for stationing groups of troops at key points along the Pylos coast against the imminent threat of invaders, or at gods and goddesses worshiped. When deciphered, one tablet at Pylos was found to record a shrine of Poseidon, a Dove Goddess, Hermes, Zeus, Hera and Artemis, while in the Knossos tablets there are references of offerings to all the gods, a Priestess of the Winds, Diktaian Zeus, Eleuthia (Eileithyia, later goddess of childbirth), Mistress Athena, Enyalios, Paian (the later Apollo, the healer god) and Poseidon.

What the tablets do not record is also of interest. There is no historical information, no names of kings or nobles, no literature or poetry. These last certainly existed in oral form, as the evidence of tradition and continuity in Homer, and frescoes like the lyre player of Pylos indicate. Mycenaean kings presumably were known by name, but not on the palace records. These are simply scribes' lists comprising a system of highly efficient book-keeping.

Art and artifacts. Although our knowledge of Mycenaean workshops is almost non-existent, the products of their craftsmen or women display the range of the civilization in the abundance of their survival. The achievements of the architects, builders, stone masons, fresco painters and scribes have been discussed. We turn now to the potters, metalworkers, ivory carvers, lapidaries, jewelers and seal carvers of the palace period.

Pottery workshops were in production at all the main Mycenaean centers. Analysis of the proportions of residual or trace elements in fired clay is beginning to show distinct groups, corresponding to different clay sources and manufacturing centers. Further analyses of samples should eventually allow important conclusions to be drawn about the quantity, direction, distribution, areas of origin and variety of provenances at any one receiving center of

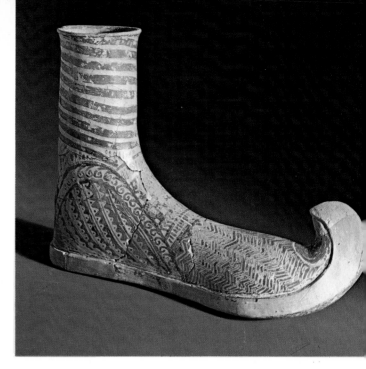

exported Mycenaean pottery. Products for local use would have been made at places like the potter's kiln at Berbati in the Argolid, which was producing many fine vases with pictorial scenes, perhaps distributed from stores like those in the large house at Zygouries or else exported in quantity to major recipients like Cyprus or Taranto in south Italy. Within the Mycenaean world proper, that is, central and southern Greece and the Aegean islands (not Crete), there is a remarkable uniformity both of shape and painted decoration during the 14th and earlier 13th centuries.

Shapes and decorative patterns, in lustrous paint, varying from red to black in color, on a lightly polished, creamy buff surface, developed from the early Mycenaean styles of Late Helladic I and II. The pottery of the Palace Age is called Late Helladic III A (14th century) and Late Helladic III B (13th century). The basic open shapes in fine decorated ware are the krater, a large deep bowl with handles used for mixing wine and water, the one-handled drinking cup with an elegant profile, the kylix or stemmed goblet, again for drinking, and several types of deep, open bowl for holding food. Conical, funnel-shaped or animal-head rhytons were used for pouring liquid offerings in religious rituals. Closed shapes include collared jars with handles on the shoulder and stirrup jars. All these jars were for storing liquids, probably wine and oil as in the House of the Oil Merchant at Mycenae. Globular and piriform (inverted pear-shape) jugs with elegant necks and handles were the pouring vessels in fine ware, and alabastrons of two types, low and spreading or cylindrical, straight-sided, were for holding oils and perfumes. The small mouth prevented spillage. Globular flasks must also have held precious liquids. Religious rhytons in the shape of a bull's or goat's head were for pouring offerings.

This household and tomb pottery was either plain or decorated with a variety of abstract, geometrical designs. Some shapes, bowls, jars, jugs, kraters and stemmed goblets had the patterns placed on the upper part, with plain

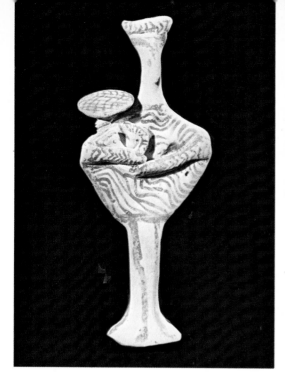

Mycenaean pottery. *Far left*: a remarkable libation vessel in the shape of a winged boot from Voula in Attica. 14th century BC. *Center*: the appealing statuette from a chamber tomb at Mycenae of a mother suckling her child, which is shaded by a little parasol. *Right*: a figurine, recently found by Lord William Taylour in a shrine store on the acropolis of Mycenae. 13th century BC.

horizontal bands below. On alabastrons, cups, flasks and rhytons the decoration covered all or most of the body. The abstract, linear motifs usually had their origin in early Mycenaean and ultimately Minoan designs. In the 14th and 13th centuries, though rather schematic and dry, motifs show a careful relation to the shape and proportions of the pot. Spirals, whorl-shells, stylized flowers, ivy and other plants, net patterns, chevrons and loops, sometimes grouped into an elaborate antithetical design or into panels, are all popular.

An animal figure style is also used on kraters, many being exported to Cyprus and the Near East. On these we find bulls and birds (occasionally the latter pecking fleas from the backs of the former) and, rarely, scenes with human figures and chariots. These luxury wine-mixing bowls must have been painted for chiefs who loved horses and chariots. One krater from Cyprus goes further and bears a scene appearing to depict the weighing and distribution of copper, oxhide-shaped ingots for Mycenaeans, as Porphyrios Dikaios argued. The human figures are stiffly and spikily rendered, often amusingly to modern and perhaps even Mycenaean eyes.

The finely decorated wares were for table and tomb. In addition there were large numbers of coarse ware vases, three-legged pots for cooking, flat, shallow baking dishes, braziers, lamps and large store-jars or pithoi for wine, oil, grain and water.

The potters were also adept at modeling and firing terracotta figurines of animals, like a little donkey from Rhodes with a flask strapped to each side, just as one sees in villages today, or a horse and rider from Attica, or a goddess riding sidesaddle, as well as scores of schematic little human figures shaped like the Greek letter Φ or Ψ, painted with red patterns and deposited in graves. Occasionally they are more explicit, such as the appealing statuette from a chamber tomb at Mycenae of a mother suckling her child, which is shaded by a little parasol.

The metalworkers excelled themselves in the 14th and 13th centuries. They had learned the techniques of their craft from the Minoans at the time of the Shaft Graves, particularly in the manufacture of bronze swords and vessels of bronze and other metals, while the inlaid daggers were their own achievement. The chances of survival have not produced comparable deposits from the Palace Age, but groups of metalwork from tholoi, chamber tombs and hoards buried on the acropolis at Mycenae, at Tiryns and elsewhere display the wide range of products. The Linear B tablets tell of the issue of quotas of copper to the bronze workers in carefully detailed quantities. The material probably came from Cyprus or southeastern Turkey in the form of oxhide-shaped ingots, as it went earlier to Crete. The rich deposits of copper in Cyprus were worked in the Late Bronze Age and would have been transported in merchantmen like that which sank off Cape Gelidonya in southern Turkey around 1200 BC. Its cargo, brilliantly recovered and published by George Bass and his team, consisted of copper, bronze and tin ingots and bronze scrap, destined for a Mycenaean port and presumably loaded in exchange for a delivery of fine Mycenaean pottery to Cyprus and the Levant coast.

Other sources of Mycenaean metals are not certainly known; the Gelidonya shipwreck indicates an eastern origin (not Cypriot) for at least some of the tin used; silver was being worked in the Attic mines at Lavrion and gold may well have been coming from Nubia, through Egypt, the nearest large source. Copper oxhide ingots have been found in Sardinia, presumably destined for Mycenaean use, and Etruria and Albania, with both of whom the Mycenaeans had contacts, may also have been supplying copper from their adequate deposits.

The metal industry produced three main classes of artifact, body armor, tools and weapons, all these of bronze, and vessels of bronze and silver, and a few of gold. Our knowledge of armor is derived almost exclusively from the

The astonishing find of a suit of bronze armor in a tomb at Dendra, datable to around 1400 BC. Our knowledge of Mycenaean armor derives almost exclusively from this unique exemplar.

astonishing find of a panoply in a tomb at Dendra, datable to around 1400 BC. Here was an ungainly suit of bronze consisting of separately made pieces originally stitched together, a cuirass, a high collar or neck-guard, shoulder pieces and broad encircling bands to protect the abdomen and groins. This warrior also had a boar's tusk or metal helmet with bronze cheek pieces, and he wore bronze greaves. The Dendra armor is unique today but it is most unlikely that once the techniques were known and the protection apparent this set alone was produced. Many of the details correspond to descriptions in Homer.

Swords, daggers, socketed spearheads and javelin tips are relatively common in bronze. The typical Mycenaean long sword of the palace period has prominent horns to protect the hand and is flanged on the hilt to receive a handle fitting of wood or ivory, which was attached by large rivets of gold, silver or bronze, while a hemispherical pommel of fine stone or ivory was fitted at the top. Towards the end of the 13th century a new type appears in the Mycenaean world, deriving from central Europe. It is known as Naue Type II and has a fishtail top to the hilt and rounded, down-curving ears at the base to protect the hand. The hilt plates were again attached by rivets. A short sword with a T-hilt instead of an attached pommel was popular through the whole Mycenaean period. In addition to offensive weapons, agricultural and carpentry tools were also made in bronze, especially the double axe and flat chisels. There were toilet articles like mirrors, pins and tweezers and there would have been scores of bronze fittings and attachments for chariots, boxes, furniture, buildings and ships.

Bronze vessels included large rounded cauldrons on three legs, many varieties of open bowl with riveted handles, pans with low, vertical sides, basins with one strap handle, hydrias and jugs for pouring, one-handled cups and tankards, hand lamps with a long stick handle and sometimes a link-chain for holding the wick-trimmer, and pairs of scale pans for weighing material or for symbolic use in tombs. Linear B tablets have ideograms confirming and extending this range of vessels. In more precious metal we have a beautiful set of stemmed goblets, a spoon and one-handled basin in silver from a tomb of about 1400 BC at Dendra, fragments of a silver bowl from Pylos with gold and niello male heads separately made to be inlaid, as well as two complete bowls of this type with inlaid bulls' heads, one from Dendra, the other from Enkomi in Cyprus, a luxury Mycenaean export.

In ivory carving, Mycenaean artistry finds perhaps its surest and most delicate expression. A wide range of styles and types of object is mastered with absolute confidence. We find little cutouts of fish, helmets, shells and rosette and spiral decorated strips, all for inlay, miniature figure-of-eight shields and beautifully carved plaques with lions, bulls, griffins and heraldically opposed sphinxes, as well as little plaques of warriors with boar's tusk helmet and figure-of-eight shield and female figures in rich dress. All these were for attachment to boxes. There are also cylindrical pyxides carved from a section of the whole tusk, with relief scenes of marine nautiluses or deer and griffins, and combs and mirrors with animals carved in relief on the handles. Plaques, carved boxes and handles, as well as exquisite ivory sculptures in the round, survive too.

The best known of these is the triad found at Mycenae with two seated female figures wearing jewelry, richly embroidered skirts and bodices with the breasts exposed in Minoan fashion. The women's arms are across each others' shoulders while in front a small child stands on the skirt of one lady, leaning across on to the knee of the other. The group has been thought to represent two goddesses with a divine child. Also at Mycenae the House of Columns was named after little model columns of ivory with detailed renderings of base, downward tapering shaft and molded capital. Recently two superb sculptures in the round were found by Lord William Taylour in the Citadel House, again at Mycenae. These are a powerfully carved lion, 18 centimeters long, which may have been the end of the arm of a throne, and a delicately sculpted human head with carefully defined eyes, nose and lips, and hair rendered in neat, regular strands. Further evidence is supplied by the Linear B tablets with their records of ivory inlays for footstools and other articles of furniture.

Other miniature arts were those of the jeweler and gem carver. Necklaces of mold-made pendants in faience, blue glass paste or gold are found in tombs. Argonauts, stylized papyri, flowers and abstract designs are used for their decoration. Beads of glass or brightly colored stones like carnelian are plain or carved into a variety of shapes. The necklace and four bead bracelets of the new Mycenae fresco shows what an aristocratic lady, or a goddess, would wear. Engraved seals and gold rings may have survived from the earlier Mycenaean period, but the craft continued, albeit with declining representational quality, into the 14th and 13th centuries. But recent finds at Thebes,

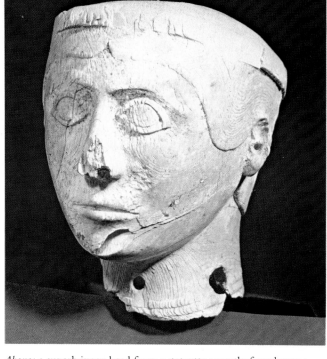

Above: a superb ivory head from a statuette recently found near a shrine at Mycenae. 13th century BC.

Left: an ivory head of a Mycenaean warrior wearing a helmet of cut boars' tusks. 13th century BC.

in part of what is probably the palace complex, are of much interest for both palatial gem-carving and inspiration from the Near East. A hoard of 30 Near Eastern cylinder seals was discovered, many in lapis lazuli, and nearby a large group of cut and polished, but not yet engraved, agate and crystal stones. Here was a workshop of high quality, contrasting with the clay sealings (from lost engraved seals) found in the destruction debris of the Pylos palace.

Stone vases were another luxury product of the Mycenaean Palace Age. In the Shaft Grave period bowls and lamps of gabbro, serpentine and other fine stones had been imported from Crete, there being as yet no distinctive Mycenaean stone types. The craft may have been learned during the Mycenaean occupation of Knossos in the late 15th century. The great gypsum alabastrons found in the destruction debris of the throne room of the Palace of Minos are a Mycenaean shape, as is their compass-drawn spiraliform decoration. Then in the 14th and 13th centuries Mycenaean lapidaries were carving graceful jars, perhaps to hold oils or perfumes, from lapis Lacedaemonius, limestone, serpentine and other rocks. Complete specimens were found in the rich houses outside the citadel of Mycenae and in tombs in Attica. Serpentine lamps from Eleusis and the palace of Pylos are probably Minoan heirlooms, but the Mycenaean craftsmen were themselves skilled in working the hardest materials. Vases of amethyst and an exquisite milky white and brown-banded agate have been found at Mycenae, the latter stone also being used for seals and a dagger haft. A fragmentary vase from Epidauros, with a relief scene of marching men and dolphins, may be Minoan or a Mycenaean copy of the well-known Minoan type.

The stone-carvers also produced beautiful friezes decorated with split rosettes, relief slabs with bull scenes and decorated columns and capitals for the "Treasury of Atreus," all in the red marble rosso antico, as well as the limestone ceiling slabs for the "Treasury of Minyas" at Orchomenos, carved with an exquisite design of spirals.

Religion. The importance of the relevant Pylian and Knossian tablets for our understanding of Mycenaean religion can hardly be overemphasized. They indicate not only a fully developed polytheism with particular offerings, priests, priestesses and cults for different divinities, but show further that the divinities are often those of later Greece, with Zeus, Hera, Athena, Poseidon and others actually named. This evidence contrasts with a curious dearth of religious locations, buildings or shrine rooms with appropriate apparatus. A shrine with terracotta figures on a bench at Asine belongs to the period after 1200 BC. For Mycenae, Emily Vermeule set out a convincing case that the building called Tsountas' House on the acropolis was a shrine, with its hollows and channels for libations. Recently remarkable finds made by Lord William Taylour near Tsountas' House have thrown new but weird light on the material aspect of Mycenaean religion.

A group of small rooms makes up two 13th-century cult areas. That to the east consisted of a room with tall male and female idols, much jewelry in pots, perhaps to adorn the figures during ritual, as well as lamps, braziers, offerings tables and terracotta snakes. This room was reached from a shrine or temple with columns and raised platforms. On one was a grim female figure with an

A silver bowl with wishbone handles inlaid with gold and niello figures of bulls' heads. The inlaying of metals on cups was a Mycenaean speciality, and a cup similar to this one, from a rich tomb at Dendra, was exported to Enkomi in Cyprus. 15th century BC.

offerings table before her. Beside the room of the idols and the temple was an alcove of walled-off natural rock containing more idols and snakes. To the west was a separate cult area with a little inner shrine having a dais on which was a gently painted female idol, portrayed wearing jewelry and a long robe, with elaborate real jewelry before her. The shrine opened into a cult room with a central hearth, a raised platform and on the east and south walls highly interesting remains of cult frescoes. In the main scene there is a goddess faced by a female worshiper, priestess or another goddess, who holds a spear, and, in a lower panel, a seated goddess apparently holding sprays of corn with an animal in front of her. A pair of sacred horns are shown and confirm the religious setting of the fresco.

The idols or cult statues comprise two groups, 19 being tall (up to 0.6 meters high) with wheelmade, tubular bodies and strikingly painted, if not intentionally gro-

tesque heads. There are males and females. The second group has four smaller figures, all female and much more delicately painted, indicating a clear difference in nature from the tall figures. One of each type of figure was on display in the two shrine rooms, with offerings before them. Possibly the other figures were brought out for ritual at appropriate times of the year. One carried something on a pole attached to its front, perhaps a double axe, another bore a hammer-axe, and differences of portrayal within the tall group suggest that these quite unhuman faces represent different divinities. But whether they were intended as major deities like Zeus and Poseidon or local gods and goddesses it is impossible to say. The 17 realistic, curled terracotta snakes clearly show that the cult of the beneficent household snake, popular in Crete, was also practiced here.

The Mycenae statues, like those from the temple of Late

Minoan I date on the island of Kea, thus fit well into the polytheistic pattern recorded on the tablets.

Several points suggest that Mycenaean religious beliefs and practices were similar to Minoan ones. The Knossos tablets show that the Mycenaean occupants made offerings to many local Cretan deities, including Mistress Athena and Poseidon, also found at Pylos. The domestic snake cult we now know was common to both peoples, and much of the Mycenaean apparatus of cult originated in Crete. In the palace at Pylos were movable plaster tables for offerings, and frescoes with shrine facades, all like those of the Minoans. The sacrifice of animals was basic to the religion of both areas; it was made on altars in Crete, as gem engravings and the Aghia Triadha painted sarcophagus show, and carried out at the ancestral hearth in the great Mycenaean megarons, like that of Pylos with its channels for liquid offerings at the side of the adjacent throne. Mycenaean iconography was largely taken over from Minoan, as cult scenes of goddesses and attendants, sacred trees, flowers and animals engraved on sealstones and gold rings found on the mainland, indicate. If these scenes were not just decorative but meaningful to the Mycenaeans it follows that the largely female aspect of Minoan religion was also adopted. Attention to the fertility of land and people, however, had presumably always, since Neolithic times, been as deeply rooted on the mainland as in Crete.

But while there was an apparent fusion of belief and practice, what part of each was in origin specifically mainland or Mycenaean is difficult if not impossible to determine. The local deities recorded and worshiped at Knossos are obviously Minoan, just as those of the Pylos tablets are Mycenaean, but what of Knossian Athene and Poseidon, Zeus and Hera? Were all or some of these, again known later at Pylos, introduced by the Mycenaeans as new to Crete, or introduced and assimilated to similar but older Cretan divinities? Zeus is usually considered an Indo-European, and so the Mycenaean sky-god, but against this must be set legends of his birth on Mount Dikte, and death and burial on Mount Juktas in Crete.

The salient features of Mycenaean religion seem then to be a flourishing polytheism, including worship of the later Greek gods and goddesses, the adoption and assimilation of divinities, especially female, and of cult, its apparatus and iconography from Minoan Crete, attention to fertility and the worship of many local gods and goddesses, Greek and pre-Greek, like the later cult of Hyakinthos at Amyklai.

By contrast, ritual and belief about death and burial show differences from those of Crete. The offering of little clay figurines is a common Mycenaean practice, as is the sacrifice of a dead man's pair of horses in the passage of his tholos tomb at Marathon. But new finds in the Mycenaean cemetery of Tanagra in Boeotia show a fusion of beliefs and practices. The tombs contained clay burial chests, a normal Late Minoan custom, with painted scenes depicting worship of a sacred pillar, and mourning and lying in state of the dead. The last two scenes suggest a direct continuity of practice with later Greece, where they are found again on the great Geometric burial amphoras of 8th-century Athens.

Society. The evidence of the Linear B tablets and of the material remains shows that Mycenaean society was elaborately hierarchical. The tablets refer to the king (of the Pylian state); to lawagetas (possibly leader of the war host), ranking next to the king in the distribution of land; telestai, who are officials probably in some kind of feudal service; kamaeus, a holder of kama (land), a particular

Above: fresco of a goddess holding sprays of corn, found at Mycenae.

Right: terracotta figurine of a goddess from Mycenae. 14th–13th century BC.

A painted terracotta burial chest from the Mycenaean cemetery at Tanagra in Boeotia. Such burial chests are unknown in Greece outside Tanagra, but are standard for Late Minoan III burials in Crete.

feudal service; eqeta, a companion or follower of high rank; kerosia (Greek geronsia, gerousia), a council; as well as to the many occupations and crafts noted above. Slavery in some form is attested; some were religious personnel (slaves of the god), others were owned by eqeta. There were several types of land-tenure, depending on the status of the holder, but apparently including both public land and private estates.

The material remains confirm aspects of these details of social structure. The palaces and large houses imply rulers, local chiefs and an aristocratic or rich merchant class. The artifacts betoken craftsmen of many kinds, whose obligations, food supplies and work quota requirements are detailed in the tablets. The Mycenae shrines suggest a priestly group, as do the tablets. Rulers and those immediately below them traveled and hunted in light, two-wheeled chariots, for which there were suitable roads and low stone bridges in populous areas. Horses and donkeys were used, though apparently not carts. Most people went by foot, as is natural on Greek terrain.

The Mycenaeans abroad; the 14th and 13th centuries.
The Mycenaean Palace Age was also a time of international peace in the eastern Mediterranean, with a balance of power maintained by the Hittites and Egyptians. Within this context Mycenaean commerce expanded rapidly from the time of the fall of Knossos around 1400 BC – and doubtless in part consequent upon it. The best surviving index of this commerce is the wide distribution of Mycenaean III A and III B pottery.

Vases went to several sites on the coast of Anatolia, from Troy southwards. At Miletos, Minoan ceramic contacts seem to have been replaced by an actual Mycenaean settlement with a defense wall. Mycenaean pottery of standard shapes – particularly the stemmed drinking goblet and the three-handled jar – was produced all over Rhodes. Vases were exported to Cypriot coastal settlements like Kourion, Hala Sultan Tekke and Enkomi, especially kraters with pictorial scenes of bulls, men and chariots. Over 60 sites in the Syro-Palestinian coastal region received imports, from Mersin and Tarsus in southern Turkey through Ras Shamra, Byblos and Megiddo down to Lachish and Tell el-Ajjul. In Egypt Mycenaean ware has come from nearly 20 sites on or near the Nile, down to Amarna, Thebes, Armant and further south, whence gold could have come in return. The Near Eastern communities were so attracted by the fine decorated pottery that they made imitations of stirrup jars and other shapes in calcite and blue glazed faience.

In the central Mediterranean the Mycenaeans had been sending pottery to Pazhok in Albania and the Lipari islands as early as the 16th century, while at least one Middle Helladic vase had reached or been copied at Monte Sallia in Sicily earlier. From 1400 BC Taranto and other sites in Apulia, Thapsos and several more communities in eastern and southern Sicily all received imports. Much of the pottery from Scoglio del Tonno at Taranto is known by style and confirmed by clay analysis to have come from Rhodes, and Lord William Taylour has argued convincingly that this site was a Rhodian trading station. Further west Mycenaean pieces have been found at Ischia and Vivara in the Bay of Naples, extensively in the Aeolian isles and, furthest of all, at Luni sul Mignone in Etruria and in Malta. Sardinia, as we saw above, has produced oxhide ingots, surely from its own sources, while from Palermo in western Sicily came imitations of Mycenaean terracotta figurines.

The exported pottery consists of small, closed shapes

like straight-sided alabastrons, little one-handled jars and taller piriform ones, jugs and stirrup vases. Within the ranges of Near Eastern and central Mediterranean pottery these technically excellent and finely-decorated pieces were clearly thought attractive in their own right and their ceramic appeal must have been as important as their contents, presumably perfumed oils. Other types of Mycenaean exports are rare, such as bronze knives and swords found in Albania, or hypothetically, the textiles known from the tablets to have been produced in quantity from the wool of countless Mycenaean sheep. Possible Mycenaean exports to the far west (Brittany, Britain and Scandinavia) have recently been much discussed. It would seem that faience beads in these areas (to which may be added Italy and Hungary) were locally made, but a few Mycenaean bronze double axes and swords and Cypriot rattanged blades may have reached the west, perhaps via middlemen along the west Mediterranean sea route or through Italy and Germany.

The explanation for Mycenaean trade is, in broad outline, fairly straightforward. In the Aegean Late Bronze Age, especially in the 14th and 13th centuries, the Mycenaean kingdoms had developed their economies and societies with enormous energy and success and it was an obvious course to voyage out with their best products. These were in any case much admired by their Mediterranean and Near Eastern neighbors. In turn the Mycenaeans had one vital need – metal, particularly copper and tin. Gold, ivory and a few other luxury items like amber and fine stones for seals and weapon fittings were also sought. Their neighbors were able to supply these products and, in the case of the eastern region, artistic motives and religious ideas along with them. Usually the Mycenaeans made simple voyaging visits; sometimes they planted settlements, or left a few merchants, as in south Italy, western Anatolia and perhaps Ugarit, the more efficiently to organize the exchange mechanisms. They were the precursors of the even grander Hellenizing movements of the 8th and 7th, and 4th and 3rd centuries BC, with the difference that their motives were those of commercial exchange rather than colonization for land.

The destruction of the Mycenaean world. The florescence of Mycenaean civilization came to an end with a series of burnt destructions of the main centers in the second half of the 13th century. The determination of the dates of the destructions depends on the styles of Mycenaean III B and III C pottery in use, and it is important to

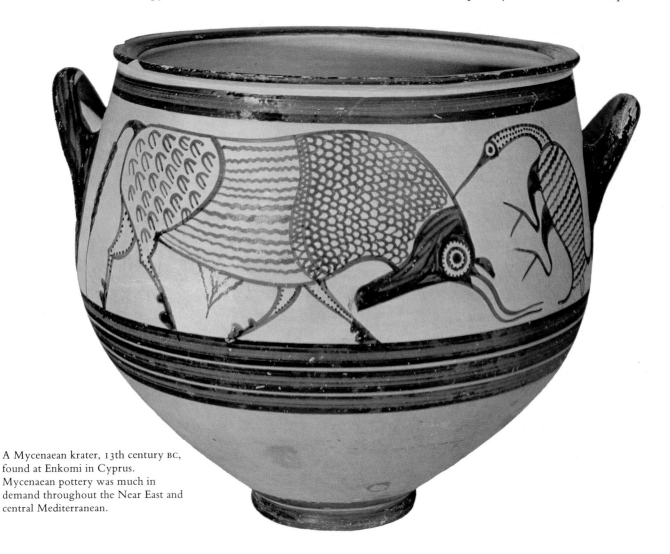

A Mycenaean krater, 13th century BC, found at Enkomi in Cyprus. Mycenaean pottery was much in demand throughout the Near East and central Mediterranean.

The most impressive of all Mycenaean fortified citadels is Gla in Boeotia. The well-preserved walls, 3,000 meters long, and gates enclose an area of some 240,000 square meters. The palace within was enclosed in a rectangular circuit wall. 13th century BC.

note, in offering any explanation for the catastrophes, that the events were not simultaneous.

The settlement at Zygouries and the houses outside the citadel at Mycenae were burnt and destroyed well before the end of Late Helladic III B, possibly around or before 1250 BC; the palace at Pylos came to a similar end about the same time or only a little later. Then around 1200 BC, at the end of Late Helladic III B, came a much greater wave of destruction in which great centers like Dendra, Mycenae and Tiryns in the Argolid, Krisa in Phokis, Gla and Thebes in Boeotia and Teikhos Dymaion in Achaia all fell, while Berbati. Eutresis and Prosymna were abandoned. Some important sites, however, were not destroyed at this time, notably Argos, Asine, Athens, Iolkos in Thessaly, Korakou, Lefkandi in Euboea and Nikhoria in Messenia. Some of these perished or were abandoned at other points in the 12th century, but not before they had enjoyed, along with an extensively rebuilt Mycenae and Tiryns, a final vigorous and wholly Mycenaean period of occupation.

Although various explanations have been proposed for this eclipse of Mycenaean civilization, one fact stands out. In the period immediately following the destructions, that is during the greater part of the 12th century, the culture of central and southern Greece is still wholly Mycenaean. The scale of life is impoverished, as we shall see below, but there is little evidence of new features in the archaeological record until the later 12th century. It is therefore difficult to see external invaders as the actual cause of the destructions, though for Pylos John Chadwick has stressed the group of tablets concerned with an early warning system of carefully numbered units all along the west Messenian coast, in anticipation of a sea-borne attack.

Climatological and natural causes have been suggested, although there seems no evidence for drought in Greece at this time, since the Pylian and Theban tablets indicate a richly flourishing agricultural production. A natural cause, the great volcanic eruption of Santorini, which Leon Pomerance would put at this date, is again unlikely, given first the time-span of the destructions, second the geographical location of the settlements in relation to Santorini – for example, distant, inland Pylos and Thebes – and third, the flourishing life at great sites like Lefkandi and Tiryns in the period immediately following 1200 BC. Both sites would have been easily exposed to Santorinian effects.

The likeliest cause of the destructions seems to be that advocated by ancient authorities and some modern scholars, namely *stasis*, internal, interstate wars. Such an explanation can be supported on four grounds: it accords with the absence of any trace of invaders, is feasible in terms of the rich economic rewards to be gained, relates well to the gradual construction of deliberately imposing fortifications by certain kingdoms which reached a peak of economic power in the 13th century and desired both to protect it and to extend it further, and lastly is of a piece with the recurrent pattern of internal, basically economic wars among the later city states of Greece.

Tradition also supports this explanation since one major story recorded two big wars from the Argolid against Thebes. The Trojan War story, for which much evidence suggests at least a historical basis, could imply a similar possibility of attack for material reward by a confederation of Aegean kingdoms against a powerful neighboring center.

Groups sometimes considered important for Aegean history around 1200 BC are the Sea Peoples. This was a term used by the Egyptians in the late 13th and early 12th centuries to describe mixed bands of raiders, including other named groups who were also active, though not collectively called Sea Peoples, in the 14th and 13th centuries. These raiders reached Egypt and were repulsed, first by Merenptah about 1220 BC and finally by Ramesses III about 1190 BC. They may have been responsible for destructions in Cyprus around 1200 BC, while similar groups on land destroyed Levantine towns and may have played a part in the collapse of the Hittite empire to the north at the same date.

Some of the sea raiders have names connecting them with Anatolia (Lukka, like later Lycians, and Danuna, land in Cilicia), others have names close to those of later central Mediterranean peoples, who probably derived from them (Sherden – ? Sardinians; Sheklesh – ? Sikels; Tursha – ? Etruscans), while two others were the Aqaiwash and Pulisati. These are usually thought to have been Achaeans (Ahhiyawa being the corresponding Hittite form) – that is Mycenaeans – and Philistines. The latter settled in Palestine after their defeat by Ramesses, and it is interesting to note that archaeologically their culture in pottery and tomb types seems to have derived from the Aegean. Little or nothing in the evidence about the Sea Peoples suggests connections outside the eastern Mediterranean, such as with central or eastern Europe.

What part, if any, the Sea Peoples played in the Mycenaean destructions of the later 13th century is impossible to determine fully, but one or two points seem clear. The Sea Peoples as a whole, a mixed bag including Anatolians, are unlikely to have been responsible for the Mycenaean destructions, though Aegeans among them could well have been involved in internal Mycenaean wars, and the kingdom of Pylos, as we saw above, was expecting an attack by sea at the time of its destruction. As far as the Mycenaean states were concerned, groups of sea raiders seem likely to have been as much a result as a cause of the internal breakdown of civilization. Essentially the raiders were operating outside the Aegean area and in the eastern Mediterranean during the disturbed conditions around 1200 BC.

The end of the Bronze Age (1200–1100/1050 BC). With the destructions of about 1200 BC the civilization based on palace centers ended. With it went the palatial arts, writing, fresco painting, the carving of ivories and stone vessels. Many sites were abandoned, especially in the southern Peloponnese. Nevertheless, 12th-century Mycenaean society flourished. Large Late Helladic III C settlements existed at Lefkandi in Euboea and on the sites listed above. A rich treasure, including gold and amber ornaments, was found in the ruins of a house at Tiryns, while extensive cemeteries at Perati in eastern Attica, on Naxos, in Achaia and on the Ionian islands of Kephallenia and Ithaka indicate considerable occupation. The homogeneity of Mycenaean III B pottery was broken, but a series of distinct and attractive regional styles developed: a Close Style in the Argolid, with rosettes, octopuses, flowers and other filling ornaments covering almost the whole surface; a Pictorial Style in traditional dark paint on a light ground with lions, sphinxes and humans – well known from the Warrior Vase at Mycenae – and in new white on black, richly evidenced at Lefkandi with griffins; an Octopus Style popular in the

islands, with the luridly decorated creatures swimming over stirrup jars; and a Fringe Style in Crete, with little fringes attached to the abstract patterns. This decorated pottery, with the plain wares, stemmed goblets, deep bowls, large amphoras, jars and jugs, was of excellent fabrication.

External trade continued, although on a lesser scale than in the Palace period. Late Helladic III C pottery went to the Near East and to Taranto, amber came south to Achaia and Kephallenia, Near Eastern and Egyptian trinkets reached Lefkandi in Euboea and Perati in Attica and, most important, first iron objects and then iron technology were introduced into the Aegean from Cyprus.

During this period and down to the final fading of Mycenaean culture in the early 11th century, several developments are important. First, after the destructions of about 1200 BC there is a notable change in the settlement pattern. Although the Argolid sites continued to be occupied, dispersion also took place on a large scale, especially to Achaia and the Ionian islands, to Lefkandi in Euboea, to Naxos and probably other Cycladic islands and, most significantly, to Cyprus, where a series of coastal settlements received Mycenaeans early in the 12th century, bringing with them all the details of their bronze technology, their language and oral ballads of former exploits. A few Mycenaeans also went to Crete, as we noticed in the previous chapter. Second, the century is punctuated by further destructions and abandonments, at Korakou and Iolkos early on, at Mycenae and Tiryns in mid-century, at Lefkandi and Teikhos Dymaion by the end.

Third, new features of material culture appear in central and southern Greece in the later 12th century and in the 11th. These are principally long dress pins, arched fibulae and finger rings with two spiral terminals, all of bronze; a certain amount of dark, hand-made pottery with decorative knobs; and stone cist graves with single burials. None of these are Mycenaean. The graves are prominent in western Attica and occur also in the Argolid, Elis and at Thebes, and the bronzes and pottery appear here and there on the mainland. These features suggest that new people were arriving, but their area of origin, beyond the fact that it was certainly to the north, is obscure. Cist graves appear earlier in Greek Epeiros, from where they could have spread south. The type of ring with spiral terminals is also found before 1100 BC in the same northwestern region, and its spread over the Pindos range to Thessaly and Lokris might indicate movement to the central regions further south. But there is no compelling evidence at present to indicate that long dress pins or fibulae came specifically from Epeiros. The situation in that region appears to have been complex and is difficult to reconstruct; but it seems (according to Nicholas Hammond) that people could have been pushed out southwards, as the evidence noted above suggests, by extensive population movements from the north into Epeiros itself, since many new metallurgical features of central European origin appear there and in

A stirrup jar, with a stylized flower pattern, from a tomb at Makresia near Olympia. 13th century BC.

of life continued from Mycenaean times through the Dark Ages, but Minoan and Mycenaean building styles, wall-painting, writing, pottery types and decorations, metal-work and other crafts passed away around 1100 BC, or were thoroughly transformed. Yet the material remains are far from being the only achievements of a culture. Several fundamentals of Classical civilization were in fact inherited from the peoples of the Bronze Age.

The first of these was language, possibly the most important binding factor in the development of ideas, which comprises the essence of a culture. The Greek language, an early form of which was widely used in Mycenaean times, cannot have died out on the mainland and was, moreover, transmitted to Cyprus and many east Aegean and west Anatolian cities through migrations at the end of the Bronze Age and during the early Iron Age. It was these places which in turn produced the first great empirical philosophers, thinking and writing in Greek.

Second, there were the myths and legends which became the basis of so much Greek creative literature and art. There can be little doubt that the traditional stories of the Homeric poems are, like many Homeric artifacts, a genuine survival in an oral tradition of poetry stretching back to the doings of Mycenaean warrior princes – just as Homeric geography in its main lines fits only into a Bronze Age situation. Mycenae, Pylos, Ithaka and Troy were of little importance after the Bronze Age. Similarly, other stories in Greek literature, about Theseus, Ariadne and the Minotaur, Jason and the Argonauts, Kadmos and his descendants, must have been formed in the knowledge, if only dim, of the traditional greatness of Bronze Age Knossos, Volos and Thebes.

Finally, there is religion. It is impossible to overestimate the importance of religion in Classical Greek life, whether the Olympian religion of Zeus or the mysteries of Diony-sos or the scores of small local cults for local deities. Classical religion can now be traced back in almost every aspect to the Bronze Age. Most of the Greek pantheon are mentioned in the Linear B tablets as recipients of offerings. Shrines in Cretan caves like that of Eileithyia at Inatos or on Cretan sites like the acropolises of Gortyn and Prinias, or in the rich and newly-found sanctuary of Hermes at Kato Syme seem to exhibit, in the material objects offered, a continuity of worship from the Bronze Age to the Iron Age. This may be true also of the temple at Aghia Eirene on Kea, and on Delos. In Minoan and Mycenaean art there are many representations of a Mistress or Master of Animals, important aspects of Artemis and Apollo in later times; and local cults of Classical times, like that of Hyakinthos at Amyklai near Sparta, are of essentially Bronze Age deities. Thus in language, oral poetry, the legends and mythology of creative literature and in religion, all fundamental parts of Classical (and thus European) civilization, we find a profound continuity from the brilliant Minoans and Mycenaeans of the Bronze Age to their successors in the same lands.

southern Yugoslavia and Greek Macedonia at this time.

The tradition received by Thucydides spoke of Dorian tribes arriving in the Peloponnese 80 years after the Trojan War, which would mean sometime during the 12th century, and this in turn could be equated with the new later 12th-century features in central and southern Greece. The later distribution of Greek dialects also suggests that the northwestern region was the formative area for Doric. The archaeology of the period, however, is fraught with problems and a relative lack of evidence, and any equation of objects, events, people and language must remain at present extremely hypothetical.

Fourth and last we turn to Athens and her environs. Here, and perhaps here alone, there was firm, unbroken continuity of existence which, while not spectacular in these Dark Ages, was never moribund either. The cemeteries of Salamis and Athenian Kerameikos show in their gradual but continuous transition from Mycenaean to sub-Mycenaean and then Protogeometric usage (late 12th–10th centuries) how the communities of Athens transformed the old Mycenaean ceramic tradition, absorbed the new northern or northwestern features, and mastered and developed the new iron technology to produce a culture which was to flow out from 9th-century Athens as the originator of the material side of Hellenic civilization.

The Greek heritage. What, finally, was the Greek heritage from the Aegean Bronze Age? Materially, very little. The artifacts of 10th- and 9th-century Greece, which develop with some Anatolian and Near Eastern influences into those of the Classical period, have almost no links with those of the Bronze Age. Of course the agricultural basis

Further reading

Barber, R.L.N., *The Cyclades in the Bronze Age* (London, 1987).

Bass, G.F., "Oldest known shipwreck reveals splendors of the Bronze Age," *National Geographic* 172, no. 6 (December 1987).

Betancourt, P.P., *The History of Minoan Pottery* (Princeton, N.J., 1985).

Blegen, C.W., *Troy and the Trojans* (London, 1963).

Branigan, K., *The Foundations of Palatial Crete* (London, 1970; Amsterdam, 1988).
—— *The Tombs of Mesara* (London, 1970).

Buchholz, H.-G., and **Karageorghis, V.,** *Prehistoric Greece and Cyprus* (London, 1973).

Cadogan, G., *Palaces of Minoan Crete* (corrected ed. London, 1980).

Chadwick, J., *The Decipherment of Linear B* (Cambridge, 1967).
—— *The Mycenaean World* (Cambridge, 1977).

Desborough, V.R.d'A., *The Last Mycenaeans and their Successors* (Oxford, 1964).
—— *The Greek Dark Ages* (London, 1972).

Doumas, C., *Thera. Pompeii of the Ancient Aegean* (London, 1983).

Graham, J.W., *The Palaces of Crete* (Princeton, N.J., 1962; repr. 1988).

Hägg, R., and **Marinatos, N.** (eds.), *Sanctuaries and Cults in the Aegean Bronze Age* (Stockholm, 1981).
—— *The Minoan Thalassocracy. Myth and Reality* (Stockholm, 1984).
—— *The Function of the Minoan Palaces* (Stockholm, 1987).

Hood, M.S.F., *The Minoans* (London, 1971).
—— *The Arts in Prehistoric Greece* (London, 1978).

Jones, G., Wardle, K., Halstead, P. and **Wardle, D.,** "Crop storage at Assiros," *Scientific American* 254, no. 3 (March 1986).

Krzyszkowska, O., and **Nixon, L.** (eds.), *Minoan Society. Proceedings of the Cambridge Colloquium 1981* (Bristol, 1983).

Luce, J.V., *The End of Atlantis* (London, 1969).

Marinatos, N., *Art and Religion in Thera* (Athens, 1984).
—— *Minoan Sacrificial Ritual* (Stockholm, 1986).

Marinatos, S., and **Hirmer, M.,** *Crete and Mycenae* (London, 1960).
—— *Kreta, Thera und das mykenische Hellas* (Munich, 1973).

Mylonas, G., *Mycenae and the Mycenean Age* (Princeton, N.J., 1966).
—— *Mycenae Rich in Gold* (Athens, 1983).

Nilsson, M.P., *The Minoan-Mycenaean Religion in its Survival in Greek Religion* (2nd ed., Lund, 1950).

Pendlebury, J.D.S., *The Archaeology of Crete* (London, 1939; repr. New York, 1965).

Renfrew, C., *The Emergence of Civilization. The Cyclades and the Aegean in the Third Millennium BC* (London, 1972).

Rutkowski, B., *The Cult Places of the Aegean* (New Haven, Conn., and London, 1985).

Snodgrass, A., *The Dark Age of Greece* (Edinburgh, 1971).

Stubbings, F.H., *Mycenaean Pottery from the Levant* (Cambridge, 1951).

Thimme, J., and **Getz-Preziosi, P.** (eds.), *Art and Culture of the Cyclades in the Third Millennium BC* (Chicago and London, 1977).

Vermeule, E., *Greece in the Bronze Age* (5th impression, Chicago and London, 1972).

Wace, A.J.B., *Mycenae. An Archaeological History and Guide* (Princeton, N.J., 1949).

Warren, P., *Minoan Religion as Ritual Action* (Göteborg, 1988).

Zervos, C., *L'Art de la Crète néolithique et minoenne* (Paris, 1956).
—— *L'Art des Cyclades* (Paris, 1957).

Acknowledgments

Unless otherwise stated all the illustrations on a given page are credited to the same source.

Ashmolean Museum, Oxford 20, 21, 22, 85 top left and right, 86 top left

R. Barnard, London 28 center, 31, 57 top, 70, 71, 88 top, 96

C. W. Blegen and M. Rawson, *The Palace of Nestor at Pylos in Western Messenia* (1966), reprinted by permission of the Princeton University Press 122

Brooklyn Museum, New York, Charles Edwin Wilbour Fund 110

J. L. Caskey, University of Cincinnati 52

E. Dodwell, *Cyclopean or Pelasgic Remains* (1834) 2, 17, 32 bottom

Ekdotike Athenon S. A., Athens 9, 19, 24 top, 26–27, 29 top right and center right, 33, 35 left, 37, 44, 47, 48, 51, 53, 54, 55 left, 56, 67, 68, 72, 73, 76, 77, 78, 82–83, 85 center right, 86 bottom left, 87 top and bottom, 88 center left and bottom right, 89 top left, 95 left, 97, 98, 99, 100, 101, 106, 109, 112 top, 114, 115, 116, 117, 118, 121, 123, 124 top, 126, 127 right, 129, 131, 132

Elsevier, Amsterdam 10, 41 top, 46 top, 55 right, 69 top, 112 bottom, 113 bottom left, 127 left

J. Fuller, Cambridge 7, 8

R. Gorringe, London 65 top and bottom left, 80, 84, 86 bottom right, 93, 113 right, 125

Greek National Tourist Office 43 bottom, 45

Archiv G. Hafner, Mainz 29 top left, bottom left and center left, 32 top, 50 top, 79, 102, 133

D. A. Harissiadis, Athens 15 left, 38, 75 bottom, 90–91, 94 bottom, 111

Photo Dimitrios Harissiadis, copyright George Rainbird Ltd. 40, 41 bottom, 45, 119, 128, 136

A. A. M. van der Heyden, Amsterdam 69 bottom, 85 bottom right, 87 center, 124 bottom

Hirmer Foto-Archiv, Munich 49

Holle-Bildarchiv, Baden-Baden 89 top and bottom right, 107

Italian School of Archaeology, Athens 75 top

N. Kontos, Athens 130

J. A. Lavaud, Paris 15 right, 104

H. Loxton, Oxford 113 top left

G. Perrot and C. Chipiez, *Histoire de l'art dans l'antiquité* (1882–1914) 30 bottom

N. Platon, Athens 108

H. Schliemann, *Ilios* (1880) 13

H. Schliemann, *Mykenae* (1878) 28 top, 30 top

C. Schuchhardt, *Schliemann's Excavations* (1891) 12

Spectrum, London 14, 86 top right

Lord William Taylour, Cambridge 25

P. de Tournefort, *Relation d'un voyage du Levant* (1717) 11

P. Warren 23, 24 bottom, 34, 35 right, 39, 43 top, 46 bottom, 57 bottom, 58, 59, 61, 62, 63, 64, 65, 66, 74, 81, 88 bottom left, 94 top, 95 right, 134

The Publishers have attempted to observe the legal requirements with respect to the rights of the suppliers of photographic materials. Nevertheless, persons who have claims are invited to apply to the Publishers.

The author wishes to acknowledge the assistance of the following: Professor Stylianos Alexiou, the late Professor J. L. Caskey, Dr. Oliver Dickinson, Professor J. D. Evans, Dr. Elizabeth French, Dr. Angelike Lembessis, Professor Doro Levi, the late Professor Sp. Marinatos, the late Professor G. Mylonas, Professor Nikolaos Platon, Lord William Taylour and the late Mrs. Alan Wace.

Glossary

The glossary lists only persons and terms referred to in the book. The definitions of terms are based primarily on usage in Aegean prehistory. Some may of course have slightly different or wider meanings in other contexts. Entries of modern scholars refer primarily to their work in Aegean prehistory and are not intended as biographical vignettes encompassing all work in other fields, such as Classical archaeology.

Achaeans In Homer the usual name for the Greeks; the same people are probably meant by the name Akaiwasha in Egyptian texts of the 13th and 12th centuries BC, when they fought among the Sea Peoples against Egypt. The name Ahhiyawa in Hittite texts of c. 1400–1200 BC may well also refer to the Achaeans, although the location of the Ahhiyawa is disputed. In the 12th century there was an influx of population into the central area of the north Peloponnesian coast. This area is Achaea in later Greek times and may have received its name from the Mycenaean peoples settling in the 12th century, if not from the earlier Mycenaean population. Another group of Achaeans inhabited southeast Thessaly in Classical times and since this was earlier an area of thoroughly Mycenaean culture the name of the district probably arose then. Support for this lies in the fact that in Homer one of the main groups of Achaeans is that under Achilles, from southeast Thessaly. The historical reality of the Achaeans as the Mycenaean Greeks, as they are in Homer, is supported by the fact that the Arcado–Cypriot dialect, one of the main branches of Achaean, is closely related to the Mycenaean Greek of the Linear B tablets.

Agamemnon In the *Iliad* King of Mycenae and its adjacent territory, and leader of the Greek chieftains in the war against Troy. Some of those who accept the Trojan War as in essence historical would think a historical Agamemnon also likely, as a Broze Age ruler of Mycenae in the 13th century BC.

Agrimi (pl. **Agrimia**) The Cretan wild goat, a variety of ibex with very long horns curving right over to the back. Common in Minoan times and frequently depicted with complete realism in Minoan art.

Aigina Treasure A hoard of jewelry, mostly gold, with many elaborate beads and pendants. It was found on the island of Aigina in 1891 and is thought to have come, in part at least, from Minoan Crete originally, perhaps from the Khrysolakkos tomb at Mallia, and to have been hidden in the 1880s in a Mycenaean chamber tomb in Aigina. Now in the British Museum.

Aigisthos See under **Atreus** and **Klytaimnestra**.

Akhenaten Name adopted by the Egyptian Pharaoh Amenophis IV (1368–1351 BC), son of Amenophis III and Nefertiti. He transferred the royal capital to Amarna and instituted there a new religion (or reinstated an earlier one), the belief in the sun, the Aten, as the source of all prosperity. His successors reverted to the cult of Amun and considered him a heretic. Politically his reign was disastrous for Egypt, but trade prospered and hundreds of Mycenaean vases went to Amarna. The brief occupation of that site thus provides a cornerstone in the absolute dating of Mycenaean pottery. Wall paintings at Amarna display elements of Aegean style and might have been painted by refugee craftsmen from Crete after the fall of Knossos c. 1400–1350 BC.

Alabastron Vessel of clay or stone (often Egyptian alabaster, whence the name), either low and squat or taller and more rounded, in each case with a small mouth the better to keep in the contents, which were probably perfumed oils. The tall form was a favourite shape among Egyptian lapidaries while both shapes were imitated by Late Minoan and Mycenaean potters.

Alexiou, Stylianos Greek archaeologist and scholar whose major excavations have been rich tombs at Minoan sites (Kanli Kastelli, Katsamba (the harbor town of Knossos) and Lebena) and who has written widely on the Minoan civilization, especially Minoan religion, and on Cretan poetry and scholarship in the Venetian period (1204–1669 AD).

Amphora Storage vessel around 1½ to 3 feet tall. In Minoan and Mycenaean pottery amphoras are roughly barrel-shaped or piriform with a neck and lip and were usually decorated with rich patterns.

Amulet An object worn on the person as a lucky charm or as an imagined protection against sickness or magic.

Andronikos, Manolis Greek archaeologist who has specialized in the archaeology of northern Greece, especially in the huge Iron Age cemetery at Verghina in Macedonia. He has also written on Mycenaean and Homeric burial customs.

Aphrodite The Greek goddess of sexual love and beauty. In origin she is related to the Semitic Ishtar and Astarte. A goddess with some of her characteristics may have been worshiped in Bronze Age Crete. Several birds were sacred to her, the dove, sparrow, swallow and swan.

Apollo Paian A Master of Animals, venerated in Crete as a lesser counterpart of the great Minoan goddess, the Mistress of Animals (see **Artemis Eileithyia**). He may therefore, like her, have been worshiped in peak sanctuaries and one of his functions may have been healing, in view of votive terracotta figurines of parts of the body in the sanctuaries. The Greek god Apollo, brother of Artemis, had a healing function and was an averter of pestilence. Although Apollo is not known in the Linear B religious tablets, Paiawon, an early form of Paian, is found there and the name later became an epithet of Apollo as healer.

Argonaut See **Nautilus**.

Arsenical Used to describe Early Bronze Age bronze tools where arsenic rather than tin has been alloyed with copper.

Artemis Eileithyia A single Minoan goddess probably combining the attributes of the later Artemis and Eileithyia, who were in any case often considered identical by the Greeks. For the Greeks Artemis was the patron goddess of hunting and of chastity. At the same time she was goddess of childbirth. The apparent contrast lies in her origins, since much that was believed of her was derived from Minoan belief in a great goddess who was Mistress of Animals and Nature. The Minoan goddess may have been

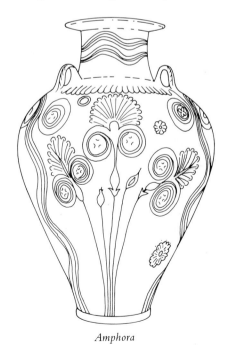

Amphora

identical with a goddess worshiped at stalactites in caves. This was Eileithyia, who had a cave at Amnisos near Knossos, and is mentioned both in the Linear B tablets and in Homer. Since Eileithyia was a goddess of childbirth in Classical Greece she probably had the same function in the Bronze Age.

Ashlar Term used to describe Minoan and Mycenaean masonry in which the blocks, rectangular in elevation, have a smoothly dressed external surface and fit exactly against one another. The palaces and mansions of central and southern Crete have many external walls of limestone blocks in the finest ashlar technique.

Athena One of the leading goddesses of the Greeks and the patron deity of Athens. Her origins lay in Minoan–Mycenaean religion as a domestic, snake goddess, protectress of the household, palace and town. For the Greeks she was also goddess of crafts, of wisdom and war.

Atreidae The sons of Atreus and Aerope, Agamemnon and Menelaos, legendary kings of Mycenae and Sparta.

Atreus In legend the son of Pelops, brother of Thyestes and father of Agamemnon and Menelaos. The story of this family is replete with incest and murder, including Atreus' killing of Thyestes' two sons whom he served up to Thyestes at a banquet. When king of Mycenae, Atreus married his third wife, Pelopia, already pregnant by her father Thyestes. The child was Aigisthos, who later murdered both Atreus and Agamemnon.

Awl Pointed tool of bone, or of bronze or stone set in a handle, used for boring small holes in hides, wood and other materials.

Axe-adze Bronze tool with a central hole for a wooden handle and two blades, opposite each other, one vertical for use as an axe, the other horizontal (the adze), for use in planing down timber, hollowing earth or working stone.

Baldric An ornamented belt passing over one shoulder and under the opposite arm to hold a sword at the waist.

Batter Architectural term meaning a wall deliberately built not vertically but leaning inwards as it rises, or the slope of such a wall.

Beehive Tomb A tomb resembling a domed beehive in shape, built of stones and, in Mycenaean Greece, set mostly below ground level. The protruding top of the dome was covered with earth. The entrance to the tomb was by a long passage cut into the hillside. See also **Corbeling** and **Dromos**.

Belon, Pierre (1518–64) French traveler in Greece and the Near East. His book, published in 1553, contains many acute and interesting observations on the antiquities, botany and topography of Crete.

Bent, James Theodore (1852–97) English explorer and traveler who in addition to work in Arabia and Africa produced a delightful book in 1885 (*The Cyclades or Life among the Insular Greeks*) treating of their people, folklore, religion, economy and antiquities.

Bichrome The use of two colors on a surface of a different color, especially the use of red and black on a buff ground in Middle Helladic, Middle Cycladic and Cypriot Iron Age pottery. Compare **Polychrome**.

Blegen, Carl W. (1887–1971) American, one of the greatest Aegean archaeologists, excavator of Korakou, Zygouries, Prosymna, Troy and the Mycenaean palace at Pylos in Messenia.

Bouleuterion Building in Greek cities for meetings of the council.

Boyd, Harriet (Mrs. Boyd Hawes) (1871–1945) American archaeologist who directed excavations at Gournia, in 1901, 1903–04, uncovering what is still one of the most fully visible prehistoric towns in the Aegean. She also organized and largely wrote the monumental publication which appeared only four years after the excavations.

Bronze Age Convenient label used by archaeologists for period of time during which the predominant metal employed by a culture was bronze (3000–1100 BC in the Aegean). Usually succeeds Stone Age and is followed by Iron Age. Often divided into Early, Middle and Late. In the Aegean bronze did not come into general use until Early Bronze II (c. 2600–2200 BC).

Bull's Horns The bucranium, an ox-head with its horns, often shown in Minoan art. A bull cult and bull sacrifices seem to have been common. Bulls' horns are sometimes found

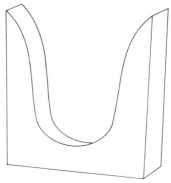

Bull's horns

in excavated buildings and they may have been the origin of the so-called horns of consecration, which are made of stone, terracotta or plaster, and are one of the commonest Minoan religious symbols.

Burnish The rubbing or polishing of the surface of a pot with a smooth piece of stone, bone, pottery or wood after it had dried in the sun but before it was fired in the kiln. This technique produced an attractive glossy surface after firing.

Carination A profile, common on vessels, where a concave and a convex curve meet to produce a ridge or sharp edge like a keel (Latin *carina*).

Cartouche Egyptian hieroglyphic inscription set within an elliptical area and giving the name and titles of a pharaoh or divinity.

Caskey, John L. American archaeologist whose major Aegean prehistoric excavations have been at Troy (with **Blegen**), Lerna and, currently, at Aghia Eirene on the island of Kea. In addition to Troy the discoveries at Lerna and on Kea have made these sites fundamental for understanding the Aegean Bronze Age.

Cassandra A daughter of Priam and Hecuba, endowed by Apollo with the gift of prophecy. Taken as a concubine by Agamemnon, she was killed along with him by Klytaimnestra on their return to Mycenae from the Trojan War.

Chadwick, John English Classical scholar and Greek philologist. Collaborated with **Ventris** immediately after the latter's decipherment of the **Linear B** tablets and has produced many leading publications on the tablets. The actual story of the decipherment is graphically told in his book, *The Decipherment of Linear B*.

Chamber Tomb An underground chamber for burial, hollowed out of soft rock and approached by a passage cut into a sloping hillside. Used successively for family burials, chiefly in the Aegean Late Bronze Age.

Chased (noun: **Chasing**) Term used for surface decoration on metal vessels executed with a hammer and punches which produce indented lines. Occurs on gold vessels from the Shaft Graves of Mycenae. Contrast **Repoussé**, which was often finished off on the outside by chasing.

Cistern In Minoan Crete a large pit with plastered stone walls, used to collect and store water. Some Mycenaean palaces had underground passages leading to springs where water collected in a hollowed-out pool or cistern.

Cist Grave Rectangular grave cut in the earth, its sides lined and its top roofed with stone slabs. The body and offerings were placed within on a layer of pebbles. Common in Early Cycladic and Middle Helladic times and at the end of the Bronze Age and early Iron Age in mainland Greece.

Clay Bar Small terracotta bar, usually square in section, used for inscriptions in the Minoan hieroglyphic or Linear A script.

Corbeling Architectural term in the Aegean for masonry constructed in overlapping courses to bring the walls of a building inwards as it rises, as in the domed vaults of tholos tombs or the gabled passages within fortification walls.

Cycladic Describes the Bronze Age cultures of the Cyclades, the central islands of the Aegean sea. The Early Cycladic or Early Bronze Age cultures of the third millennium BC were particularly rich in their production of vessels and figurines in white marble.

Cyclopean A term used for walls at prehistoric sites like Mycenae, built of blocks so enormous that it was later believed only the giant **Cyclopes** could have constructed them.

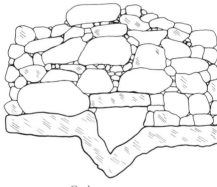

Cyclopean masonry

Cyclopes In Homer giant shepherds with one eye in the center of the forehead. Polyphemos was their chief and one of Odysseus' adventures was to blind him in his cave before escaping, with his men, tied to the underbellies of Polyphemos' sheep, so that the latter would not realize what was happening.

Cylinder Seal Sealstone in the shape of a small cylinder. Unlike Oriental cylinders, which were engraved round the side, Early Minoan ivory cylinders were engraved with a design on each end and were pierced through the side for suspension. Late Minoan cylinder seals in semi-precious stones were rare, but were engraved with beautiful designs round their sides.

Dark Ages The period in Greek history

from the end of the Mycenaean civilization (c. 1125–1050 BC) to the re-emergence, especially at Athens, of a materially prosperous and literate society in the 9th and 8th centuries BC. In consequence of their material poverty Greek communities have left relatively few traces of life in the Dark Ages, save in the modest pottery and metal objects in their tombs. See also **Fibula**, **Iron Age**, **Protogeometric** and **Geometric**.

Death Mask A mask made of thin gold sheet or electrum and placed over the face of some of the dead in the Shaft Graves at Mycenae

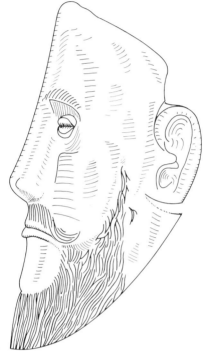

Death mask

(c. 1550–1500 BC). Although some details are stylized the masks give a clear general impression of portraiture and two family types are discernible.

Dionysos Greek god (also called Bacchus) of an emotional religion and, by Classical times, of wine and the drama. His origins and the early history of his cult are complex and disputed. The majority of ancient writers thought he and his cult originated in Thrace, with bull worship, orgiastic rites, communing with wild life, both animal and vegetable. Others thought he came from Asia Minor. In both cases his introduction to Greece was placed later than the Bronze Age, but the name Dionysos does occur on a Linear B tablet from Pylos, though it is uncertain whether it refers to the god or is simply a proper name.

Dodwell, Edward (1767–1832) English traveler in Greece (1801–06) and Italy. He was an antiquarian writer and an

accomplished draughtsman. The watercolors in his published works illustrate the condition of sites on mainland Greece later to be made famous by archaeology as centers of Bronze Age culture.

Dorians Tribes speaking the Dorian dialect of Greek who by the 8th century BC inhabited most of southern Greece, the southern Cyclades, Crete and the Dodecanesian islands such as Rhodes. They probably came from northwestern Greece, arriving in groups from the late 12th and 11th centuries BC onwards, reaching the Peloponnese first and spreading eastwards and southwards from there. Politically they became merged with the previous population in Corinthia and the Argolid, but in Sparta and Crete they maintained a rigid, ruling military aristocracy with local peoples kept as serfs or dependants.

Dörpfeld, Wilhelm (1853–1940) One of the greatest German archaeologists in the Aegean. Before joining **Schliemann** at Troy in 1882 he had taken part in the German excavations at Olympia. His work at Troy did much to help understanding of the history of the superimposed cities. He also excavated Tiryns with Schliemann and discovered and meticulously published rich prehistoric tombs on the Ionian island of Lefkas, which he always believed to be the site of Homer's Ithaca.

Double Axe Bronze double-bladed axe with a perforation between the blades for the handle. Common Minoan and Mycenaean tool and one of the commonest Minoan religious symbols, perhaps from its use in

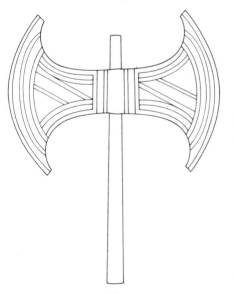

Double axe

animal sacrifices. It is constantly depicted by the Minoans on vases, gold rings, stone blocks and pillars in the palaces, while large models made of decorated sheet bronze were set up in shrines on poles fixed into stone bases. See also **Labyrinth**.

Dressed Stone Stone blocks used in masonry, their surfaces worked with tools into regular shapes, sometimes as ashlar.

Dromos Passage cut into sloping ground, leading to a chamber tomb or tholos.

Duck Vase Pottery vessel a bit like a duck in appearance; found in the Cyclades at the end of the Early Bronze Age and in various parts of the Aegean, emanating from Cyprus c. 1050 BC, at the very end of the Late Bronze Age. The former has at one end a little vertical cylinder with an open spreading lip; the latter usually has a bird's head at one end and a cylindrical spout and affixed handle in the middle of the back and little feet. The functions are unknown but are unlikely to have been of a practical or domestic nature.

Einkorn Variety of wheat, grown by the farmers of Neolithic Greece. Wild forms are found in Greece today and it was probably from these that the Neolithic people domesticated einkorn, not needing to introduce it from outside the Aegean.

Emmer Variety of wheat cultivated in Neolithic Greece. Its wild progenitors are not found in Greece today and it was probably introduced as seed corn by the earliest Neolithic settlers in the 7th millennium BC, coming from Anatolia or the Near East.

Evans, Sir Arthur John (1851–1941) Excavator of the great Bronze Age palace at Knossos and, through his many writings, discoverer and exponent of the Minoan civilization of Crete.

Fibula Type of pin shaped like a modern safety pin or like a deeply pulled bow or arch. Usually of bronze, though sometimes of iron in the Iron Age. The first type appears in Mycenaean Greece in the 13th century BC, the arched type later, becoming common in the following centuries. It probably indicates a change in clothing, pinning a long robe at the shoulder, and perhaps supports climatological evidence that the weather was becoming wetter and colder.

Flask Late Minoan or Mycenaean pottery vessel, almost globular and made as two bowls joined at the rim. A flask stood on its edge, with a small ring-shaped foot, and had a small neck with little handles. Circular patterns covered the surface. It would hold scented oils safely and some were exported.

Fluting Shallow, concave grooves, normally in architecture, as on columns, or in metalwork, especially on vessels of gold, silver and bronze.

Fringed Style A type of painted decoration on pottery of many shapes, including Octopus Style stirrup jars, at the end of the Bronze Age, 12th century BC, chiefly in Crete. The geometrical patterns frequently have little fringes added to them.

Furtwängler, Adolf (1853–1907) A German Classical archaeologist who excavated at Bronze Age Orchomenos. Two of his masterpieces were volumes on ancient gems, including Minoan and Mycenaean, and (with Loeschke) on Mycenaean pottery, the first such study.

Furumark, Arne Swedish archaeologist who produced the fundamental study of Mycenaean pottery and its dating in 1941. He has also published on Mycenaean links with Cyprus and on Aegean religion, and has written a basic monograph on Minoan and Mycenaean history from the point of view of their foreign connections.

Fyfe, Theodore Evans' architect in the first years of the excavations at Knossos. He was responsible for the proper recording and drawing of the early plans in the palace.

Geometric Term used to describe abstract patterns in regular and repeated arrangements, most commonly on vase painting. A geometric style is found at most periods and places in the Aegean but the Geometric style proper and its forerunner Protogeometric also gave their names to the art of a specific period in Greece, c. 1050–700 BC.

Gortyn Law Code A very large and remarkably well-preserved legal code, discovered in 1884, inscribed on limestone blocks now in the Roman odeion (singing hall) at Gortyn in Crete. The code, written in the Dorian dialect of Crete, was set up c. 450 BC, though its contents include and refer to many earlier laws. It is concerned with the legal position of the family, adoption, heiresses, family property and with slaves, who had rights, could own property and even marry free women. Procedure at trials is carefully defined. Generally the code has been considered a mixture of primitive and developed, often liberal regulations. Some aspects seem non-Dorian and may derive from Minoan Bronze Age society. It is one of the most important sources of our knowledge of Greek law and was first brilliantly read and published by Halbherr and his Italian colleagues.

Graham, J. Walter Canadian archaeologist who has specialized in the architecture, elevations, planning and functions of Minoan and Mycenaean buildings. See **Minoan Foot**.

Grave Circle A group of graves enclosed by

a low circular stone wall, as in the royal burial circles at Mycenae.

Haft Wooden handle for a stone or metal tool such as an axe, or the metal hilt of a dagger, knife or sword to which plates and sometimes decorated goldwork were added to complete the handle.

Halbherr, Federico (1857–1930) Italian archaeologist and explorer of Crete who inspired and helped **Evans** in the latter's early reconnaissances in the island. Evans dedicated *The Palace of Minos* to him. Halbherr took a leading part in the excavations of Aghia Triadha, Phaistos and the Idaean Cave but his great work was his study and edition of the huge Law Code inscribed on the odeion at Gortyn and dated 500–450 BC.

Hammer-axe Tool, or model of one, with a central hole for the handle and on one side of the hole an axe blade, on the other a blunt hammer head. A terracotta deity from Mycenae holds a crude object which is apparently a hammer-axe.

Hatzidhakis, Joseph (1848–1936) Cretan scholar and archaeologist. He greatly assisted **Evans** in the purchase of the Knossos site from its Turkish owners and he formed the first collection of Cretan antiquities, later to become the Herakleion Archaeological Museum, of which he was the first Director. He began the excavations of the palace at Mallia, which he ceded to the French School. His main discovery was at Tylissos, where he excavated and published the three Minoan country mansions.

Helladic Term used to describe the Bronze Age of mainland Greece (c. 3000–1050 BC), which is divided into three periods, Early, Middle and Late Helladic (EH, MH, LH), of which the last is synonymous with Mycenaean.

Hellenistic Term used for the period of Greek history and the art styles and products thereof from the death of Alexander the Great to the Battle of Actium (323–31 BC), when Rome defeated the last of the Ptolemies in the persons of Cleopatra and her Roman lover Anthony.

Hera In Greek mythology sister and wife of Zeus and mother of Ares, Hephaistos and Hebe. For the Greeks she was the patron goddess of marriage. She is mentioned already on the Linear B tablets, coupled with Zeus, so was worshiped in Mycenaean times. She may have been a pre-Greek or Minoan goddess whom the Greeks connected to their chief god, Zeus.

Hermes In Classical mythology a son of Zeus and Maia and herald or messenger of the gods, whence he also became the patron god of travelers and commerce and escort of the souls of the dead. He was always thought of as a young or junior god. His name occurs on the Linear B tablets so he is known to have been worshiped already in the Bronze Age. A mountain shrine of the Classical and Roman periods recently found in Crete belonged to Hermes and some representations there show him as a vegetation god. He may therefore have been a young male companion of the Mistress of Animals in Minoan times, since cult at the shrine goes right back to the Bronze Age.

Hieroglyphic A system of writing in which the symbols consist of pictures (eg man, fish, plant), realistic or stylized, and abstract signs to convey an idea or to refer to a material object. A hieroglyphic script was used on clay tablets and sealstones in the First Palace period in Crete, 1900–1700 BC, and perhaps early in the Second Palace period. The idea for such a system, though not the form of it, may have been taken by the Minoans from the great hieroglyphic script of contemporary Egypt.

Hogarth, David (1862–1927) English archaeologist who excavated in Greece and the Near East. As Director of the British School at Athens at the beginning of the century he uncovered houses in the Minoan town of Knossos while **Evans** was excavating the palace, conducted excavations in the sacred Dictaian Cave and revealed several large houses in the Minoan town of Zakro, without finding its palace.

House of the Tiles The main building of the Early Bronze Age II settlement at Lerna, so called because it had a pitched roof made of terracotta and stone roof tiles.

Hyakinthos A pre-Greek god worshiped at Amyklai near Sparta. In Classical times his cult was subordinate to Apollo's, who is said to have loved him and killed him accidentally. But this was probably a Greek development since Hyakinthos had a distinct cult and a pre-Greek name, which was attached to Artemis. Hence in origin he was probably thought of as a young male consort of the Mistress of Animals (for whom see **Artemis Eileithyia**).

Hydria A vessel of jug shape with a vertical handle from lip to shoulder and one or two horizontal handles on the body.

Hyksos Asiatic invaders who ruled Egypt from about 1670 to 1570 BC (Second Intermediate period). They arrived in chariots and first dominated the eastern Delta of the Nile, then gradually all Egypt. They were finally driven out by the Theban prince Ahmosis, founder of the 18th Dynasty or New Kingdom.

Iakovidhes, Spyridon Greek archaeologist whose major works have been a study of the acropolis of Athens and the excavation and publication of the huge late Mycenaean cemetery at Perati in Attica.

Iconography The ways in which a subject and its meaning are worked out, as a whole and in details, in works of art. To be distinguished from style. For example iconography would be concerned with the presence or absence of wings on Mycenaean sphinxes, and any meaning attached to this; style with the technique by which the wings are represented.

Ideogram A sign consisting of a simplified (often unrecognizable) picture representing a word, as in Chinese characters. In the Linear A and Linear B tablets ideograms are for words representing material objects or substances, such as man, wheat, sword. For a scribe reading a tablet they provide a visually quick way of seeing the subject he wants to study. They are usually followed on tablets by numeral signs giving the numbers or amount of the object or substance.

Iron Age In the Aegean a term sometimes used for the period when iron became as important as bronze for metal artifacts, namely from c. 1050 BC onwards. It is most commonly used for the centuries following the 11th in regions peripheral to the central Greek area, such as northern Greece or Cyprus.

Jamb base A base, usually of limestone or gypsum, for a door frame or jamb.

Kadmos In Greek legend the son of Agenor, King of Phoenicia, and brother of Europa (see **Minos**). When Europa was carried off to Crete by Zeus Kadmos was sent to search for his sister. The oracle at Delphi told him to settle where a certain cow lay down. This was at Thebes, where he founded the city, first called Kadmeia. Since Thebes had a rich Mycenaean culture the legends may reflect the establishment of the Mycenaean palace and kingdom controlled from it. But the tradition that Kadmos introduced writing to Greece probably arose from a confusion with the much later (8th century BC) introduction of the alphabet to Greece from Phoenicia, rather than being any memory of Mycenaean writing.

Kalokairinos, Minos A well-named Cretan businessman and amateur archaeologist who in 1878 excavated in what came under **Evans** to be the Minoan palace at Knossos. He found ten of the terracotta store jars (see **Pithos**) in two of the West Magazines. He gave some to foreign museums (one to the British Museum in 1884), but the rest were destroyed in his house in the Cretan Revolution of 1897.

Kamares Ware Middle Minoan I–II pottery with polychrome decoration in red, orange and white on a black surface (c. 2000–1700 BC). Named after its first discovery in the Kamares Cave on the south side of Mount Ida in Crete.

Karo, Georg (1872–1963) German archaeologist whose major contributions to Aegean prehistory were his work on Minoan libation vases and his huge, definitive publication in 1930–33 of the Shaft Graves of Circle A at Mycenae and their thousands of precious objects.

Keel-vaulted Tomb Late Bronze Age rectangular tomb built of stone with a pitched or gabled roof like the inverted keel of a boat. The best examples are in Grave Circle B at Mycenae and, earlier, the royal tomb at Isopata north of Knossos.

Keftiu Egyptian name (in full, Princes of the land of Keftiu and of the isles which are in the midst of the sea), found painted in Egyptian nobles' tombs, mainly in the earlier 18th Dynasty, from c. 1490 to 1405 BC, most commonly taken to refer to the Minoan people of Crete. Sometimes in tombs with these inscriptions people are shown dressed in short kilts like the Minoans and bearing gifts of Minoan type, such as bull's-head rhytons, as an offering to the pharaoh. The Egyptian tombs thus give evidence of Minoan embassies to Egypt at the height of Minoan overseas influence in the Aegean.

Kerameikos An area of Athens a little to the northwest of the agora or market place. In Classical times it was the potters' quarter, but both then and earlier many tombs were placed there, especially of the latest Mycenaean, Protogeometric and Geometric periods. The cemeteries lined the road to Eleusis outside the city gate located at this point.

Klytaimnestra Wife of Agamemnon and paramour of Aigisthos during Agamemnon's absence at the Trojan War. The bloody history of the family, begun with Atreus, continued when Klytaimnestra and Aigisthos murdered Agamemnon on his return, in revenge for which they were murdered by Klytaimnestra's and Agamemnon's children, Orestes and Elektra. The tragic story is immortalized by Aeschylus, Sophocles and Euripides in their dramas.

Krater A large, open, deep bowl, usually of pottery, with handles on the side. Common in Mycenaean times. In Classical Greece such bowls were used for mixing wine and water, so Minoan and Mycenaean pots of similar shape to Classical ones may have had the same function.

Kylix Goblet with a shallow bowl on a narrow stem, which grows taller as the type develops in Late Minoan and Mycenaean pottery. The normal vessel for drinking wine; many hundreds were found in the palace at Pylos. Decorated gold and silver copies of the clay form were placed in the royal Shaft Graves and richest tombs.

Label Small flat piece of fired clay (if circular called a roundel) with a hole for tying to a container and incised with Minoan hieroglyphic or Linear A signs.

Labyrinth The legendary home of the Minotaur built by Daidalos for King Minos at Knossos. It was full of winding, complicated passages like a maze. Here Theseus is said to have come to rescue the seven maidens and seven youths sent as tribute from Athens to Minos. Ariadne gave him a ball of thread to tie at the opening and thus find his way out after killing the Minotaur. Medieval travelers were shown an underground area near Gortyn in Crete, honeycombed with passages, and told it was the labyrinth. In fact this was the stone quarry for Roman Gortyn. The discovery of the complex palace at Knossos by Evans suggested that the idea of a place full of winding passages survived in folk memory after the Bronze Age palace had been abandoned, while one of the Linear B religious tablets from Knossos actually refers to a "lady of the labyrinth." The coins of Knossos bore a labyrinth as a symbol of the city, maintaining the ancient belief. The word itself may be of Bronze Age date, perhaps meaning the House of the Double Axe, so often inscribed on walls at Knossos.

Lapidary Maker of stone objects, especially vessels.

Larnax (pl. **Larnakes**) Terracotta chest. Oval types were used by the Minoans as bathtubs and sometimes for burials. Rectangular ones, standing on four or six feet, with a gabled lid, copied wooden prototypes and were regularly used for burials in Late Minoan Crete and at Tanagra in mainland Greece. Their sides are decorated with abstract patterns, octopuses and scenes of hunting and cult.

Levi, Doro Italian archaeologist who has discovered much of the First Palace and Bronze Age town at Phaistos and published its innumerable contents. His other work in Crete includes excavation at the Archaic city of Arkadhes, a Minoan villa near Gortyn, a rich Minoan circular tomb at Kamilari near Phaistos, all published, and currently the excavation of the Bronze Age town at Iasos on the coast of Asia Minor.

Libation

Libation The pouring of liquid offerings, often through rhytons, in religious rites.

Linear A and Linear B Scripts consisting of simple linear signs apparently derived from older hieroglyphic or pictographic script evolved by the Minoans by 1700 BC. The first script, Linear Script A or Linear A, was regularly used for the Minoan language in the Second Palace period (1700–1450 BC) on clay tablets and religious vessels of stone. The script and language are undeciphered, but about two-thirds of the signs were taken over, probably c. 1450–1400 BC at Knossos, and used by the Mycenaeans for their script, Linear B, presumably because those signs had the same sound value for the Mycenaeans as for the Minoans. Fewer than 400 Linear A documents survive, but there are several thousand Linear B tablets. The latter script, with 87 signs, was deciphered in 1952 as an early form of Greek, expressed in syllables, by Ventris. Tablets in both scripts are mainly concerned with quotas of produce of all kinds issued by or due to the palaces. See also **Chadwick, Ideogram, Ventris**.

Lithgow, William (c. 1583–1660) Scottish traveler who visited Crete in about 1610. His extraordinary, vivid style describing the places he saw and people he met in his long-suffering adventures, and the excruciating tortures he suffered under the Inquisition, has drawn many readers to his book, *The Totall Discourse* (1632).

Lolling, Habbo (1848–94) German archaeologist and epigraphist who spent much of his life in Greece and whose excavations of the Late Bronze Age beehive tomb at Menidhi, just north of Athens, in 1880 produced remains of Mycenaean burials and revealed the true purpose of these

monuments. He also excavated Mycenaean tombs at Nauplion.

Macehead Polished spherical or solid oval stone with a cylindrical hollow right through for mounting the stone on a stick or shaft. Attractively colored stones were used and the objects are common in prehistoric Egypt and Neolithic Crete. Copper maceheads are found in Palestine in the 4th millennium. Their function in Crete is in fact unknown and they could have been used as weapons (as by the pharaoh in Egypt) or as marks of office.

Mackenzie, Duncan (1859–1935) Scottish archaeologist who played an important part in the first British excavations in the prehistoric Aegean, at Phylakopi in Melos (1896–99), and then worked as assistant to **Evans** at Knossos throughout the excavations. His fine stratigraphical sense and his detailed recordings of pottery in relation to find places and levels helped in large measure towards the understanding of the architectural, and so historical sequences at each of these sites.

Magazine A room in a palace or house, or a separate building, used for storage and containing large jars (see **Pithos**) to hold cereals and liquids. The best known are the long, narrow chambers on the ground floor of the west wing of the palace at Knossos.

Marinatos, Spyridon (1901–74) Greek archaeologist, Director of Herakleion Museum and Director General of Greek Antiquities, excavator of many Bronze Age sites in Crete, Kephallenia and Messenia, and, to the moment of his recent death, of the Bronze Age settlement on Thera.

Matt-painted Ware Pottery decorated with dull, lusterless, dark paint on a buff surface. Characteristic of Middle Helladic Greece.

Meander A winding pattern, often curving back on itself, as on the seals of Early Helladic

Meander

Lerna. In vase painting it is a repeated pattern of interlocked lines, often in a key formation.

Megalithic Used to describe masonry constructed of large, usually dressed stone blocks, as in the walls of Mycenaean citadels or the dromos and entrance of a tholos tomb.

Megaron A type of long house in the prehistoric Aegean with a porch area leading to a main room, which often contained a hearth and which led into a small storage room at the far end. This last room was straight-ended, making a rectangular

Megaron

building, or curved like an apse. Megarons were common at Troy, appear in Greece by 2000 BC and form the central unit of the Mycenaean palaces.

Mesolithic The Middle Stone Age or period immediately preceding settled Neolithic occupation in the 7th millennium BC. The hunters used much smaller stone tools than in the Palaeolithic period but such groups are as yet scarcely known or understood in Greece.

Minoan Foot Minoan unit of measure calculated by **Graham** at 30.36 centimeters ($11\frac{15}{16}$ inches). He showed that the major dimensions of Minoan palaces were planned and laid out to specific whole numbers of Minoan feet, thus greatly advancing our knowledge of Minoan design abilities.

Minos In legend the king of Knossos, son of Zeus (the king of the gods) and Europa (daughter of Kadmos), to whom Zeus came in the form of a bull. Minos' name was used by Evans for the Bronze Age civilization of Crete. The name may have been a title in Crete, like pharaoh in Egypt or Caesar for Roman emperors.

Minotaur See also **Labyrinth**. The Classical Greeks often portrayed Theseus killing the bull-headed man on their vase paintings. This later concept of the monster may be a distant memory of Bronze Age religious rites in which bulls, precious vessels in the shape of their heads and perhaps bull headdresses are known to have played an important part.

Minyan Ware Name given to the wheel-made, gray, polished pottery of the Middle Bronze Age on the Greek mainland, after its discovery at Orchomenos in Boeotia, capital of the legendary King Minyas. Very similar pottery is found in the Sixth City of Troy. The style in fact has no special connection with Boeotia but seems to have evolved in Greece around 2200–2000 BC, perhaps under the impetus of settlers from northwest Asia Minor.

Minyas Legendary king of Boeotia, with his capital at Orchomenos. This site has produced important Mycenaean buildings and one of

the finest tholos or beehive tombs (the so-called **Treasury of Minyas**), so that it probably did have powerful kings in the Bronze Age. Minyas and his people, the Minyans, were credited by later Greeks with the draining of the adjacent Lake Kopais to produce fertile land and there is some archaeological evidence that this was first done in Late Bronze Age Mycenaean times.

Mortuary House Tomb apparently built above ground level, as at Mochlos in Crete; its rectangular plan with one or more compartments was perhaps a small-scale imitation of the houses of the living.

Myres, Sir John (1869–1954) Classical scholar, anthropologist and prehistorian. Traveled with Evans in the latter's earliest journeys in Crete, excavated and published the Minoan peak sanctuary at Petsopha in 1903 and organized Evans' notes and studies to produce a publication of the Linear B tablets from Knossos in 1952.

Nautilus Type of mollusc with a large arched shell. Minoan artists found these and other sea creatures attractive and painted them realistically on their vases in the Marine Style (1500–1450 BC) as well as making models of the shell in faience. Nautili, sometimes also called Argonauts, appear in inlay on Mycenaean daggers and were represented in stylized forms on Mycenaean pottery.

Neolithic New or Late Stone Age. Term used for that period of Aegean prehistory from the first establishment of settled farming communities in the 7th millennium BC to the introduction of metals in the 4th millennium.

Nestor In the *Iliad* the king of Pylos in Messenia and a delightfully garrulous old man. A great Bronze Age palace has been excavated near Pylos and was reasonably called the Palace of Nestor by **Blegen**.

Octopus Style A type of painted decoration on globular stirrup jars at the end of the Bronze Age, 12th century BC, in which octopuses fill most of the surface and are rendered in a lurid but completely unrealistic manner. Abstract patterns and stylized birds and fishes fill in spaces around the octopuses. The style is found in the central Aegean area, especially the Argolid and the Cycladic islands.

Offset In Aegean architecture used of a wall built not with a continuous surface but with straight sections forming a polygon, each section projecting out slightly from the previous one, the line of the projection being vertical. Used in the facades of Minoan buildings and on the walls of the Sixth City at Troy, where the function may have been

to ease the transition and prevent cracks between each section of wall.

Orthostat Large slab set upright on its side or end and used as the lowest or penultimate course of a wall. Used in Neolithic Thessaly to protect mud-brick walls and in Minoan palaces, such as the western wall at Knossos, and in an important tomb at Mallia.

Ossuary A building below ground level, usually an annex to a tomb, for the storage of human bones moved out of the tomb to make room for fresh interments. Used in Early and Middle Minoan times in Crete.

Palaeolithic The Old Stone Age or period before c. 8000 BC in the Aegean, when the mainland of Greece was populated by hunters and gatherers of wild foods, who lived in caves and rock shelters and used flint and bone tools. Such occupation has been traced back to 40,000 BC in Epeiros.

Palmer, Leonard Former Professor of Comparative Philology at Oxford University and a leading worker on the Linear B tablets. He has also written several books about Knossos, proposing that the date of the final destruction of the palace, including the tablets, frescoes, stone vessels and other major finds, occurred about 1200 BC, not 1400 BC, the date which Evans proposed and which most archaeologists before and since Palmer's work have considered correct.

Pantheon The divinities of any culture conceived of as a group. In Classical Greece the family of 12 gods believed to reside on the summit of Mount Olympus: Zeus, Poseidon, Apollo, Ares, Hermes, Hephaistos, Hestia, Demeter, Hera, Athena, Aphrodite and Artemis. Most of these the Linear B tablets show to have been worshiped already by the Mycenaeans in the Late Bronze Age and the frequent listing of groups of them suggests that the Mycenaeans may have thought of them collectively as a group. Certainly they were worshiped separately, indicating Mycenaean polytheism. The evidence suggests that many of these divinities, or at least many aspects of their cults, had been taken over from the Minoans and that the Minoans too worshiped many distinct divinities, especially goddesses. But there is no indication of a Minoan pantheon or collectively conceived group of divinities. See also gods and goddesses listed individually.

Papyrus Tall, rushlike plant formerly common on the Nile. The frequent depiction of the whole plant on Minoan vases and frescoes suggests it was well known and may have been grown in Crete also. It grows today in Sicily, which has a climate similar to that of Crete. Whether it was used in the

Aegean as a material for writing on is unknown, but clay seal impressions with very fine string marks on the reverse suggest the sealing of documents made of some delicate material like papyrus.

Pashley, Robert (1805–59) English traveler in Crete in 1834. His two volumes, *Travels in Crete* (1837), are an unsurpassed exposition of contemporary Crete, its people, their political condition, way of life, their folklore and the identification of the island's Classical cities.

Petrie, Sir William Flinders (1853–1942) The greatest of British Egyptologists. He excavated and published a large number of predynastic and pharaonic buildings and cemeteries, devised a system of sequence dating for prehistoric Egypt based on the stylistic development of basic pottery jar forms and on what objects were found with them in graves, and he published many basic works on individual classes of objects from Egypt.

Picture-writing See **Hieroglyphic**.

Piriform Pear-shaped. Applied to vessels, chiefly pottery, which are somewhat like an inverted pear in shape, with a small neck and broad shoulder running down to a smaller base.

Pisé Rammed clay and small pebbles forming a wall. Used in Neolithic buildings at Knossos.

Pit Grave A simple oval or rectangular pit dug in the ground for a grave, its sides sometimes lined and roofed with slabs. Especially common in the Early and Middle Bronze Ages on the Greek mainland and in the Cyclades.

Pithos Large storage jar of terracotta made in the Aegean in a continuous tradition and by the same method from the beginning of the Bronze Age to the present day. Giant pithoi at Knossos stand well above the height of a

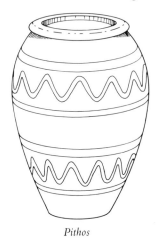

Pithos

man and needed ladders for entry. Some pithoi were for dry substances such as cereals, others have a bung hole near the base and were for liquids, especially wine and oil.

Platon, Nikolaos Greek archaeologist, formerly Director of the Archaeological Museum, Herakleion, Crete, excavator of many Cretan sites of all periods and discoverer and excavator of the Minoan palace of Kato Zakro.

Polychrome Term applied chiefly to the decoration of pottery in more than one color, for example red and white on a black ground as in Middle Minoan ceramics.

Polykrates Ruler of the Greek island of Samos from c. 535 to 522 BC. He was an aristocrat who assumed personal control of the island, established a powerful Samian fleet and controlled the eastern Aegean. He became an ally of Egypt or Persia as circumstances required. Like a Florentine Medici he encouraged poets and thinkers at his court and his architect constructed a remarkable mountain tunnel and a huge temple of Hera on Samos. He was murdered by a Persian governor c. 522 BC.

Pommel Knob to fit in the hand on the top of a sword or dagger hilt. Minoan and Mycenaean weapons have pommels of ivory or attractive stones, sometimes covered with decorated gold sheet.

Poseidon In Classical mythology the brother of Zeus and Hades, husband of Ge (Earth) and god of earthquakes, streams, horses, bulls and, principally, the sea. His name and that of his shrine are found on the Linear B tablets so he was known and worshiped already by the Mycenaean Greeks, especially at Pylos.

Priam Legendary king of Troy at the time of the Achaean campaign under Agamemnon against the city (see **Trojan War**). An old man at the time of the war, he was held by Homer to have had 50 sons, 19 by his second wife Hecuba. Hector, who conducted the defense of Troy, was one of these sons and his body was afterwards ransomed by Priam from Achilles.

Prism Seal Sealstone, usually of the Middle Minoan period, made with three or four sides or faces like a prism, with engraved decoration on each face and pierced for wearing on a cord.

Protogeometric See **Geometric** and **Iron Age**.

Proto-urban Term used to describe, in the Aegean, Early Bronze Age settlements like Troy or Lerna in which stone-built houses and walls, stored wealth in metalwork or

food, the probability of specialized groups of craftsmen and of some degree of communal organization give the impression of an emerging town rather than a purely agricultural village as in the Neolithic period.

Pyxis (pl. **Pyxides**) Name used for vessels of ivory, pottery, stone and probably wood which are essentially boxes with close-fitting lids. Shapes vary from cylindrical to curved (with a C profile) and rectangular. Pottery pyxides have painted decoration, stone ones incision or relief, while Late Minoan and

Pyxis

Mycenaean cylindrical pyxides of ivory have relief scenes of human figures or animals or attached objects such as little shields. Pyxides probably served as jewelry boxes and are seen carried in procession on frescoes, doubtless with the idea that they contained offerings.

Quadrant A quarter of a circular face. Circular seals often have a design emphasizing the four quadrants on the engraved face.

Radiocarbon Dating Measurement of the amount of radioactive carbon (C-14) left in organic matter, usually wood charcoal, since it died and stopped taking in carbon dioxide. From the remaining amount of C-14 the time since the organic matter lived, that is the age of the sample, can be calculated. In the last 20 years it has proved an invaluable means of dating early cultures all over the world and in the Aegean from c. 2000 BC backwards in time.

Relief Decoration consisting of human figures, animals or patterns which has been raised by the carving away of the surrounding surfaces and which is then finished off by sculpting or engraving.

Renfrew, Colin English archaeologist who has excavated Neolithic settlements at Saliagos in the Cyclades and Sitagroi in Macedonia and is currently continuing the old excavation at Phylakopi in Melos. He has specialized in the application of scientific techniques, especially **Radiocarbon Dating**, to Aegean prehistory.

Repoussé Metalworking technique in which the design of human figures, animals, vegetation or abstract patterns, is gently beaten out or beaten into a mold from behind, that is from what will become the interior surface or underside of a vessel. Contrast **Chased**.

Rhadamanthys In legend a son of Zeus and Europa and brother of Minos and Sarpedon. In Homer, for his justice on earth, he has become a judge in Hades. Rhadamanthys has a pre-Greek name and was traditionally associated with Phaistos in Crete. In fear of Minos he is said to have fled to Boeotia in Greece. It is therefore interesting that tombs with larnakes of Minoan type have recently been found there.

Rhyton Vessel with a small hole for liquids to flow out of, in addition to a normal mouth or opening. Used for libations and usually made of terracotta or fine stones such as

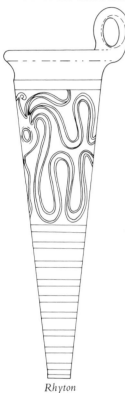

Rhyton

alabaster, marble or serpentine; often conical or piriform in shape or in the form of an animal's head with an exit hole through the mouth and entrance on top of the head.

Ribbing Usually a form of decoration on clay or metal vases, consisting of one or more horizontal, convex ribs. Compare **Carination** and **Fluting**.

Ring Vase Pottery vessel shaped like a ring or inflated tyre. It is found especially in the Cyclades at the end of the Early Bronze Age. Decorated with incision it also has on one part of the surface a little vertical cylinder with an open spreading lip.

Roundel See **Label**.

Sarcophagus Burial chest of terracotta or stone, and probably wood, though none has survived. Common in Late Minoan Crete, although the famous limestone sarcophagus from Aghia Triadha, with painted religious scenes, is unique. See also **Larnax**.

Sarpedon In legend a son of Zeus and Europa and brother of Minos and Rhadamanthys. He is said to have quarreled with Minos over the town of Miletus and to have fled to Asia Minor, where Miletus was later a great city. Its history extends back to the Bronze Age and its earliest connections are with Minoan Crete. In Crete there was a Classical city of Milatos near the Minoan palace of Mallia, so perhaps there was an actual king Sarpedon who ruled at Mallia in Minoan times.

Sauceboat Modern name for frequently found pottery or metal vessels of the Early Helladic and Early Cycladic cultures. The shape is distinctive and resembles a modern

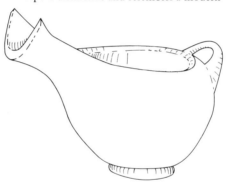

Sauceboat

sauce- or gravy-boat with a rising spout on one side. It usually has a ring or pedestal foot and a handle opposite the spout. Its purpose was probably for drinking or for pouring liquids like wine and oil.

Scarab Egyptian sacred beetle or, commonly, an Egyptian seal cut in the shape of this beetle, engraved on the oval base and worn as an amulet. The development of the designs and the presence of royal and official names and titles often enable scarabs to be closely dated, so that those which found their way from Egypt to the Aegean are sometimes valuable for dating purposes.

Schematic Abbreviated or sketchy; often of linear designs whose original form was more realistic or natural.

Schliemann, Heinrich (1822–90) German merchant and archaeologist who discovered the Aegean Bronze Age through his great excavations at Mycenae, Orchomenos, Tiryns and Troy.

Seager, Richard (1882–1925) American excavator of Mochlos, Pachyammos, Pseira and Vasilike in eastern Crete and as such one of the founders of Minoan archaeology. Seager had an excellent sense of stratigraphy and published many of his finds in detail.

Sealstone A small piece of semi-precious stone such as agate, carnelian or jasper carved into a disk, lens, cylinder or other shape, with an engraved pattern on one or more faces.

Sealstone

Hundreds of exquisite seals were made by the Minoans and Mycenaeans and were worn as personal identity disks and were impressed on clay to seal documents and containers.

Shaft Grave A type of grave in Late Bronze Age Greece and Crete in which the body and grave goods were lowered on to a layer of pebbles at the bottom of a rectangular shaft. In the most elaborate graves, such as the famous six at Mycenae, the shaft was lined with stones and roofed over with beams and slabs, the rest of the shaft filled with earth and a sculptured stela set on top as a marker.

Sherd Broken piece of pottery.

Signet Sealstone or ring with engraved bezel used like a stamp for impressing the design on to clay to seal documents or containers.

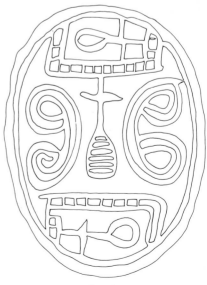

Scarab

Snake Goddess The Minoan household or domestic goddess, one of whose attributes was the snake, which was thought of as a beneficent, protecting spirit. Terracotta images of the goddess are found in Minoan shrines with or without snakes attached to her. The famous faience statuettes from Knossos include an image of the goddess, or her votaries, or are models of priestesses taking part in the snake cult. The Greek goddess Athena had her origins in the Minoan household goddess and one of Athena's attributes was the snake.

Sphinx Mythological monster with the body of a lion and a human head, probably originating in Egypt and known widely in the Near East and to the Mycenaeans. It appears in Mycenaean art on ivories, sealstones and gold rings and in some representations the head looks female, which it was regularly in Greek literature, though not always in Greek art. Its function in Mycenaean art is unknown; it may have been purely decorative or have had its later Greek function of averting evil.

Staes, Valerios (1857–1923) Greek archaeologist who excavated mainly Classical sites but investigated a Mycenaean beehive tomb at Thorikos and prehistoric remains on Aigina.

Stamatakis, Panaghiotes (died 1885) A leading Greek archaeologist in the later 19th century. Apart from excavations on Classical sites he discovered and excavated the sixth shaft grave within Circle A (Schliemann's) inside the citadel of Mycenae. He also made important discoveries in the entrance passages of the tholos tombs at Mycenae and found the beehive tomb at the Heraion (Temple of Hera) at Argos.

Stamp Seal Sealstone with one engraved surface and a handle above to enable the seal to be used to impress or stamp the design on clay.

Stasis The Greek word for dissension and fighting between or within cities or city-states. Perhaps applicable likewise to Mycenaean Greek kingdoms.

Stela A stone slab set upright over a grave as a marker. Some of the famous stelae set over the Shaft Graves at Mycenae bore sculptured decoration of spirals and chariot scenes.

Stirrup Jar A pottery jar, of piriform, globular or flattened globular shape, much favored by Late Minoan and Mycenaean potters. The name comes from the distinctive top part, a little neck with a handle on each side, looking like a stirrup. The spout is separate, a little cylinder on the shoulder. The larger jars held oil and other valuable liquids,

the small ones, which had painted decoration, perfumed oils, which were frequently exported thus by the Mycenaeans.

Stratigraphy Study of the history of a site by examination, during excavation and afterwards in excavated vertical sections, of the formation of levels, often superimposed, from accumulated occupation debris and natural deposition.

Tankard A Late Bronze Age pottery or stone vessel shaped like a mug with slightly concave sides and, in pottery, a handle. Mycenaean pottery tankards are not uncommon and must have been for drinking.

Taylour, Lord William British archaeologist who has worked chiefly on the Mycenaeans, having excavated in Lakonia and at Mycenae, where he recently found Mycenaean shrines on the acropolis, with many terracotta figures of divinities and snakes.

Thalassocracy From two Greek words (*thalassa* and *kratos*) meaning command of the sea. Used by Greek writers of various maritime powers, King Minos of Crete being cited as the prototype. The tradition of Minoan sea power is probably accurate, since Crete exercised much influence and established many settlements in the Aegean in the Second Palace period (c. 1700–1450 BC), but the form of the sea power, whether, for example, mainly military or commercial, is not known.

Thermoluminescence Means of dating pieces of terracotta, such as pottery or figurines, by measuring the amount of radioactively accumulated energy in the clay since it was fired. The energy is emitted as a form of light (luminescence) when the sherd is again heated (thermo-). The development of the technique is still at an early stage but is potentially of enormous value to archaeologists.

Stirrup jar

Theseus Legendary hero who became king of Attica after the death of his father Aigeus. His story is one of remarkable adventures and exploits of which the freeing of Athens from her tribute to Crete by killing the Minotaur (see **Labyrinth**) is the most famous.

Tholos See **Beehive Tomb**.

Tod, Marcus (1878–1974) Distinguished epigraphical scholar and ancient historian. As Assistant Director of the British School he excavated an Early Minoan burial cave near Palaikastro in 1903 and produced an exemplary publication.

Tournefort, Joseph, Pitton de (1656–1708) French botanist and antiquarian who traveled in the Aegean and Levant on the orders of Louis XIV. By his excellent systematic work he brought the number of scientifically described plants in Crete to 306. His book, *Voyage du Levant* (1717), also describes political conditions and peasant life and customs in Crete.

Treasury of Atreus Pausanias' name for the greatest of the tholos or **Beehive Tombs** at Mycenae, probably built in the 14th century BC. In Pausanias' time (2nd century AD) these domed vaults had long been ransacked and their function was unknown, hence they were thought of as the treasuries of the legendary kings. Their function as burial places was rediscovered through excavation in the late 19th century.

Treasury of Minyas Traditional name for the great Mycenaean tholos or **Beehive Tomb** at Orchomenos in Boeotia, which was the home of the legendary King Minyas (see also **Minyan Ware**). Apart from its superlative architecture the building has a side chamber with a ceiling of beautifully carved spiral patterns. Compare **Treasury of Atreus**.

Trilithon Generally a construction with two upright posts and a horizontal one set on top of them. Often the lintel slab set over the doorway of a tholos tomb or over those of Early and Middle Minoan round tombs.

Triton Shell Also called conch shell and found in the Mediterranean. A vividly colored shell spiraling up from a point to a large open mouth. The Minoans cut off the pointed end and used the shell as a ritual trumpet.

Trojan War The background of the *Iliad*. The poem is concerned only with a part of the last year of the ten during which traditional, oral stories said the Greek heroes under Agamemnon fought against the Trojans, because they had stolen Helen, wife of Agamemnon's brother Menelaos. A kernel of historical truth may well lie behind the poems, but is unlikely ever to be proved objectively, namely that a confederation of Mycenaean Greek states attacked Troy in the 13th or early 12th century BC.

Tsountas, Christos (1857–1934) One of the most successful Greek archaeologists. Tsountas uncovered many rich Mycenaean chamber tombs at Mycenae, the untouched princely burial in the tholos tomb at Vapheio and hundreds of Early Bronze Age graves in the Cyclades. He also excavated at the great Neolithic sites of Dhimini and Sesklo and published his work there in a major book.

Ventris, Michael (1922–56) English architect who in 1952 deciphered the **Linear B** tablets from Knossos and Pylos as written in an early form of Greek. How Ventris arranged the signs, each representing a syllable, that is a vowel or consonant plus vowel, into a grid to work out their sound values is told by John **Chadwick**, with whom Ventris collaborated soon after the decipherment to produce the book, *Documents in Mycenaean Greek*. He was tragically killed in a car accident at the age of 34.

Vermeule, Emily American art historian and Classical archaeologist who writes about the Aegean Bronze Age (mainly the Mycenaeans) and on Mycenaean and Homeric religion. Has also excavated at Morphou, a Bronze Age site in Cyprus.

Vinça Period Late Neolithic period (4th millennium BC) in the Balkans, chiefly Yugoslavia, where the great mound of Vinça is situated on the Danube near Belgrade. The farming peoples of that time and region had a rich figurine art and had already begun to mine copper and produce copper tools.

Votary Human participant in religious ritual.

Votive Figurine or other object dedicated or vowed to a divinity at a shrine.

Wace, Alan (1879–1957) English archaeologist who, with M. S. Thomson, excavated in Neolithic Thessaly and produced in 1912 what is still a standard handbook for that region. In addition to excavations at Sparta he carried out his main work at Mycenae, excavating cemeteries of Late Bronze Age chamber tombs, investigating all the beehive tombs and the palace and other buildings inside the citadel.

Xanthoudides, Stephanos (1864–1928) Cretan scholar and archaeologist of the highest caliber. His main excavations were in the Early Bronze Age communal round tombs of southern Crete, published in a large book in 1924. He also uncovered and published the Middle Minoan oval house at Khamaizi in eastern Crete, the mansion at Nirou Khani, the Pyrgos burial cave and important tombs dating from the end of the Bronze Age at Mouliana.

Zeus All-powerful father of the Greek gods, with temples all over the Greek world. His name occurs on the Linear B tablets, so he was worshiped in some form by the Mycenaeans. Thought to have been in origin an Indo-European sky and weather god, bringer of rain and storms. He appears to have taken over characteristics of a Minoan earth god, which probably influenced a tradition that he was born and brought up in Crete.

Index

Page numbers in *italics* refer to illustrations or their captions.